ARCHIBALD STURROCK

PIONEER LOCOMOTIVE ENGINEER

ARCHIBALD STURROCK

PIONEER LOCOMOTIVE ENGINEER

TONY VERNON

TEMPUS

First published 2007

Tempus Publishing Limited
The Mill, Brimscombe Port,
Stroud, Gloucestershire, GL5 2QG
www.tempus-publishing.com

British Library Cataloguing in Publication Data.
A catalogue record for this book is available from the British Library.

ISBN 978 07524 4135 1

Typesetting and origination by Tempus Publishing Limited
Printed in Great Britain

CONTENTS

INTRODUCTION

My interest in Archibald Sturrock was inspired by his granddaughter, my grandmother. She pointed out the railway works at Doncaster and the nearby railway church of St James, as we travelled between Darlington and London on the east coast main line in the late 1940s. She gave me his copy of G.F. Bird's *Locomotives of the Great Northern Railway* and it was with her that I met briefly Sturrock's daughter Georgina, who died at the age of ninety-nine in December 1951.

Sturrock left only one written record of his life. His memorandum *For my children* is a seventeen-page handwritten note signed on 9 June 1892, when he was seventy-five. He also gave an interview to the *Railway Magazine* in August 1907 in his ninety-first year. The family has retained his 'testimonials' on completing his apprenticeship and extracts from the GNR Board minutes concerning his appointment as locomotive and subsequently as carriage superintendent of the Great Northern Railway. A few papers concerning the early history of the Sturrocks in Forfar survive, including records of the rents received from the Sturrocks' estate at Pitreuchie between 1794 and 1805. His two daughters compiled a scrapbook containing over thirty obituaries. Portraits and photographs of the Sturrock family are owned by my mother, Sturrock's great-granddaughter, by my sister, myself and our cousin Michael Brerton.

I have been greatly assisted in the research for this book by Douglas Brown, who has made available to me his own research into the Sturrock family and introduced me to another descendant of Archibald's father, John Sturrock. Douglas is an engineer, who was a LNER Premium Apprentice at the Plant, as the Doncaster railway works has traditionally been called. He accompanied me on many field trips and his engineering expertise was invaluable.

This book has been prepared largely from research at the National Archives at Kew and from archives and libraries in Bristol, Cambridge, Cardiff, Doncaster, Dundee, Forfar, Newcastle, Sheffield, Swindon, Winchester and York. I am most grateful to the archivists and librarians for the help they have provided. For information on locomotives built or designed by Sturrock, two studies published by the Railway Correspondence and Travel Society have been invaluable: *Locomotives of the Great Western Railway Part Two Broad Gauge* and N. Groves's *Great Northern Locomotive History* vol.1 *1847–1866*. Sturrock's copy of *The Locomotives of the Great Northern Railway* by G.F. Bird was of interest for Sturrock's comments in the margins. For Sturrock's life in Doncaster, the *Doncaster Gazette* and *Doncaster Chronicle* were the principle sources. Information on the Yorkshire Engine Co. was obtained largely from the company record books in the Sheffield archives.

Background information has been obtained particularly from E.T. MacDermot's *History of the GWR* and J. Wrottesley's and C.H. Grinling's histories of the *Great Northern Railway*. Niall Ferguson's *Dundee & Newtyle* provided context for Sturrock's first experience with steam locomotives. The *Diaries of Sir Daniel Gooch, Swindon Legacy of a Railway Town* by John Cattell and Keith Falconer, and A.S. Peck's *The Great Western at Swindon Works* were essential reading for Sturrock's time with Brunel and Gooch at Paddington and Swindon. John Cattell let me see a copy of Edward Snell's UK diary and advised me of the existence of his Australian diary. Commentaries on Sturrock's life and work are contained in *Twenty Locomotive Men* by C. Hamilton Ellis, pages 64-74, and F.A.S. Brown's *Great Northern Locomotive Engineers* vol.1 pages 45-112.

Four members of the Great Northern Railway Society (GNRS), Douglas Brown, Geoffrey Hughes, Paul Craig and Malcolm Crawley, were kind enough to read the manuscript and gave me many helpful comments. Alan Sibley of the GNRS and Reg Carter of the Stephenson Locomotive Society (SLS) provided substantial help with photographs. I am also most grateful to Paul Craig, Jeremy Suter, Geoffrey Hughes and Douglas Brown for supplying photographs from their collections. Any errors and omissions are entirely my responsibility.

Tony Vernon

1

SCOTTISH FOUNDATIONS

I thank God that he inspired me with the desire and gave me the health to work hard at a profession which I honestly confess I do not know why I ever entered; and I did work as hard and honestly for the two railways I served as if they had been my own property.[1]

Colonel Archibald Sturrock, VD, Hon. Colonel of the 5th Battalion King's Own Yorkshire Light Infantry … had a marked personality. Nobody having once met him could well forget him … Indeed with men and women alike it was a burst of sunshine on a chilly day to have Mr Sturrock stop and talk.[2]

Mr Sturrock, albeit a very able engineer, never appeared to like his profession. He delighted in playing the part of a country squire of the best type. He was exceedingly fond of field sports. He hunted regularly till he was seventy-three and shot and fished until he was eighty-five. His dress was always entirely appropriate, not to his profession, but to his amusements.[3]

Archibald Sturrock combined an ability to enjoy life with a capacity to work diligently for two major railways, the Great Western and the Great Northern. A love of the countryside, a willingness to serve others and an ability to innovate can be seen in his family background. His father is reported to have been horrified at Archibald's request to train as an engineer, but he consented. 'What,' John Sturrock retorted, 'you want to become a blacksmith?'[4]

Archibald Sturrock was born on 30 September 1816 to John Sturrock, a banker and linen merchant, and his wife Christian in their substantial house at 2 Park Street, Dundee. Archibald was their fifth son. His father came from a prosperous Forfar family, which had made its money from manufacturing and trading in linen. Forfar was the principal town of what is now the county of Angus. William Sturrock, Archibald's great-great-grandfather had been a Baillie or magistrate of the town in the early eighteenth century. His son John developed the family's fortune in the linen trade and acquired an estate at Pitreuchie about a mile outside Forfar. John of Pitreuchie's eldest son, also called John, was made a freeman and burgess of Forfar at the age of twenty-six in 1767 and is credited with being the first man to take the linen weavers out of their homes and group them together in a factory.[5]

Account of Rents due for Pitruchie for Crop 1804, and for house on Pitruchie, and house in Forfar from Whitsunday 1804 to Whitsunday 1805.

	£		
William Couper	160	"	"
Alexr. Mee	9	15	"
James Nicoll	5	5	"
David Wallace	7	13	1
John Michie	8	"	"
Rent of the Kirk of Forfar Whit: 1804 to 1805	1	"	8
Feu by Episcopal chapel 1804 to 1805	1	"	"
House on Pitruchie			
John Ritchie	1	9	"
John Mackay	1	5	8
David Crichton	1	10	"
Alexr. Allan	1	6	8
Amount of Pitruchie	198	5	1
House in Forfar			
Mr. Sturrock	8	10	"
Joseph Cairns	8	10	"
	£215	5	1

The rent roll for the Sturrock's Pitreuchie estate for the year to Whitsunday 1805. (Author)

Pitreuchie farm in December 2005. (Douglas Brown)

The Sturrocks were unusual in being members of the Scottish Episcopal Church. The church was formed from members of the Church of Scotland who did not want to adopt the Presbyterian form of government. The Episcopal Church suffered persecution because many members had supported the restoration of Prince Charles in 1745. Forfar church had remained Episcopalian till 1715 and, when the Episcopal Church was able to re-establish a place of worship in Forfar in 1770, John Sturrock of Pitreuchie provided the land. Supporters of the Episcopal Church were amongst the wealthier families in the Forfar community and intermarried. Such links were to remain important to the Sturrocks for both social and business reasons in succeeding generations.

Archibald's father John arrived in Dundee in 1798 at the age of nineteen to take up an apprenticeship with Peter Stirling, a merchant in the linen trade. His own father had died some ten years previously, shortly before his grandfather, the purchaser of Pitreuchie. The estate was administered on young John's behalf. It was sold, probably in 1805 when John reached the age of twenty-five, to his father's sister Anne and her husband, John Ker.[6] The young John Sturrock took steps to secure his position in Dundee society by taking on the treasurer's role for the Dundee Episcopal Church in 1800.[7] He enhanced his standing by marrying Christian, the nineteen-year-old daughter of David Ramsay, a merchant in the town, on 27 April 1803. As a result of his marriage, John was admitted a free burgess of the town and joined his father-in-law in the Guildry. John was now in a position to play a major role in the local community.

John and Christian's first child Elizabeth was born prematurely on 6 December 1803 and died two days later. Their second child and eldest son, also called John, was born eighteen months later on 26 February 1805. In the meantime his father had become an ensign in the Dundee or Fifth Forfarshire Corps of Volunteer Infantry. Twins David and Silvester were born on 22 December 1806 and their sister Christian Sandeman on 28 August 1809. After a gap of almost six years, Robert was born on 6 July 1815 and Archibald just over a year later on 30 September 1816. The final child of the marriage, John Binny, arrived on his mother's fortieth birthday in 1823.

Dundee was, by today's standards, a modest town of 30,000 when Archibald was born. It was suffering from a downturn in the coarse linen trade as a result of the ending of the Napoleonic wars, when coarse linen had been much used for making tents. There were riots in the town, when the mob attacked the shops of meal sellers. Highway robberies were commonplace and there was no police force. Many merchants, attracted by the profits of banking, reduced their dependence on trade and became bankers.[8] John Sturrock was no exception and in 1815 was elected treasurer of the newly formed Dundee Savings Bank. In 1827 he became the local agent for the Bank of Scotland, a role he undertook for the rest of his working life.

John's public duties helped advance his business career. He served as Dean of Guild on the Town Council, where he dealt with warrants to build in the town. He was appointed to the Harbour Board at a period of rapid expansion and became a convenor or chairman of the Harbour Trustees. He served on the Gas Board, joined the Police Board when it was established and was a director of the Orphan Institution. He wrote papers on Dundee Harbour trade for the *Journal of the London Statistical Society* and expressed his views on the disadvantages of the Corn Laws. He served as a JP.

Archibald and his siblings grew up in a comfortable household, largely insulated from the poverty of the mass of the population of Dundee in the immediate aftermath of the Battle of Waterloo. By the time Archibald was looking for an apprenticeship, trade had recovered and the number of ships visiting the enlarged Dundee Harbour had increased from 157 in 1815 to 284 in 1833. Steam-driven ships were taking their place amongst the sails in Dundee Harbour and steam was driving the spindles in the mills. Dundee's population had increased by 50 per cent to 45,000 in the sixteen years since Archibald's birth.

Archibald was educated in the town where schooling was available only to those who could afford to pay. Eighty small private schools taught the basic skills of reading, writing and arithmetic. Three larger schools provided what we would call secondary education. The Grammar School had two staff teaching Latin and Greek; the English School, which shared a building with the Grammar School, had a master for English and a Master for writing. The Academy, the largest of the three, had four masters who taught Maths, Logic, Drawing, Natural Philosophy, Moral Philosophy, Chemistry and Modern Languages between them. The three schools came together as the Public Seminaries in 1833–34 the year after Archibald finished his education, and were subsequently known as Dundee High School.

Archibald needed to decide on a career. His eldest brother John had followed his father into banking. Through family connections, David had secured a position as an assistant surgeon with the East India Co. Silvester was unfit for work and Robert had entered the linen trade. As Archibald reached the age of fifteen, he will have noticed the impact of the steam engine in the mills and harbour of Dundee. Forty-eight steam engines of increasing size had been installed in the town and its surroundings by 1832. Archibald was attracted by the potential of the new technology.

The earliest steam engines had been brought in from Boulton & Watt, Fenton & Murray, Robert Napier and G.&J. Rennie. Foundries were established in Dundee from 1800 onwards to meet the need for machinery for the linen mills and, in due course, for the production and repair of steam engines. Charles Carmichael arrived from Glasgow in 1805 and was joined by his brother James in 1810. Their firm J.&C. Carmichael was one of the first to produce steam engines locally.

Archibald Sturrock chose the Dundee Foundry for his apprenticeship. It had commenced operations about 1790 and was owned by James Stirling and his brother, the Revd Robert Stirling. The brothers had experimented with air engines, where hot air was to be the motive power rather than steam, and taken out patents in 1816 and 1825.

Above left: John Sturrock Senior, Archibald's father, in 1865, three years before his death. (*History of Dundee Savings Bank*)

Above right: John Sturrock Junior, Archibald's eldest brother. (*History of Dundee Savings Bank*)

Right: Robert Sturrock, the brother who was closest in age to Archibald. (*History of Dundee Savings Bank*)

Archibald Sturrock started his apprenticeship on 1 September 1832, twenty-nine days before his sixteenth birthday. The main business of the firm was the manufacture of machinery for the linen trade, but in 1829 the firm had secured orders from the Dundee Perth & London Shipping Co. for engines and boilers for a tug, the *William Wallace*. Patrick Stirling, Robert's son and Sturrock's successor at the Great Northern Railway, commenced his apprenticeship with the firm as Sturrock's time was drawing to a close.

Two events in Archibald's apprenticeship were critical to his future career. The first was the chance to work on a locomotive for the Dundee & Newtyle Railway. The second was the opportunity to develop a friendship with Daniel Gooch, the future locomotive superintendent of the Great Western Railway.

The Dundee & Newtyle's inaugural meeting had taken place in Dundee Town Hall on 16 June 1826, when Archibald was rising ten.[9] The line ran from the north of Dundee in Ward Road through a tunnel under the Law as far as Newtyle, about 10 miles away on the edge of the Vale of Strathmore. The railway was expected to make its principle revenue from the transport of linen to Dundee. Construction was slow, partly due to difficulties with the short tunnel under the Law, and the line was not opened until December 1831. The carriages and wagons were pulled up the three inclined planes by stationary steam engines and pulled along the two flat sections by horses. Such a complex array of motive power was bound to be expensive. Ropes on the inclines had to be regularly replaced. Enginemen in the stationary engine houses were provided with telescopes to monitor the progress of trains. Travel on the line proved immediately popular with the locals.

As traffic grew, the directors realised they would have to increase speeds on the line and a decision was made to buy two locomotives from J.&C. Carmichael, who had supplied two of the stationary engines. Carmichaels had already built one locomotive for the Edinburgh and Dalkeith. The two engines, one for each level section of the line, were delivered in September and October 1833 and were called the *Earl of Airlie* and *Lord Wharncliffe*. The directors of the Dundee & Newtyle had been advised that there was a need for a spare, as engines were liable to break down, and the two Carmichael engines were no exception. The directors decided to purchase a third engine from the Dundee Foundry and this provided Archibald with his first opportunity to be involved with locomotive construction. The locomotive, named *Trotter*, was delivered in March 1834.

Ward Road Station in Dundee, the original terminus of the Dundee & Newtyle Railway, looking north to the Law Hill. (Dundee Central Library)

Trotter was built for the Dundee & Newtyle Railway when Sturrock was serving his time at the Dundee Foundry. (John Boyle)

Sturrock's testimonial on completing his apprenticeship at the Dundee Foundry in 1852 is signed by the manager, James Stirling. (Author)

Trotter was a 4-2-0, with the 4ft 8in driving wheels to the rear, just in front of the firebox. The two vertically acting cylinders were at the front of the boiler and connected to the driving wheels by long connecting rods. A water cask was carried on a small four-wheeled tender.[10] According to Archibald's interview with the *Railway Magazine* in 1907, he was personally involved in setting up the locomotive to work on the railway. He recalled it was only 6 tons in weight, but company records suggest it was 8 tons 10cwt. Archibald helped with repairs to *Trotter* following a fatal accident in June 1834, when the tender was derailed and a man travelling illegally on the tender was crushed by the locomotive. Subsequently Archibald helped with a major overhaul of *Trotter* in April 1836, when the line was being extended to the harbour.[11]

The Dundee Foundry also built three locomotives for the Arbroath & Forfar Railway. A tender for £1,145 each was accepted in 1834; the first locomotive was not ready for operation until January 1839, by which time Archibald had completed his apprenticeship. These engines were 5ft 6in gauge 2-2-2s with inclined outside cylinders adjacent to the smoke box and 5ft driving wheels.[12]

Archibald Sturrock aged twenty-one. (Mrs N.E.Vernon-Harcourt)

Daniel Gooch arrived in Dundee on 17 February 1835.[13] He wanted to work at the Dundee Foundry because it 'did a class of work I had not had the opportunity of seeing, such as marine engines, flax and other general machinery'. Gooch noted that James Stirling was very pleasant. Day to day running of the works was in the hands of a Mr Leslie Meldrum, whom Gooch found difficult. Gooch was paid £1 a week and found he could easily live on this without the support of his widowed mother He took a room with a Mrs Stephens for 7s a week, but found the place noisy and had to use a poker on the ceiling to quieten the family above.

Gooch knew the manager of the Dundee & Newtyle Railway, a Mr Nicholson, from his days at the Bedlington ironworks in Northumberland. Mrs Nicholson introduced him to 'some of the best families'. Daniel Gooch recalls in his memoirs: 'The Sturrocks also lived here. Archie who afterwards served under me on the Great Western … was serving his time at the foundry, so that I had plenty of pleasant society.' Gooch's comments on Dundee society were echoed by another writer of the time:

> From the number of wealthy families in the town, either engaged in business or enjoying the fruits of their hard and honourably earned affluence, the society of the place is extensive and pleasant. As business is now transacted chiefly before dinner, the evening is often devoted to domestic enjoyment, to useful instruction, to social parties or to the club.[14]

Archibald Sturrock recalled that Gooch had worked in the drawing office and had given him instruction in mechanical drawing. They attended lectures together at the Watt Institution, which had been established in 1824 principally to give lectures on engineering and scientific subjects to tradesmen and others interested in furthering their education. In the 1835–36 session, when Gooch attended with Archibald, there were fifteen lectures on physical science subjects, ten on natural history and six on other subjects. The benefits they both received from attending the Watt Institution encouraged Gooch and Archibald to support similar ventures in Swindon and Doncaster in later years. Gooch left Dundee on 6 January 1836 and Archibald completed his apprenticeship in August the following year.[15]

> Dundee 5th December 1837
> These are to certify that the bearer Mr Archibald Sturrock served a regular apprenticeship as an Engineer in the employment of the Dundee Foundry Company, namely from the first day of September one thousand eight hundred and thirty two to the thirty first day of August one thousand eight hundred and thirty seven inclusive, during which period he conducted himself with uniform propriety and acquired for himself the character of a good workman, having had opportunity also during the last two years of his engagement of showing an extensive and accurate knowledge of his profession – much beyond what is generally acquired during an Apprenticeship.
> Jas. Stirling
> Engineer & Manager for the Dundee Foundry Company.

Having celebrated his twenty-first birthday at the end of September 1837, Archibald looked to widen his engineering experience and broaden his education. He also took out his first game licence. He wrote in his memoir:

> I then went to Manchester and worked as a journeyman mechanic for six months in the firm of Messrs. William Fairbairn and Company. That took place during the autumn of 1838 and the beginning of 1839. I then went abroad in the autumn of 1839 to travel and study for nearly 6 months in Brussels. I then visited Paris for about six weeks and returned early in 1840 to Scotland. Afterwards I studied geology and chemistry at Edinburgh University for six months.[16]

Fairbairns provided Archibald with essential additional experience. William Fairbairn had established his firm in Mattier Street, Manchester, in 1816. Like the Dundee Foundry, Fairbairns had extended their activities to include the design and construction of stationary steam engines and the manufacture of canal boats. By the time Archibald joined, its activities included locomotive manufacture. The largest customer was to be the Manchester & Leeds Railway for which Fairbairns built at least sixty-nine locomotives. They also supplied parts and undertook subcontract work for other locomotive manufacturers.[17] Archibald received 34*s* per week and his overtime was paid at time and a quarter.

During his time in Belgium and Paris, he developed his fluency in French. His period of study in Edinburgh may have arisen due to his difficulty in finding a job in Scotland, which he put down to his youthful appearance. He extended his search into England and persuaded his old friend Daniel Gooch, who was now Locomotives Superintendent of the Great Western Railway, to give him an assistant's role in the locomotive department at Paddington in the autumn of 1840. He never returned to live in Scotland.

2

PADDINGTON AND THE
ESTABLISHMENT OF SWINDON

The Great Western main line to Bristol was incomplete when Sturrock joined Gooch at Paddington in the autumn of 1840. The line had opened to Maidenhead in June 1838 and reached Reading by March 1840. During July the line was extended to Farringdon Road, east of Swindon. In August the detached section from Bath to Bristol commenced operation.

Isambard Brunel, the engineer for the GWR, had appointed Gooch locomotive superintendent of the GWR in 1837. Unfortunately for Gooch, Brunel had already ordered locomotives to a specification which resulted in the manufacturers producing locomotives with excessively large driving wheels and small boilers and cylinders. Only the locomotives from the Vulcan Foundry and *North Star*, which had been designed by Robert Stephenson for another railway, were of use. Gooch notes: 'For many weeks my nights were spent in a carriage in the engine house at Paddington, as repairs had to be done to the engines at night to get them to do their work the next day.'[1] As a consequence of the problems with the locomotives, Gooch was required to report directly to the Board and not through Brunel. Gooch's report criticised Brunel's designs and alarmed the directors. However, Gooch gained the confidence of the Board and was permitted to design his own locomotives. He prepared drawings for two Classes of engines to be known as the Firefly and Sun Classes. The Great Western was probably the first railway to adopt a policy of standardisation.[2]

The Firefly Class of 2-2-2 express engines had 7ft driving wheels and were to be used on the relatively level line from Paddington to Swindon.[3] The Sun Class engines were also 2-2-2s, but with 6ft driving wheels to give extra power for the undulating line west of Swindon. Both Classes owed much to Stephenson's Star Class, which continued to be ordered alongside Gooch's own designs. The first *Firefly* was delivered in March 1840 from Jones Turner and the first *Sun* was delivered a month later from R.&W. Hawthorn. By the time Sturrock arrived eleven Firefly Class and four Sun Class locomotives had been delivered, in addition to the nineteen engines built to Brunel's specification and six Star Class locomotives from Robert Stephenson. Some of the early Brunel specification engines were already out of use.

Gooch appointed Sturrock without Brunel's consent. On 6 October 1840 Brunel wrote to Gooch:

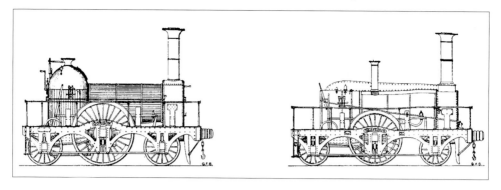

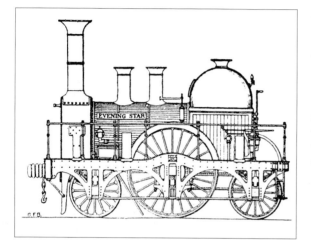

Above: Gorgon and *Hesperus* are examples of Firefly and Sun class 2-2-2s designed by Gooch and built by outside manufacturers between 1840 and 1842.

Left: Evening Star is one of Stephenson's Star class locomotives on which the GWR largely relied prior to the delivery of engines designed by Gooch.

Please let me know directly you come home that I may fix a time for our meeting, as on my return to this end of the line I find several things in the Locomotive department requiring explanation and which are at present quite unintelligible to me and very unsatisfactory.

The Directors disapproving some of the arrangements of the engines, on Sunday last and wishing for an explanation I sent for Andrews. I was surprised to find that he considered he was not responsible but referred me to Mr Sturrocks [sic] or some such name; he may or may not be a proper person and Andrews may or may not have proved himself efficient, but it can not be right that a man whose name neither I nor any of the Directors heard before should be appointed to any responsible situation or that any such important change should be made without my sanction and I should not have done it without the Directors' sanction, but that is a matter between the Directors and myself – you should look to me – A practical evil has resulted the probable consequences of which I am frightened to think of.

On Saturday I saw an engine on the line near the Scrubs sent to look for the 3 o'clock up train in which I was and which was very late; this engine started after the 6 out and without any special order from anybody but in consequence of some general order which Sturrock tells me is sufficient and returned on the wrong line. I cannot contemplate the dreadful results that might, I do not say it is probable, happen from such a general order and from such a particular case, without feeling the necessity of a total revision of our locomotive system and the necessity of taking the management more into my own hands than I have hitherto done, partly from my great confidence in you and partly from the necessity of devoting so much of my time to the works on the line.[4]

Top: The forecourt of the original Paddington station built under Bishop's Bridge. (Bourne's *Great Western Railway*)

Above: Interior of the engine shed at Paddington in Sturrock's time. (*Railway Magazine*, August 1907)

Sturrock's first and difficult meeting with Brunel took place at Paddington station, where the locomotive department was based. Paddington was a modest structure, for the GWR had planned to run its trains into Euston, a joint station with the London and Birmingham. Negotiations broke down in December 1835 and the GWR opted for an independent approach to London. The 1838 station used the arches of the new Bishop's Bridge to accommodate booking hall and office, waiting rooms and parcels depot. Carriages could pass through two of the central arches to be loaded onto and off the trains. When goods traffic started to develop, modest facilities were provided adjacent to Eastbourne Terrace in the station approach.

One of Gooch's first tasks on joining the GWR in August 1837 had been to prepare plans for engine houses at Paddington and Maidenhead.[5] The central portion of the Paddington engine house was a 130ft diameter roundhouse with a pair of straight sheds at each end. A series of workshops was situated to the north of the engine house between two sidings with connections to the arrivals platform. Eight radial roads on which engines could be stored were accessed through a 35ft central turntable. This engine house was Sturrock's first place of work with the GWR.

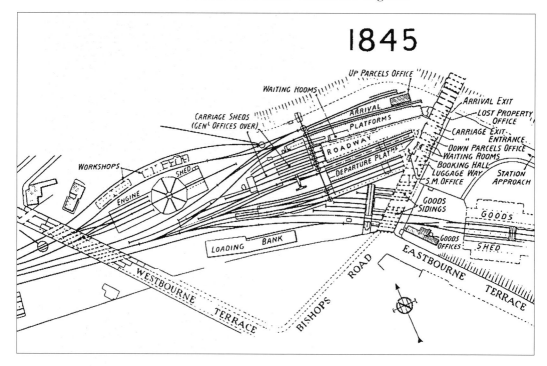

Paddington station layout around 1845. (MacDermot's *History of the Great Western Railway*)

With locomotives arriving at a rate of two per month, Sturrock supervised the testing of new locomotives and the training of drivers and firemen, a role he shared with Thomas Crampton, who had worked originally for Marc Brunel, Isambard's father, and joined the GWR in 1839. Crampton was born in Broadstairs on 6 August 1816 and was the same age as Gooch and Sturrock. He took out his first patent in 1843, the year before he left the GWR to work for Rennie. His locomotives were to be widely used in northern and eastern France, in Belgium and Germany; Sturrock was to adopt one of his patents on the Great Northern in later years. [6]

By July 1841 Sturrock and Crampton were training drivers in the use of the bank engine through the Box Tunnel. The missing link between Chippenham and Bath had opened on 30 June 1841. Sturrock wrote to Frederick Clarke, the traffic superintendent:

> Will you have the goodness to send instructions to Dixon to permit the Bank Engine to pop through the tunnel without the presence of Mr Crampton or myself, as we go to London tomorrow? Would you also authorise the policeman at Box station to allow the trains to proceed, without stopping, through the bridge at the crossing before arrival at Box, as for the future the trains are to be pushed by the Bank Engine? Instructions have been sent to all the enginemen so that they understand exactly how to conduct the train, as to speed etc, and today I am to show them personally how to drive.[7]

The opening of the Box Tunnel was not without mishap. As Gooch's memoirs indicate:

> Only one line of rails was completed through the tunnel the day we opened and the trains had therefore to work on a single line. I undertook to accompany all trains through the tunnel, and did so the 1st day and night, also the second day, intending to be relieved when the mail came down on the second night at about 11 o'clock. That night we had a very

Interior of Box Tunnel. (Bourne's *Great
Western Railway*)

narrow escape of a fearful accident. I was going up the tunnel with the last train up when
I fancied I saw some green lights (danger) placed as they were in the front of our trains. A
second's reflection convinced me it was the mail coming down. I lost no time in reversing
the engine I was on and running back to Box station with my train as quickly as I could,
when the mails came down close behind me. The policeman at the top of the tunnel had
made some blunder and sent the mails on when they arrived there. Had the tunnel not been
pretty clear of steam we must have met in full career and the smash would have been fearful,
cutting short my career also.[8]

On the same day in October 1840 that Brunel wrote to Gooch to complain about Sturrock's
appointment, the Board passed the following resolution: 'That the principle locomotive
station and repair shops be established at or near the junction with the Cheltenham and
Gloucester Union at Swindon.'[9] Gooch had convinced Brunel and the Board that the site
at Swindon was the best location. It was a central point for the repair shops and, although
nearer to Bristol than to London, was the best place to change engines and for servicing
the locomotives to be provided to work the Cheltenham line. The only likely drawback was
the absence of a water supply other than from the canal. A contract for the construction of
Swindon was approved by the Board in April 1841.[10] Bertram, one of Brunel's engineers,
was to supervise the construction and Sturrock to install the machinery.

During this period, Sturrock made the acquaintance of Caroline Sophia Fullerton, his
future wife. Her family came from Carstairs in Lanarkshire. Her father had been with the
East India Co. and had died in 1824. Sophia Fullerton, Caroline's mother, had returned to
London following her husband's death and lived in Marylebone, no great distance from
Paddington. Her brothers, William and Charles, who were born in June 1816 and October
1817, were out in India.

Caroline Fullerton, Sturrock's wife as a child, with her two brothers William and Charles in 1827. (Author)

The engine shed, engine house and erecting shop fitted out by Sturrock were described in detail by Bourne in 1845, some two years after the formal opening of the works in January 1843:[11]

> At some distance west of the passenger station, on the north side of the line, is the engine depot: its arrangements are upon a large scale, and capable of accommodating about a hundred engines: these consist of the engines in actual use, of the stock of spare engines, and of those undergoing repair. At this station every train changes its engine, so that from this circumstance alone, at least twice as many engines are kept here as at any other part of the line.
>
> The engine shed is a rectangular building, 490 feet long by 72 feet broad, and capable of holding upon its four lines of rails 48 engines and tenders... The engines standing here are all in serviceable condition, and a sufficient number of them are ready, with their steam up, to carry on the business of the Railway. In the centre of it and at right angles to this shed, and abutting against its northern side is the Engine house; this is an oblong room, 290 feet by 140 feet, and divided by two rows of columns into three compartments; the engines stand in the side compartments, transversely, as horses in the stalls of a stable; and the central part, 50 feet broad, is occupied by a large platform, travelling on wheels from one end of the house to the other, and by means of which an engine can be readily transferred between the central part and any one of the stalls.

To the east of the engine house or main repair shops were two blocks. The southern block immediately opposite the engine house contained the offices and stores. Gooch had his own office, bedroom and drawing office at the northern end of the top floor of this block.

The interior of the engine house at Swindon in 1845. (Bourne's *Great Western Railway*)

The northern block, which was closest to the line to Cheltenham, was also of two stories and housed the fitting shops. Tucked under the stairs of this block was a small office, about 10ft by 10ft, which Sturrock used and where he nearly lost his life.[12] A party of labourers was lugging a heavy piece of metal along the landing of the stairs, which formed the roof of Sturrock's office. A plank gave way; the piece of iron disappeared and, passing through the roof, fell on and smashed up the desk at which Sturrock was sitting.

Sturrock's relationship with Brunel was, for the most part, improving. In September 1842 Brunel invited Sturrock to draw up a specification and price list for a twenty-engine repair facility. However, a month later Brunel complained to Gooch about Sturrock taking action without proper authority:

> I understand from Mr Spiller today that he was about to make some alterations in the forge work as supplied by him under a contract in consequence of directions I think given by Sturrock. I have told him not only will I not pay for but I will not allow any alterations to be made without my written instructions. Let Sturrock understand this … take care that anything is done out of the ordinary without my first sanctioning it … I should not have objected as it happens but I might have had reasons for not having it tried or not thinking it worth the expense …

The Swindon works machinery was put into operation in November 1842, although the official opening did not take place till January 1843. Brunel was concerned that Sturrock should not see himself as permanently based at Swindon and sent Gooch another longwinded but considerate letter:[13]

I forgot to mention yesterday that it appears to me that Sturrock is settling himself at Swindon as if he were regularly appointed or were sure of being so as the head of the establishment. Such is by no means the case – I once inquired of you what you thought of Sturrock's capabilities for it – but I subsequently told you that the appointment of Swindon must come before the Board and that Sturrock must not consider himself as otherwise than merely erecting the tools and putting the shop to work – perhaps he does so understand his position but several little things have led me to think otherwise – and if I am right it would be a kindness in you to correct him – so far from his appointment being certain I have not myself made up my mind on the subject and have great doubts whether the directors are not likely to come to the conclusion that you yourself reside there. I have always assumed perhaps incorrectly that you would prefer remaining in London and have not broached the subject but remarks have been made which convince me that, when the question comes before the Board, they will all be of that opinion – and if that has not occurred to you before, it is well you should now think of it, but, while thinking of it, do not forget Sturrock and do not let him consider himself appointed and settled in a berth where certainly he is not.

Whether Sturrock was officially in charge or not, he was left to find the Swindon workforce. Swindon works was about a mile from the 'old' town of Swindon and Sturrock needed cottages close to the new works. An agreement with the contractors Rigbys required them to build 300 cottages at their own expense on land owned by the company. The cottages were to be leased to the company, which planned to recover the costs in rent from the employees.[14] The cottages were to be completed by December 1842 in time for the opening. The schedule was over-ambitious and about 130 were eventually built. The shortage was ameliorated by speculative private building, but there was general overcrowding in the village.[15]

Railway workers' cottages in Swindon New Town. (Images of England)

Caroline Fullerton in 1841, four years
before her marriage to Archibald. (Mrs
N.E. Vernon-Harcourt)

Railway workers had to be mobile in those days and an early recruit was Edward Snell,
who came to work at Swindon on 28 February 1843 at the age of twenty-two. Snell kept
a diary which gives a flavour of life at Swindon in Sturrock's time. Snell had served an
apprenticeship with Henry Stothert in Bristol and joined Swindon as a fitter. On his first
day he was introduced to Sturrock and records, 'Went over to the shops – introduced to
Mr Sterrick [sic] the foreman – young fellow and rather swellish.'[16]

In July Snell asked Sturrock for time off to see the launch of Brunel's iron ship at Bristol:
'The Great Britain steamship [is] to be launched today, so asked Sturrock's permission to go
down to Bristol to see it. Obtained leave and left the works at 7, cleaned and dressed and
proceeded to station. The train with Prince Albert reached Swindon about ¼ to 9, waited
3 minutes and on again – driven by Gooch and engine embellished with Royal Arms, Union
Jack etc'.[17] Snell did not bother to go to the launch but spent the day with friends in Bath.

In spite of the company's efforts to make Swindon a more attractive place to live and
work, it was not always successful. Snell handed in his notice:

> I had been heartily tired of Swindon for some time and had written to Mr G. Stothert to say
> so and he kindly applied to Mr Penn on my behalf, who agreed to employ me whenever I
> came to Greenwich, so I gave Mr Sturrock a week's notice last Friday week – on the Saturday
> last but one he sent me to Box to examine the bank engine…I slept on a bench till the steam
> was blown down and the fire dropped – I examined the firebox.

Snell did not find Greenwich quite as enjoyable as he had hoped and four months later
was back working for Sturrock as a draughtsman:

> Have been offered a situation as draughtsman at Swindon – spent time in London – on
> Friday left London by the 2 o'clock train and arrived at Swindon at 5. Called on Mr Sturrock
> and on Saturday at half past 6 commenced drawing a locomotive – full size in the pattern
> shop with Hawitt.

On Christmas Eve 1844 Sturrock gave Snell a pass to go and see his friends in Bath. Over subsequent months Snell progressed well and was made head draughtsman on £2 2s per week plus 'plenty of overtime.'[18] The fast expansion of the works in subsequent years gave good opportunities for promotion for many of the skilled craftsmen and children of railway workers.

Sturrock was established as manager of the Swindon works by April 1844, for his salary was brought up for consideration by the Board. Brunel was asked to prepare a report, but no decision on Sturrock's salary is recorded. The Board had considered building a house for Gooch at Swindon the previous year, but had been persuaded by Gooch that the new train service meant he could get to Swindon easily when needed and should remain in London. Sturrock was, therefore, sufficiently confident of his position to plan marriage. Caroline Fullerton and Archibald Sturrock were married on 30 January 1845 at St Marylebone Parish Church. Sturrock was recorded as living in Swindon and his future wife with her mother in the parish of St Marylebone.

With a growing workforce of over 300 and their accompanying families, the Board decided to provide for the educational and spiritual welfare of the people of New Swindon. Both Gooch and Sturrock were devoted churchmen, but the Board agreed that 'the company cannot feel justified in employing the funds of the company to any purpose connected with church and schools at Swindon unless sanctioned at general meeting.'[19] Even in a church-going age, the Board realised the shareholders were unlikely to support such a move other than in a personal capacity. Gibbs, an early director, had left £500 towards the construction of a church at Swindon. The Board agreed to set up a committee to seek subscriptions directly from shareholders for both church and school. By August 1843 £3,907 had been raised towards the cost of the church and £1,256 for a school. The company agreed to lend money to get the projects off the ground. The Chairman stated the new church was the 'best means of obtaining a sober, industrious, happy and contented class of worker'.[20] The church and school were completed by May 1845.

St Mark's Church, New Swindon, in October 1951; the church designed by Scott & Moffatt was opened in 1845. (Images of England)

The company was also conscious of the need to provide for the education of the men. In December 1843 the Board agreed to pay for books to the value of £30 for the Mechanics Institute library.[21] Gooch and Sturrock recalled the benefits they both obtained from the Watt Institution in Dundee. A full institute, of which Sturrock was treasurer, was established in 1844 'for the purpose of disseminating useful knowledge and encouraging rational amusement amongst all classes of people employed by the Great Western Railway.' A Locomotive Carriage and Wagon Sick Fund was established in the same year.

3

EXPANSION AND CONTRACTION AT SWINDON

During the period 1845–1847 Swindon works almost doubled in size, locomotive manufacture commenced on site and the gauge controversy preoccupied the senior officers of the company. As a consequence Sturrock had greater freedom to run the works than might normally have been expected. Expansion was followed by a period of recession, which, in 1850, caused Sturrock to look elsewhere to advance his career.

The substantial increase in the size of the works is illustrated in the accompanying 1849 plan. Most of the new buildings were completed between 1845 and 1847. Sturrock had responsibility for the installation of the machinery, with Bertram again handling the physical construction of the new buildings. Locomotive manufacture commenced whilst the works was being extended.

With the creation of the new turning shops in the block immediately to the left of the engine repair house, the old facilities were reserved for repairs and the new for locomotive manufacture. Sturrock was given a larger office in the bottom right-hand corner of the iron stores. This building and the office still exist today.

Perhaps the best indication of the size and scale of the facilities at Swindon is given in an article in the *Illustrated Exhibitor* of 1852. The machinery in use in the works at that time was largely installed between 1843 and 1847:

> The Smithery is a long range of buildings, containing the astonishing number of 176 forges, with all the appliances required for their full efficiency. Here all parts of a locomotive which are of wrought iron – as axles, piston-rods, connecting rods and the smaller pieces… are produced… One branch of this department is appropriated to the spring-makers, who forge and nicely temper the parts of which a spring is composed, and then fasten them together by an iron band.
>
> Close to the furnaces are two of Nasmyth's steam hammers, which are invaluable in forging large masses of iron… Our illustration shows the back of one of these furnaces, with the opening through which the men put the coal; the crane by which the iron is brought to the steam-hammer; and that vast congeries of 'sledge hammers' itself.[1]

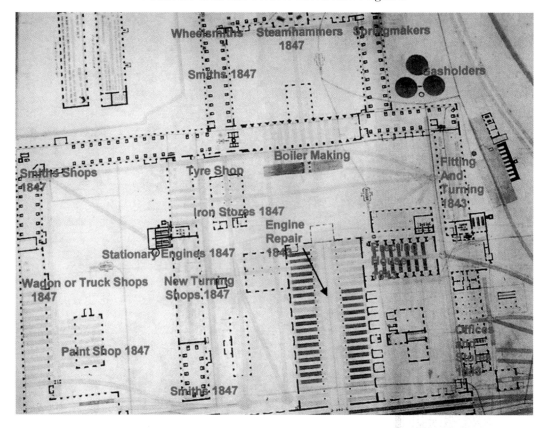

Plan of Swindon works in 1849 showing how the plant expanded between 1843 and 1847.

The decision to expand the works and to start locomotive manufacture was influenced by the railway mania which gripped Britain in 1844. The enthusiasm for new railways resulted in the mileage increasing from around 2,000 in 1844 to around 6,000 miles by the end of the decade. The GWR doubted whether the existing manufacturers could meet demand and a decision was taken to build six goods engines. Construction started in late 1845 with boilers supplied from outside. The Premier Class locomotives had sandwich frames, 5ft driving wheels and 16in by 24in cylinders. The last of the Class, *Jason*, entered service in May 1847.[2]

By building its own engines, the GWR could prove the advantages of the broad or 7ft ¼in gauge locomotives over the narrow or 4ft 8½in gauge engines in the 'gauge wars', which had commenced when the two gauges met for the first time at Gloucester in 1844 and the problems of transhipment of goods and passengers became evident. The narrow gauge won the first contest; the Birmingham & Bristol Railway was built to the 'narrow' gauge. In July 1845 a House of Lords decision favoured the broad gauge for lines from Oxford to Rugby, Worcester and Wolverhampton.[3]

A Commission was established in August 1845 to examine the relative merits of the two gauges. There were many witnesses for the narrow gauge, but it was left to Brunel, Gooch and Saunders, the company secretary of the GWR, to defend the interests of the broad gauge. The broad gauge representatives proposed a test in which the broad gauge engines proved their superiority and the selected narrow gauge engine came off the track. Fortunately Gooch and others who had been on the engine were not seriously hurt. The accident put an end to all further trials.[4]

The interior of Swindon works in 1852. (*Illustrated Exhibitor,* 1852)

Premier and *Bellerophon* were the first and fourth 0-6-0 locomotives built at Swindon under Sturrock's management using bought-in boilers. (Bird)

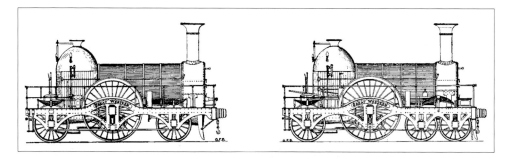

Great Western was built by Sturrock in 1846 to Gooch's design to prove the superiority of the broad gauge engines during the gauge controversy; due to too much weight on the leading axle, it was rebuilt as a 4-2-2. (Bird)

In January 1846, whilst the gauge commissioner's deliberated, Brunel and Gooch persuaded the GWR Board to build a larger engine to convince Parliament of the merits of the broad gauge. Time was short if the engine was to have proved itself by the next Parliamentary session. Gooch and Sturrock had a major challenge ahead with Sturrock bearing most of the day-to-day responsibility. *Great Western*, as the engine was to be called, was completed in thirteen weeks. Gooch states:

> I arranged for night and day work upon her and had her finished in 13 weeks from the day of getting the order, probably as quick a job as ever was done. She was first tried at the end of April 1846 and on 13th June we made a sensational trip with her to Bristol with a load of 100 tons.' The trip from London to Bristol was completed in 3 hours and 30 minutes.[5]

The 77 miles to Swindon were completed in seventy-eight minutes.

Great Western was originally built as a 2-2-2 with 8ft driving wheels and 4ft 6in carrying wheels, an outside slotted sandwich frame and a large 'Gothic' firebox. There proved to be too much weight on the leading axle, which broke whilst hauling a down train near Shrivenham. The frame was lengthened and two pairs of 4ft leading wheels added, making it in effect a 4-2-2. The boiler pressure was 100lb. *Great Western* continued to work till 1870 and completed 370,687 miles.[6] All parts for the *Great Western* were made in Swindon under Sturrock's overall guidance.

In his interview with the *Railway Magazine* shortly before his death, Sturrock recalled the gauge controversy:

The broad gauge of 7ft proved very superior to the narrow one of 4ft 8½in; the broad gauge engines, with their larger fireboxes, being able to drag much heavier loads, and having staying power to continue at higher speeds than those of the narrow gauge. Such was the information gained by the contest, but the greater length of railway having been constructed on the narrow basis, it was found impossible to adopt the wider one. I need hardly say I was much impressed by the facts elicited.[7]

Sturrock noted that Gooch visited Swindon every three or four weeks and described how they worked together:[8]

During 1847 to 1850 the improved engines were all built at Swindon under my supervision, Mr Gooch and myself having, after discussion, had the plans made in the offices at Swindon. I may mention that at that time Mr Gooch preferred living in London, though Swindon was the headquarters of the railway, and hence the whole authority over the offices as well as the engineering, was conferred upon me and was of great advantage to me as an education in my business.

Sturrock's notes are faulty. Manufacture of locomotives began in 1846. Swindon was the headquarters of the locomotive department, not of the company as a whole.

Between February 1846 and March 1850, Sturrock built forty-four locomotives at Swindon. Only one locomotive, *Avalanche*, was purchased from an external supplier, Stothert & Slaughter. The six coupled saddle tank was used as a banking engine. Premier and Prince Class locomotives continued to be produced during 1846, but in April 1847 Iron Duke was completed. The Iron Duke Class locomotives became the standard express locomotives of the GWR until 1892, when the broad gauge ended. Classic GWR broad gauge features including a domeless boiler, firebox with mid-feather and raised casing, first appeared on these engines. The 18in by 24in cylinders were enclosed in the smoke box casing with the steam pressure at 100lb, later raised to 115lb.

The introduction of locomotive manufacture required a larger workforce and Sturrock found the current pay rates were inadequate. In April 1845 Brunel was authorised to allow such an increase in wages to the fitters and other men at Swindon as, 'under existing circumstances of the trade, and in relation to the higher wages given elsewhere, he should think necessary to retain or secure the proper supply of labor in the factory'. Many staff salaries were also increased at the same time but locomotive department salary changes were not recorded. Increases were substantial – for example from £225 to £250 for the station superintendent.[9]

Iron Duke was the first of a class of twenty-nine 8ft singles on which Sturrock's 4-2-2 No.215 for the GNR was modelled. (Bird)

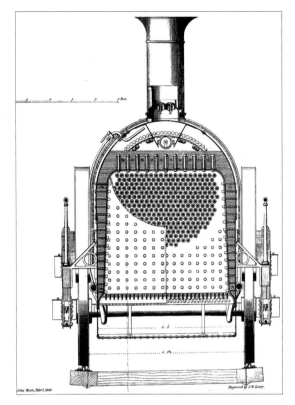

Iron Duke's boiler design. (Bird)

Gooch's contribution to the debate on the gauge question was recognised in January 1846, when he was presented with a cheque for £500 as a bonus and his basic salary increased from £700 per year to £1,000 per year. He had not had a pay rise since January 1841.[10] Sturrock had to wait another eight months for his pay rise, although the resulting increase was backdated to January 1846. His new salary was £400 per year and recognised his exceptional contribution in getting locomotive manufacturing launched. Brunel wrote to Sturrock on 13 August 1846:

I had great pleasure in recommending to the directors the increase they have made in your salary, but I need hardly say it was at the suggestion of Mr Gooch … You owe it to him as a very kind friend of yours as well as to the directors and to myself to exert yourself to conduct in the best possible manner the business entrusted to you. I have no doubt you will do so and do not suppose that I think it necessary to remind you of any such obligation but the responsibilities of your duties are very serious and the office a very important one and I feel that to pass over so natural an occasion for remarking upon them would almost be making light of a very serious subject. I believe you will continue to feel it a pleasure to devote your best exertions to the cause we are all embarked on.'[11]

The committee also agreed to construct a house for Sturrock as manager of Swindon works at a cost of £1,200.

Sturrock's pleasure at receiving a pay rise, a house and a congratulatory letter from Brunel was tempered by the death of his first child. Archibald John Sturrock was born on 7 July 1846 and died six weeks later on 14 August 1846, two days before the committee meeting which awarded his father a house and salary increase. Archibald John was buried in the churchyard of St Marks, New Swindon, on 17 August.

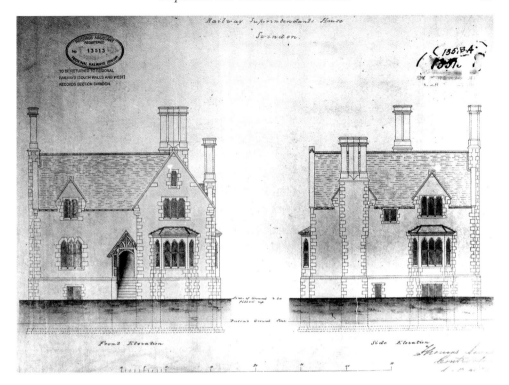

Elevations of Sturrock's house at Swindon. (Images of England)

The new house was a substantial three-storey building. The lower ground floor included a kitchen, scullery, coal and wine cellars, larder and storeroom, plus a servant's bedroom. Outside was a yard with brew house, copper, privy and further stores. The main entrance was on the first floor with two reception rooms, the master bedroom, dressing room and WC. There were five more bedrooms on the top floor. We also know from a later entry in Snell's diary that Sturrock had at least two servants.

By 1849 the recession, which had commenced in late 1847, was biting more vigorously. The workforce was reduced and production fell to six locomotives in the year. Three Iron Duke Classes were completed, plus the only two Bogie engines built at Swindon in Sturrock's time and *Bacchus*, a 0-6-0 rebuild from *Thunderer*, one of the Hawthorns ordered by Brunel.[12] The Bogie Class engines were 4-4-0 saddle tanks with inside sandwich frames. It appears these may have been intended as tender engines for the South Devon after the failure of the atmospheric system on that railway.[13] The second and last Swindon Bogie engine was produced in September 1849. No further engines were completed until March 1850, the month preceding Sturrock's departure, when Iron Duke *Hirondelle* came out of the works.

Sturrock was increasingly perceived as the company's representative in the local community. Most of the workforce was under his care; he had to deal with the social and domestic issues of concern to the people of New Swindon and took charge of the cottage estate. His wife would also have been expected to play her part in the community. In his works management role he was supported by two men, Edward Snell, whose role widened from that of head draughtsman to a general assistant manager position,[14] and Dougal Mack. Mack is described as an assistant manager.[15]

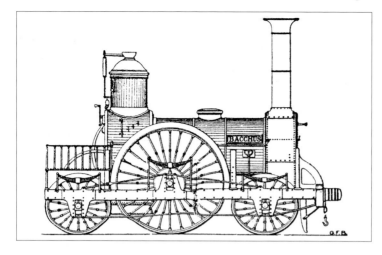

Bacchus, an 0-6-0 built in 1849 from *Thunderer* one of the unsuccessful locomotives ordered by Brunel. (Bird)

Efficient operation of the locomotives required Sturrock to concern himself with all aspects of engine efficiency. Gooch and Sturrock used the Firefly locomotive *Mentor* to conduct experiments during 1846–47 on the use of Dr Ritterbandt's method for preventing the build-up of scale by the use of Chloride of Ammonia. Sturrock's handwritten note of September 1847 appears on the original 1846 statistics compiled by a foreman.[16] Economy in all things was required, as the recession deepened.

In May 1849, Gooch wrote to Sturrock concerning repairs to *Briareus*, an 1846 Premier Class locomotive.[17]

> The fire was in Briareus when I got back on Tuesday so that I could not examine the box but I am told that the ends of the bottom row or rows of tubes have given 3/16th of an inch into the plate. This cannot happen without the tube plate is sprung and if it is so I think most likely the stays you mention are broken.
>
> I have not ordered any tubes for the bigger engines. You had better cut off the 2½ inches from those we have in stock and not order more. In fact get the stocks of everything we use worked down to the lowest possible amount, as I expect we shall be charged with interest on the value in hand. There are few cases in which we cannot wait for the delivery of tubes, after it is certain we want them.

The success of Gooch and Sturrock in reducing running costs is illustrated in the table below, which compares performance at each running shed and shows the benefits of a footplate bonus plan which Gooch had introduced.[18]

COKE CONSUMPTION	Early 1843 lb per mile	September 1849 lb per mile
Paddington	40.44	27.79
Slough	38.31	14.41
Reading	48.16	26.10
Swindon	39.63	23.70
Cheltenham	39.81	22.91
Bristol	36.91	23.80
Goods	57.50	63.25

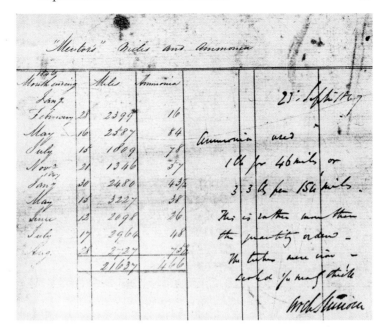

A comment from Sturrock on the impact of the experimental use of ammonia in the boiler of *Mentor*, a Firefly class locomotive, in September 1847. (National Archives)

The Slough figures were achieved by the use of a tank engine and a change in duty. The Goods figures are misleading. Many trains were double-headed in 1849 and the load per mile increased more than the fuel consumption.

The confidence Gooch and Brunel had in Sturrock's abilities is illustrated in a letter dated 31 May 1848, when Sturrock took charge in Gooch's absence. 'You have full power to give such orders as are necessary at the different stations on the line and Mr Brunel has kindly promised to give you assistance and advice in any case of importance. However I hope you will not need to interfere with the foremen.'[19]

Housing remained a major issue. A report by Sturrock showed there were still only 241 houses available. With a total of 1,735 inhabitants, there was an average of 7.19 people per house. There were five houses and two shops still incomplete and twelve houses ordered but not built. Sturrock had applications for 119 houses and the Station Superintendent needed twelve. Twenty houses were occupied by individuals who did not work in the factory.[20] However, the housing problem disappeared as the recession led to massive redundancies. In November 1847 between 300 and 400 men lost their jobs.[21] Short-time working encouraged workers to move to cheaper but less convenient housing provided by speculative builders.

Sturrock had also to deal with drainage problems on the estate. Gooch was concerned about cholera and wrote to Sturrock:[22]

> I enclose a notice for the workmen – what we must do is to give notice in writing to each of the men whose house requires cleaning the drains. You had better see what can be done with those that are stopped up, any of the houses empty in the street where you say there is a bad smell or one of the boards had better be taken up in the floor to see if any water is standing there … The rubbish heaps must be cleared away. If the regular scavenger does not do it on being told, have it done and I will get it settled who is to pay for it.

Little medical support was provided in the early years, but in November 1847 Gooch persuaded the Board to provide a free house for a doctor, who would attend accidents at the works. Gooch explained that many railway companies paid for the services of a doctor and indicated the LNWR paid £50 per year. In the light of the GWR's present difficult circumstances, Gooch suggested a free house to which the Board readily agreed. The rent of a house might have been about £30 per year; but with the numbers in the works being cut, it is probable the short-term cost was negligible, since houses are likely to have been vacant.

A formal organisation, the GWR Medical Fund Society, was founded in December 1847 along lines developed by Gooch and Sturrock. The works manager was to be ex-officio president, so Sturrock assumed the role from 1847 until he left in early 1850. All workers had to pay a subscription which varied with their status. The doctor received a free house plus a capitation fee of 10s to 13s per person depending on the numbers employed in the works, between 500 and 700. Out of this capitation fee, the doctor had to supply bandages, splints and other materials of his trade. In March 1849 a local doctor, Dr Sealy, complained that 'men were threatened with dismissal if they did not sign for the one medical man approved by Sturrock'. Gooch stated this was untrue, but that the company was only willing to pay for one medical man and workers would have to pay if they wanted Dr Sealy to attend.[23]

As the recession mounted in 1848, there was one piece of good news in the Sturrock household. Sturrock's second child was born on 21 March 1848. Caroline Christina Sophia Sturrock was baptised at St Mark's. New Swindon on 19 April 1848.

Sturrock had to involve himself in sensitive matters concerning the use of the cricket ground. The company was happy to encourage temperance but did not want to appear to sponsor meetings of a political or religious nature. Gooch wrote to Sturrock in July 1848:

> To prevent any wrong use being made of the sanction the Council of the institution have given for the meeting in the Cricket Grounds tomorrow, will you be good enough to let those interested in the meeting know that the Council can only give such sanction to lectures or meetings when their rules are acceded upon [viz] that no political or religious subjects can be introduced; it would also be better for you to see the parties who are to lecture and point out to them that these are the rules ...

The institution to which Gooch refers is the Mechanics Institute which continued to flourish. Gooch was president, the vicar Joseph Mansfield vice-president and Sturrock treasurer. During 1848, 420 volumes were added to the library to bring the total number of books up to 1,650 volumes. Newspapers and periodicals taken included *The Times*, *Illustrated London News*, *Punch*, the *Railway Chronicle* and Johnson's *Cottage Gardener*. Scots papers included the *Glasgow Citizen* and the *Edinburgh Review*. Chess and draughts were popular and the brass band, the Quadrille band and the Choral Class had been well attended. Four concerts had been given and over twenty lectures on technical and other subjects, including emigration to Australia and Texas. Classes were organised on mechanical drawing as well as art. The baths were a valued facility and over 500 members and their families went on an outing by train to Oxford. The income, derived largely from subscriptions and apprentice's fees, was £215 6s 3d. Intriguingly the printed accounts do not add up correctly, with the receipts being overstated by 5s. We shall never know whether this was a mistake by Sturrock or the printer!

The recession continued to mount during 1849 and a flavour of the changing atmosphere is given in later extracts from Snell's diary:

5 May 1849:

> Everything [is] going on the same as usual. About 200 hands employed under me building new shops – all busy and bustle – this lasted till October 1848 when our reverses began. Had to sack all the hands and had 3 or 4 sweeping sacks through the shops – since then things have been generally getting worse and worse. This present week Mr Sturrock announced his

intention of docking my pay from £2. 15s per week to £2, so today I gave him a fortnight's notice and mean to start early in June for New York.

15 May 1849:

Left the service of the company for ever having discovered that length of service was of no use and that the only recommendation on the Great Western was being a Scotchman – I found that although my wages were docked to £2, Budge's were only reduced to £2 10s and as he had been there only two years why I of course would stand it –however on the whole I have not done too badly at Swindon. I started there as a fitter on 24s per week and before I left had charge of the whole factory under Mr Sturrock. I had been successively fitter, erector, inspector of engines, head draughtsman, foreman of the various shops one after another and afterwards assistant manager of the whole factory. I received a very decent testimonial from Mr Gooch on leaving in which he regretted he couldn't offer me sufficient inducement to remain in service. He countermanded Sturrock's order for stoppage of my pay, but I wouldn't remain and made up my mind to go to New York.

In the end Snell went to Australia and continued to receive news of Swindon from his friend Routeledge. John Budge took over Snell's role as chief draughtsman and later became a sub manager. Snell records in his Australian diary:

Routeledge's letters [are] full of news principally bad –work getting slacker and slacker at Swindon – the men making only 4½ days per week and a great number of them sacked. Sewell at the stores got into a scrape for writing a letter to Herapaths journal about Gooch and Sturrock's salaries – had the sack but wouldn't take it (Scotchman like) and eventually got off with a reprimand.

Routeledge wrote again a month later in October 1849 (diary entry 12 April 1850):

Mrs Sturrock is in the family way again [Gordon Sturrock was born the following May]. The directors examining into the loco accounts pretty severely, have overhauled the accounts four times. Two of Sturrock's servants nearly suffocated by charcoal on the night of October 15th – that day spent as a general thanksgiving day on account of the cessation of cholera.

Snell also notes from one of Routeledge's letters that: 'Budge does all he can to point out any little faults in my [Snell's] drawings etc. now I have left, which Sturrock does not think very gentlemanly.' In spite of Budge's behaviour, Snell kept in touch and in September 1858, when back in England, went to see some old friends who had joined Sturrock at the GNR including Budge at King's Cross, Charles Sacré at Peterborough and Froward at Boston.

Swindon was struggling to find work. Much of the machinery bought in 1847 had never been used. Brunel tried to find work for Swindon and in December 1848 Brerton, one of Brunel's main assistants, wrote to Sturrock with an order for some springs for one of Brunel's bridge projects.[24] Gooch prepared a more comprehensive report than was usual on the state of the engine stock in November 1849. Sturrock signed off what might well have been his last report sheet on the engine stock at Swindon on 26 October 1849.[25]

With a second child on the way, Sturrock did not wish to accept a pay cut. He had received exceptional training and responsibility at Swindon. He had gained the respect of both Gooch and Brunel and shown himself capable of handling a workforce of more than 1,000. He could claim some credit for the GWR's success in building and operating locomotives. He was well equipped to look for a locomotive engineer's position and the following advertisement in *The Times* on 6 March 1850 caught his attention:

Friday October 26 1849

(see over for explanation of date)

REPORT OF THE STATE OF THE ENGINES.

Engines working in good order.	Engines which can be at work in	Days.	Engines requiring more than two Weeks repairs.	Engines come in Shed, and the Repairs required.
Damon	Stag		Pegasus	Bellerophon gone to Paddington
Orion	Thun		Hecla	Goliath — Didcot
Mentor	Gorgon		Stentor	Avalanche — Box
Peri	Falcon		Minos	
Priam			Spitfire	
Milo			Vulture	
Bright Star	Painting & Read.		Atlas	
Pollux	Ganymede		Exe	
Pyracmon	Bellona		Panther	Have no reports for
Ajax	North Star		Aurora	Wolf, Zebra, and Behemoth.
————	Sultan		Antelope	A.S.
Stock	Greyhound		Djerid	
Gt Britain	Hesperus		Elephant	
Iron Duke	Mazeppa		Lynx	
Gt Western	Virgo		Firebrand	
Lightning			Pasha	
Shooting Star			Etna	
Fire Fly	Repairs.		Royal Star	
Evening Star	Achilles	10	Proserpine	
Dog Star	Sun		Tityos	
Leopard	Eclipse }	Tank	Sampson	
Actaeon	Vesta	6	Goliah	
Castor	Medusa	10	Leo	
Elk	Teign	8	Comet	
Load Star	Arab	4	Gazelle	
Stromboli	Centaur	6	Premier	
Eagle	Javelin	8	Vesuvius	
Mercury	Stiletto	14	Wolf	
Dart	Rocket	4	Zebra	
Hercules	Swallow	6	Behemoth	
Mammoth				
Brontes				
Caliban			Signed,	
(continued in next Column.)				Foreman.

Sturrock's report to Gooch on the state of the engine stock in October 1849. (National Archives)

Swindon in 1847; *Fire Brand*, a Firefly class locomotive of 1840, is passing in front of the station superintendent's house. Sturrock's house is in the centre of the picture with the New Town cottages, rectory and church to the right. The picture illustrates clearly the unusual construction of the broad gauge line and the primitive signalling. (Swindon Museum & Art Gallery)

GREAT NORTHERN RAILWAY – To Locomotive Engineers – The directors of this company are desirous of ENGAGING a LOCOMOTIVE ENGINEER from the end of this month, who is competent to manage the whole of the locomotive establishment. His salary will be £500 per annum with a prospective advance. Applications will be received on or before Monday the 15th day of March instant. They must be accompanied by testimonials as to capability, character, and conduct and addressed under cover to the Secretary of the Great Northern Railway Company, 14 Moorgate, London, and marked on the outside 'Application for the Office of Locomotive Engineer.'

On 8 March 1850 Sturrock arranged for a private meeting with Brunel following the latter's attendance at a GWR expenditure committee. Sturrock told Brunel he wished to apply for the recently advertised vacancy for a locomotive engineer at the Great Northern. Brunel agreed to see William Cubitt, Brunel's opposite number on the GNR, for he wrote to Sturrock three days later:[26]

There can be no reason why you should not conditionally seek interest with the directors of the Great Northern Railway but I think I would delay sending in a formal application till Friday next or even the last day Monday. I have seen Mr Cubitt and have written to Mr Russell and I can see you on Friday.

Brunel met Sturrock again on Friday 12 March at his Duke Street office at 4.30 p.m. He confirmed he would support Sturrock's application. Sturrock wrote in his memoir:

Mr Brunel took a great interest in my appointment. Pending my application and the decision of the Great Northern Railway Board Mr Brunel wrote to me that I must take steps to counteract the influence of a letter which had been written by one of my competitors showing that he could construct engines that would work very economically. I replied that all Locomotive Engineers of my position knew very well how to build engines, but that the man who would succeed in producing the greatest economy was he who would use 150 lbs steam. He wrote me that I was quite right, but 'for God's sake not to tell the Great Northern Board so', for if I did so they would look upon me as a very dangerous man and would not appoint me.

Following the second meeting, Brunel wrote to the Great Northern directors:

> At the request of my friend Mr Sturrock, I address you to express my opinion of his qualifications for the appointment of General Superintendent of the Locomotive Department on your railway, for which he is a candidate.
>
> It is with great regret that I assist him in such an application as likely to deprive the Great Western Railway Company of services which I value highly, but a general reduction which has taken place in the salaries of the Officers of that company has compelled him, in justice to himself, to seek some other appointment than that which he now holds with credit to himself and advantage to the company.
>
> Mr Sturrock entered the service of the Great Western Railway Company in 1840 and since 1842 has been the Resident Superintendent of our principal locomotive establishment at Swindon.
>
> As a young man of ability, industry and integrity with experience and a perfect knowledge of his department, and a gentleman, I can strongly recommend him. Without disparagement to others who may be candidates I do not believe that you can select one who will bring so much ability and desire to ensure the utmost economy in every detail and perfection generally in the management of the Locomotive Department of a Railway.
>
> I am Gentlemen Your Obedient Servant
> IK Brunel

Sturrock was less harshly treated than the average worker in the cottage estate. He and his family stayed on in their house in Swindon till after the birth of their second child, Gordon David, on 10 May 1850. Sturrock continued to campaign to the end to keep his full salary. A Board minute of May 1850 states, 'The Secretary is instructed to inform Mr Gooch that the Directors can not feel justified in paying Mr Sturrock who quits the service at any higher scale than the amount of his reduced salary for his period of service after 31st March until he left to join the GNR.'[27]

4

ESTABLISHING THE GNR
LOCOMOTIVE DEPARTMENT

The Executive Committee of the Great Northern Board met on 19 March 1850 to consider forty-one applications for the post of locomotive engineer. The vacancy had arisen as a result of the sudden departure of Edward Bury, who had combined the role of locomotive engineer with that of general manager. Bury had been accused by a supplier of not accepting the lowest tender for carriage wheels and axles and for favouring his own firm of Bury, Curtis & Kennedy. Bury declined to explain his conduct to the Board and submitted his resignation on 18 February 1850. Fred Parker, the works manager based at Boston, was put in temporary charge of the locomotive department.

The Executive Committee selected four applicants to meet the Board on 27 March 1850. Sturrock's three rivals were: George Harrison, locomotive superintendent of the Scottish Central, with extensive experience in France prior to the revolution of 1848; Francis Trevithick, who was locomotive superintendent of the Northern Division of the London North Western; and John Dewrance, who had been locomotive engineer of the Liverpool & Manchester. Although Sturrock was the only one of the four without experience at locomotive engineer level, the reputation of Brunel and of the Great Western helped to secure him the position. The four candidates were called into the meeting. Sturrock was advised of his appointment. The others were thanked and invited to submit their expenses.

Sturrock immediately accepted the position, but indicated he would need to make up his accounts at Swindon before joining the GNR full time. He attended executive committee meetings on 9 and 23 April to discuss the requirements for locomotives for the opening of the line to London. On 16 April he agreed to take charge of the rolling stock and make a report, albeit without any uplift in salary. The secretary accompanied Sturrock to the Boston offices to take charge of the locomotive department on 24 April.

The GNR was in the course of construction when Sturrock joined. The Board had decided to concentrate first on the line from Peterborough to Lincoln via Boston, which opened in October 1848. Known as the 'Loop' line, this was extended to Gainsborough in 1849. Revenue could be generated from this line, which was relatively easy to build, while construction of the line from Peterborough to London proceeded. Additional revenue was obtained from the East Lincolnshire Railway, which the GNR had leased in 1847 and on which traffic had commenced on 1 March 1848. The East Lincolnshire ran from Great Grimsby to a connection with the 'Loop' line at Boston.

At the same time the GNR was proceeding with a section of line from Retford, north to Doncaster and on to Askern, where a connection was made with the Lancashire & Yorkshire Railway in September 1849. This provided access to Wakefield and Leeds. York could be reached via the York & North Midland Railway. From Retford a connection using the Manchester, Sheffield & Lincolnshire Railway (MSLR) enabled through running to Lincoln. By the spring of 1850 the GNR was operating 143 miles of its own track and had the use of about 50 miles of line owned by other railways. Services could be provided between Doncaster and Peterborough via Retford, Lincoln and Boston. Eastern Counties and London North Western trains provided onward links to London from Peterborough. The journey time from Lincoln to London was reduced by an hour.

The GNR's own line from London to Peterborough was in the course of construction. Due to bad weather in the winter of 1849–50, the opening of this line from a temporary station at Maiden Lane had been delayed till late summer. Sturrock's first task was to ensure the GNR had the necessary locomotives to open the through services from London to Doncaster and York via the 'Loop' line through Boston and Lincoln. Contracts had still not been placed for the construction of the major portion of the direct 'Towns' line from just north of Peterborough through Grantham and Newark to Doncaster.

The GNR had a fleet of eighty-one locomotives when Sturrock arrived.[1] Forty of an order for fifty Sharp 2-2-2 tender engines had been delivered. The 'Sharpies', as they were affectionately known, had been ordered by Bury's predecessor, Benjamin Cubitt, who had died in office aged fifty-three in January 1848. Cubitt had also ordered twenty 2-2-2 singles from R.&W. Hawthorn of the firm's standard pattern and fifteen 0-4-2 'luggage' engines, also from Hawthorns. All the goods engines and twelve of the 'small' Hawthorn singles had been delivered by April 1850. In addition Cubitt had ordered twelve 0-4-0 goods engines, six from Bury, Curtis & Kennedy and six from Fairbairns, all of which had been delivered. Bury had also built a 2-4-0 passenger engine prototype for use on the GNR main line. Numbered 100, this was an improved version of the standard Bury Curtis passenger locomotive.

Locomotives delivered by April 1850:

Class	GNR Numbers	Maker	Nos	Designer
2-2-2 Tender	1–40	Sharp	40	Firm's standard
'Small' Hawthorn 2-2-2	51–62	Hawthorn	12	Firm's standard
0-4-2 Goods	101–115	Hawthorn	15	Firm's standard
0-4-0 Goods	121–126 127–132	Bury Curtis Fairbairn	6 6	Bury
2-4-0 Passenger	100	Bury Curtis	1	Bury prototype
2-4-0 Ex Contractors	133	C Tayleur	1	Firm

Sturrock was committed to acquire four 2-4-0 locomotives from the 'Loop' line contractors, Peto & Betts, one of which had been transferred to the GNR by the time Sturrock joined. More regrettably, he was also committed to acquire twenty passenger and thirty goods engines, which had been ordered on 26 March, the day before

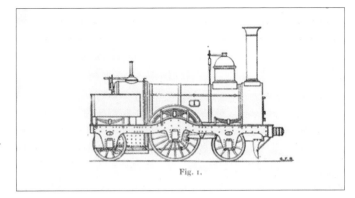

Fig. 1.

Forty out of an order for fifty Sharp 2-2-2s had been delivered when Sturrock arrived; he noted in his copy of Bird, 'raised pressure to 120lbs, lopped sides, turned round eccentrics.' (Bird)

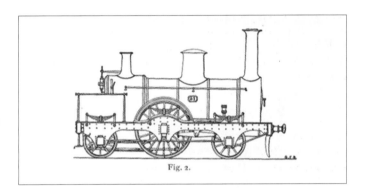

Fig. 2.

Twelve out of an order for twenty Hawthorn 2-2-2s had been delivered by March 1850; they became known as 'small' Hawthorns to distinguish them from the later Sturrock 2-2-2s also built by Hawthorn. (Bird)

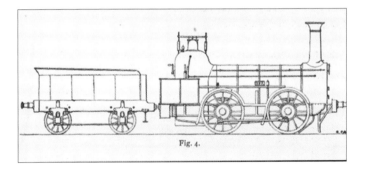

Fig. 4.

Six 0-4-0s were supplied by Fairbairn probably on behalf of Bury during 1848–49. (Bird)

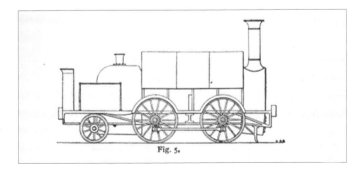

Fig. 5.

Sturrock converted the Bury 0-4-0s to 0-4-2 saddle tanks to create a more useful engine. (Bird)

his appointment was agreed. E.B. Wilson of Leeds had received an order for fifteen passenger and fifteen goods engines. R.&W. Hawthorn were to supply five passenger and fifteen goods engines. Sturrock immediately took steps to have these locomotives modified.

The thirty goods engines, numbered 116-120 and 134-158, were delivered between October 1850 and January 1851. An additional Wilson engine numbered 167 was added to the Class. Sturrock had the fireboxes enlarged, the cylinders increased to 16in diameter and the boiler pressure increased from 90 to 100lb per square inch. Sturrock reckoned the cost should be about £51 18s per engine. The manufacturers wanted £150. After three months of discussion, the Executive Committee agreed on 25 July 1850 to £100 per engine.

Sturrock made more substantial changes to the twenty passenger locomotives ordered on 26 March 1850. Sturrock had the locomotives constructed with outside plate frames. The boilers were modified to operate at a pressure of 120lb per square inch and the cylinder diameters increased. Sturrock was bringing his GWR broad gauge experience to narrow gauge locomotives. Sturrock reckoned the extra cost should be about £316 on locomotives originally priced at £1,775, a substantial increase. Hawthorns, who built five of the Class, asked for £325 and Sturrock suggested this was reasonable. Wilson demanded £350. The Class 71 2-4-0s were delivered between April and September 1851 and were used extensively for the Great Exhibition traffic of 1851. Some of the Class remained in service till the 1890s.

Sturrock's freedom to develop locomotives to his own design was, therefore, severely curtailed in his early years by the advance orders placed prior to his arrival. He was committed to a further seventy-two locomotives when he joined in April 1850, in addition to the eighty-one already delivered:

Class	GNR Numbers	Maker	Nos	Designer
Sharp 2-2-2 Tender	41-50	Sharp	10	Firm's standard
'Small' Hawthorn 2-2-2	63-70	Hawthorn	8	Firm's standard
Class 116 5 foot 0-6-0 Goods	116-120 134-143 144-158 & 167	Hawthorn Hawthorn EB Wilson	31	Bury modified by Sturrock
Contractors' 2-4-0	159-161	Tayleur and Hick	3	Purchased second hand, later 042
Class 71 2-4-0	71-75 76-90	Hawthorn EB Wilson	5 15	Bury modified by Sturrock

As Sturrock could make only limited changes to the locomotive fleet for the opening to London, he focussed on the provision of maintenance facilities. He also started to build a management team to help run his department. Appropriate pay and conditions had to be established for the workforce, which recognised the GNR's need for economy, but still secured maintenance and footplate men of the required calibre.

Ordered by Cubitt in 1842, No.112 was rebuilt by Stirling in October 1869 and received a new boiler in 1883; the tender is believed to be a Sturrock design and is now attached to the Stirling 4-2-0 at the NRM.

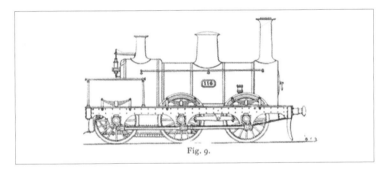

The Class 116 0-6-0s, which had been ordered the day before Sturrock's appointment, were modified by him prior to delivery. (Bird)

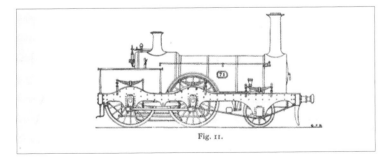

The Class 71 2-4-0s were ordered the day before Sturrock was appointed; they were substantially modified by Sturrock prior to delivery. (Bird)

Prior to Sturrock's appointment, the Board had established a committee to consider whether the maintenance of locomotives or rolling stock or both should be handled in-house or contracted out. Contracting out was a not uncommon policy on smaller railways. The committee had discussed inviting Mr Daniel Gooch of the GWR and his brother John of the London & South Western to examine the locomotives and tenders and advise on future policy. Mr A. Martin and Mr J.H. Beattie, both from the London & South Western, were to be asked to examine the rolling stock. A decision on these proposals was deferred pending the appointment of a new locomotive engineer.

Sturrock's first action on arriving at Boston was to re-arrange the existing maintenance facilities, which had been planned by Bury in 1848. To achieve better supervision, locomotive department activities were concentrated under Fred Parker, the foreman, in the main building and the permanent way team were provided with the building once used by the carriage department. He obtained permission to recruit a carriage inspector at £150 to £180 per year. He dismissed the contractors responsible for washing carriages and handed the work to the porters. Sturrock suggested better wood should be used for the sides of coal wagons and he recommended new draw gear and simpler, less expensive axle boxes to prevent overheating. He experimented with enlarging coal wagons to carry 6 tons and converted coal wagons to carry passengers on the slowest trains at half a penny per mile between Boston and Lincoln. The aim was to drive the steamers off the river Witham as they were damaging the banks. The fourth-class service ran till August 1863, many years after the steamers had been withdrawn.

In May 1850, Seymour Clarke, Sturrock's former colleague at the GWR, was appointed general manager, with responsibility for the line superintendent, minerals superintendent, storekeeper and goods manager. The enginemen reported to Sturrock, but once out on the line, had to take instructions from traffic department staff under Seymour Clarke and his line superintendent, John Denniston. The chairman advised the shareholders in August 1850 that Clarke and Sturrock were likely to turn out to be most valuable servants to the company. 'We have got two exceedingly good men for less money than we paid to one before.'[2]

The other members of the senior management team were James Mowatt, company secretary, and Joseph Cubitt, the engineer responsible for the permanent way and civil engineering. Sir William Cubitt, Joseph's father, remained consulting engineer. Co-ordination between the chief officers was achieved through their attendance at regular Board and Executive Committee meetings under the part-time chairman, Edmund Denison. There was no managing director position after Captain Laws gave up the role in 1848 and no separate locomotive committee till 1866.

In preparation for the planned opening to London on 7 August 1850, Sturrock obtained approval for the appointment of a locomotive foreman for London at a salary of up to £180 a year. At the Board meeting on 9 July 1850, Sturrock presented details of his former colleague at the GWR, John Budge, who had served his apprenticeship with Sturrock at the Dundee Foundry. Budge was appointed at a salary of £170 on the basis of a testimonial from Sturrock and joined the GNR on 23 July, a fortnight before the opening to London.

Boston was only intended to be a temporary base for the locomotive department. Preliminary discussions on the location for the main workshops took place at 11 June 1850 Executive Committee meeting. Sturrock was asked to get together with the Cubitts, Seymour Clarke and Mowatt to consider the location and scope of the workshops and report back. The officers came to a unanimous conclusion that Peterborough was the most appropriate location, due to its central position in the GNR system. There should be shed room for fifty to sixty engines and repair shops for sixty to sixty-five engines. Aware of the need for economy, the officers' committee suggested construction should be phased, with carriage and wagon facilities remaining at Boston for the present. The Executive Committee recommended the proposal to the Board on 25 July 1850, which referred the matter to a sub-committee of directors to examine the locality and check whether suitable land was available at Peterborough.[3]

In the light of the Board's apparent intention to set the main repair facilities in Peterborough, Sturrock moved his wife and family to 108 Priestgate, Peterborough in the summer of 1850. His son Gordon, his two-year-old sister Caroline, their mother and servants settled in the centre of Peterborough, a few minutes walk from the station.

A committee to report on the necessary arrangements for repairing shops was not established till February 1851. The committee took advice from the locomotive engineers of the Midland, York & North Midland, London & South Western, London North Western, Brighton & South Coast and Great Western; it heard the views of the locomotive manufacturer, E.B. Wilson, and Thomas Brassey, the contractor for the line to London. The committee met again on 9 May 1851 to hear the views of the officers, including Seymour Clarke and Sturrock. All except one director, Parker, voted for Peterborough. A number of engineers were to be invited to design the repair facilities.

Five days later the Board agreed the committee's proposals with one major exception. Eight Board members voted for Doncaster and only three continued to support Peterborough. The chairman, Edmund Denison, had lobbied on behalf of Doncaster. Sturrock and the Cubitts were asked to suggest which engineers should submit plans.

The Board also agreed to look at a proposal from Wilson to undertake all the company's repairs under contract for ten years for three pence per mile. Sturrock was to report on the proposal and tried to bury the idea. Wilson wrote twice more to the chairman in June and November 1851, when Sturrock was told to talk the idea through with Wilson. The Board rejected Wilson's proposal at its December meeting.

On 3 June 1851 the Board reaffirmed its choice of Doncaster. The Cubitts and Sturrock were instructed to draw up plans for the works for the next Board. The suggestion that external engineers should advise on the plans was dropped. It took Joseph Cubitt some three months to prepare plans, which were submitted to the 23 September Board and approved. The estimated cost of the buildings was £45,000 and Sturrock indicated his machinery needs for Doncaster would be about £33,292. The Board reviewed again the plans for Doncaster as instructed back in September. Sturrock must have despaired at the slow progress.

Tenders for Doncaster were examined in March 1852 and the contract placed with Arthur and George Holme of Liverpool, who had come in with a price 11 per cent below the estimate, on 4 May 1852. Tenders for stationary engines and boilers went to James Carmichael. Whitworths and Nasmyth received orders for tools and a steam hammer. Carmichael also secured the contract for shafting for the new repair facilities.

Clerical staff moved from Boston to Doncaster in the summer of 1852. Sturrock's Board reports were sent from Doncaster from September onwards. The annual report of February 1853 predicted the shops will be 'in full operation during the next spring'. Between June and December 1853 around 700 men were moved from Boston to Doncaster, so that by the year end the works or 'Plant' employed around 950 men and the population of Doncaster had increased by about 2,500.[4] Housing was in short supply and the Boston men did not think much of the shops and other facilities in Doncaster. In May 1853 Sturrock gave an 'entertainment' for Carmichaels' men, who had installed the 40hp plant, which had operated successfully when first fired with no need for modifications.[5] By December 1853 Sturrock was receiving his first complaints about smoke from the Plant.

The two windows of Sturrock's office from 1852 still overlook twin rail tracks used for storing locomotives; now known as Denison House much of the building was used for turning and carriage repairs in Sturrock's time. (Author)

Whilst Doncaster was being built, Sturrock also gave attention to the provision of adequate maintenance facilities at Peterborough and London. Although major overhauls would be handled in Doncaster, routine maintenance of both locomotives and rolling stock would take place in London, Boston and Peterborough. All improvements to the repair facilities, including new sidings, new sheds and new machinery had to be approved in advance by the Board or Executive Committee. Tenders for machinery had normally to be obtained through the company secretary on the basis of specifications prepared by Sturrock and his team. Sturrock attended most monthly Board and Executive Committee meetings, which involved regular travel to London. Items for discussion with Sturrock were often placed in the second half of the meetings, so he typically joined the meetings at 12 noon.

It fell to Sturrock to develop in consultation with the Executive Committee and Board all aspects of the pay and conditions of the footplate men, the workforce in the repair shops and 'Plant', the clerical staff and the management team of the locomotive department.

Sturrock prepared rules for the locomotive department and for the enginemen and firemen and submitted them to the Executive Committee in May 1850, together with proposals for a bonus for the enginemen and firemen based on fuel saved. The scheme, which was developed from a similar scheme operated by the GWR, paid a 'premium' if fuel used was less than an agreed average.

Sturrock's first draft of the rules and regulations for enginemen and firemen was agreed by the Executive Committee on 15 October 1850, subject to a review by William Cubitt. Once Cubitt had given his approval, the Board asked two directors to check them again. Sturrock must have been concerned at the delay this caused now that the line to London was open. The rules had been issued by January 1851, for Sturrock proposed that all drivers and firemen should be allowed one great coat per year provided they had signed the new rules. The rules were subject to regular review in the light of operating experience and changes in working practice.

The small green leather-bound book of rules was designed to go in a footplate man's pocket.[6] The document opens:

> Every man must be able to read and write and must devote himself exclusively to the Company's service, attending at such hours as may be approved and residing wherever he may be required. He is to obey all orders and instructions he may receive from those placed in authority over him and conform to all the general regulations of the Company. He must always when on duty have a copy of these rules with him, which rules he is required to read over frequently, so as to become thoroughly acquainted with every particular set forth therein. The daily pay which may be fixed for each man will always include his service during all such hours, whether early or late, as may be determined upon from time to time by his foreman, according to the arrangements of the trains, and which hours will be so arranged as to give each man a fair day's work.

The rules provided that fines could be deducted from wages as well as rent for company accommodation. The engineman could be required to work in the shop if there was no work on the line. He would be liable to instant dismissal for insobriety and dismissal for negligence or misconduct.

Sturrock was the channel through which locomotive department employees and their families could request help in the event of misfortune. Where a footplate man or guard lost his life in an accident or a man was injured or killed in any of the locomotive department's works, Sturrock had to present requests for assistance to the Executive Committee. Even where the driver was held responsible for an accident, the committee might make an ex-gratia payment. The widow of a driver held to blame for an accident at Hatfield was awarded five shillings per week for four weeks in October 1850. A subsequent payment of £3 was agreed in November 1850. The fireman on the same train, who broke his legs and was in no way to blame for the accident, was paid twenty shillings per week at Sturrock's discretion, until he could return to work.[7]

Bills for medical treatment in the event of an accident had to be approved by the committee. Sturrock was expected to have a close knowledge of the men in his department and their families, so any special payments would reflect the full circumstances of each case. The number of dependants, the extent to which the man was responsible for his injuries and his period of service with the GNR would all be taken into account when awards were made. Sturrock was expected to give his views on the appropriate award in each case.

In June 1852 Sturrock recommended to the Executive Committee that the company should pay drivers and firemen a weekly allowance of one shilling in lieu of the provision of actual clothing, with the tailor taking the bad debt risk. The men were unhappy with the quality of the clothing provided by the contractor. Sturrock hoped the scheme would encourage the men to look after their clothing.

> The amount paid will not quite raise the wages of the men to the standard of the LNWR – the improved system will have the benefit of not costing the company more than they would probably require to pay in premiums and I consider this is a better way of generating some bonus to that class of men than giving them money.

A salaries committee was established in May 1851 to look at senior staff and clerical salaries across all departments.[8] Seymour Clarke and Sturrock attended. Excluding Sturrock, the total annual bill for the eight senior managers in the locomotive department at 20 May 1851 was £1,454. Parker was the highest paid on £350. Owen, Sturrock's foreman at Peterborough and Coffin, the carriage superintendent at Boston, lived in company houses. Sturrock asked that these should be rent free and the committee agreed. Sturrock also persuaded the committee to build a house for Budge, the locomotive foreman in London.

The salaries committee reviewed Sturrock's £500 a year salary. Sturrock had written to the Board to ask for a salary increase in September 1850 to take account of his extra responsibilities for the carriage and wagon department. He was told he would have to wait until he had completed a year's service, when he could apply again.[9] On 20 May 1851 the committee was more sympathetic:

> Mr Sturrock on being requested stated his expectations and his views. After discussion it was resolved to increase Sturrock's salary to £900 per year, with an increase of 10% thereon in the proportion of 1% of increase of dividend beyond 3% paid to the shareholders to take effect from 1st July next. Further recommended that as remuneration for the extra duty Mr Sturrock has performed in the last year in superintending the carriage department, he be paid £200.

Sturrock's salary was now the second highest in the company. Seymour Clarke, the general manager, received an increase to £1,200. Baxter, the secretary, was to be paid £800 and the accountant and the line superintendent both received £100 increases to £600. Financial posts in the 1850s did not have the standing accorded to such positions today. Engineers were more highly regarded.[10]

The August meeting of the salaries committee had second thoughts about the bonus plan offered to Sturrock and the other senior officers. Under the revised plan the officers were to receive a 'gratuity' of 5 per cent of their salary at each half year, provided the dividend increased by 10 per cent. The plan was to apply once the dividend reached 5 per cent. The plan was subject to further changes in October 1851:

> To induce the best exertions on the part of the officers, to encourage traffic and, at the same time, to promote the economy in working expenses and general management of the railway, whenever the two half yearly dividends added together shall exceed 3% in any year, there be paid to all officers in receipt of £75 per annum and upwards and to all clerks in charge of stations though receiving a salary of less than £75 per annum, a gratuity on all such excess and proportional to such excess at the rate of 5% on every 10 shillings of excess of dividend paid to shareholders beyond three and up to 5% in that year; but no increase or gratuity be paid on any increase of yearly dividend beyond 5%.[11]

The plan operated successfully but was unpopular with some of the directors and was withdrawn in June 1855, when new salary levels were introduced.

On 28 October 1851 the salaries committee agreed an increase for Charles Sacré, who had joined Sturrock from the GWR. Sacré was the locomotive foreman at Boston works and his pay was increased from £2 10s per week to £3 or £156 per year. Charles Sacré was later to transfer to Peterborough and in due course became locomotive superintendent and engineer of the MSLR.

No further salary reviews for the senior staff of the locomotive department took place till January 1853, when the opening of Doncaster repair shops was awaited. New pay arrangements for Parker, Coffin, Budge and Sacré were implemented from the opening of Doncaster. Owen and Grinling's increases were backdated to 1 January. Grinling maintained the accounts of the locomotive department and was later to become accountant for the whole of the GNR.

Parker	Works Manager	Unchanged salary of £350 plus £40 for house
Coffin	Carriage Superintendent	From £180 to £265 inclusive of £15 for house
Budge	London Foreman	From £170 to £200 plus house
Owen	Peterborough Foreman	From £150 plus house to £200 plus house
Sacré	Boston Foreman	From £150 plus house to £200 plus house
Grinling	Chief Clerk	From £170 to £200

At the following Board meeting, Colonel Packe, a director who was later to succeed Denison as chairman, suggested a review of Sturrock's salary. He received a £100 increase to £1,000 a year.[12] His salary had doubled in less than three years and his contribution to the successful launch of the new railway was recognised.

5

OPENING THE LINE
TO LONDON 1850–51

The Great Northern locomotive engineer in the early 1850s was accountable for about 40 per cent of the expenses of the railway. In the six months to 30 June 1851, the locomotive, carriage and wagon departments spent £50,774 out of total expenses of £121,640 and the engines ran 898,000 passenger and 674,000 goods miles. The ratio was unchanged five years later, by which time train mileage had increased 75 per cent and working expenses to £305,358. Sturrock's departmental expenses in the same period were £117,093.[1]

The provision of efficient goods engines for the coal trade was to be as important to the success of the GNR as the development of powerful passenger engines. Sturrock's locomotive designs were influenced by the nature of the track and by his experience on the GWR. The 72lb iron rails, up-rated to 83lb rails from 1857 on the main line, precluded the use of heavy locomotives and restricted Sturrock's freedom to bring the power of the broad gauge to the narrow gauge. Capital shortages also influenced his locomotive acquisition policy. Plant and machinery costs, which had been estimated at about £640,000 in June 1850, amounted to £1,167,000 by June 1852, when the company had to go back to reluctant shareholders for extra funds. Of the £750,000 additional capital agreed by the shareholders in 1852, £525,000 was absorbed in plant and machinery, chiefly stock, engines, carriages, wagons and the works at Doncaster.[2] As a result the Board was reluctant to order additional locomotives sufficiently in advance of anticipated growth in traffic to ensure adequate locomotive power was always available. Sturrock had sometimes to rely on ad-hoc purchases of engines and was unable to follow the standardisation policy he had operated on the GWR.

The line from London to Peterborough opened to passenger traffic on 7 August 1850. The directors dispensed with costly celebrations and *The Railway Times* noted that the opening of the line from the temporary terminus at Maiden Lane to Peterborough was 'the greatest extent of mileage that has ever been opened at one and the same time on any railway.'[3] Sturrock had to provide motive power for a network of over 220 miles of line linking London with Lincoln, Hull, Great Grimsby and York and found the whole exercise stressful.

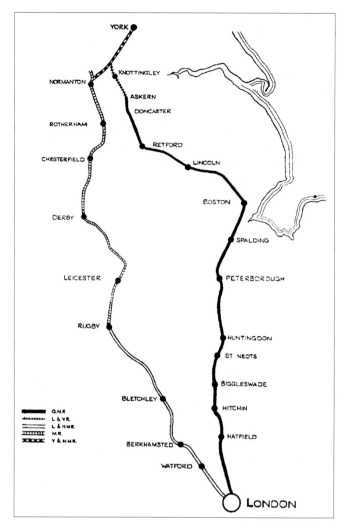

Rival routes between London and York at the opening of the GNR's line in August 1850. (O.S. Nock's *History of the Great Northern Railway*)

I opened this route for passengers one morning and, I may add, with a very inferior staff of drivers etc., as I had been unable to engage a sufficient number of men of experience. Need I add that this caused me great anxiety and that I had various difficulties in consequence; in fact I had a very bad time, being almost unable to sleep; but somehow we managed to pull through without any very bad accident.[4]

A serious accident nearly occurred three days before the formal opening. Mr Brassey, the contractor, had invited the directors and about 400 others to a trial trip down the line from London to Peterborough on 5 August 1850. A double-headed train with seventeen coaches left London at 9 a.m. with Sturrock driving. After an hour's stop at Welwyn to let the guests inspect the viaduct, the train reached Peterborough at 1.30 p.m. for a 'very elegant repast'. On the return journey at 4.30 p.m., with Sturrock still driving and the chairman also travelling in the cab, the train nearly collided with a ballast engine. Denison criticised Brassey for allowing work to continue during the trip. The train arrived unharmed at Maiden Lane just after 9 p.m.[5]

The first travellers were impressed not only by the nature of the line, including the six tunnels and the viaducts, but also by the carriages.

A train crosses the river at Peterborough on the opening of the line in August 1850. (*Illustrated London News*, 10 August 1850)

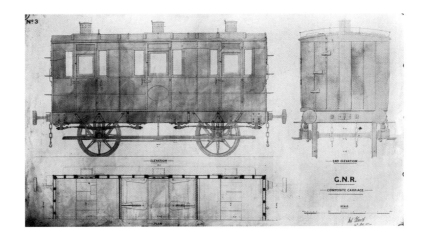

A composite carriage signed off by Sturrock in November 1853. (NRM)

> The appearance of the train was peculiar. The carriages are all built of teak by Mr Williams of Gosforth Street; and instead of being painted, the grain of the wood is polished and highly varnished, by which a great economy is affected both in the time and the expense of construction.

The Railway Times reckoned the process used by the GNR saved 10 per cent of the costs of conventional painting and decorating. What had been saved on painting had been used to provide what, in the opinion of the initial passengers, were above average second- and third-class interiors.

If the GNR was to win passenger traffic between London and the North from its established competitors, it would have to compete on comfort, quality of service and punctuality as well as cost. Until the direct or 'Towns' line from Peterborough to Doncaster was opened, the GNR route from Maiden Lane to York via Peterborough, Boston and Lincoln was as circuitous as the LNWR and Midland route via Rugby, Derby and Rotherham. The directors, therefore, gave close attention to punctuality. Sturrock noted in his report of 7 September, one month after opening, that engines were running to time and expresses arriving punctually at York. Such success was elusive, for ten days later Budge, the locomotive foreman in London, was called into an Executive Committee meeting to explain why a special on 16 September was two hours late.[6] There were also problems with the race traffic for the St Leger in the same month.

> The Committee whilst appreciating the great exertions of the Locomotive department and the servants of the Company generally during the great press of traffic in the Doncaster Race week, consider it necessary to instruct Mr Sturrock to continue to use his utmost exertions… to prevent delays in the trains, reporting specially and immediately any act of inattention on the part of any individual and the cause of delay.[7]

On 15 October 1850 Sturrock was given permission to order ten new passenger engines and to hire additional goods engines, till those on order had been delivered. The GNR was anxious to start the coal trade to London and deliveries of the Class 116 0-6-0s had been delayed as a result of the modifications made by Sturrock on his arrival. However, shortly after the meeting Sturrock learnt that there were some suitable goods engines for sale. Purchasing these engines would avoid the need to hire goods engines and would provide sufficient locomotive power for the anticipated early coal trade, since deliveries of the Class 116 0-6-0s were to start in mid-October.

Sturrock's discussions at the traffic committee convinced him that the thirty Class 116s on order, plus the additional off-the-shelf goods engines, would be insufficient to meet the GNR's ambitious mineral traffic plans. On 20 October 1850 the Board agreed to let Sturrock advertise for thirty goods engines, once drawings had been prepared. These were to be the first goods engines to be wholly designed by Sturrock, who was also working on the new passenger locomotives sanctioned on 12 October.

The first of the off-the-shelf 0-6-0s was delivered by R.&W. Hawthorn on 21 October. It differed only marginally from the Class 116 0-6-0s due for delivery from the same manufacturer. This engine numbered 163 and a Class 116, numbered 145, were involved in an accident at Barnet on 9 December 1850. A Sharp single on a pick-up train overshot Barnet station and, in the act of reversing, hit a double-headed coal train. Both 163 and 145 were derailed. Budge was first on the scene and Sturrock followed shortly thereafter. They re-railed both engines and established safe single line working.[8] The drivers of the two coal train engines were dismissed.

Two off-the-shelf goods engines from E.B. Wilson were delivered in late October and November. Numbered 164 and 165, Sturrock was satisfied they were sufficiently similar to the Class 116s to meet GNR requirements. A third Wilson engine, numbered 167, was ordered sometime after the first two for delivery in February the following year.

Sturrock was at first reluctant to take a fourth locomotive offered to him. Manufactured by C. Todd, it was less well proportioned than the others. Its boiler was much smaller than the GNR 0-6-0s on order. Sturrock, always in favour of large fireboxes, had had the Class 116 fireboxes increased in size when he first joined. Sturrock recalled a conversation in 1850 with Sir John Fowler, subsequently engineer of the Metropolitan Railway and designer of the Forth Bridge. Sir John had accused Sturrock of making his fireboxes the size of drawing rooms. Sturrock replied, 'You may call them that if you wish, but wait until you see what those fireboxes will do.'[9] Sturrock had learnt from Gooch the value of a large firebox.

Goods traffic should have started on the line from Peterborough to London in mid-November, but was deferred due to the absence of sufficient locomotives and incomplete handling facilities at stations. Delays built up in the existing local goods traffic. The traffic committee complained that there were 306 wagons full of coal at Doncaster, which needed to be cleared swiftly.[10] The Bury 0-4-0s were inadequate for the task and Sturrock had to rely on the Class 116s, of which twenty had been delivered by the end of the year, plus the first four of the five off-the-shelf 0-6-0s. Goods traffic to London, using a single train a day, did not start till 1 March 1851.

The traffic committee recognised the problems Sturrock was facing and instructed Middlemiss, the superintendent responsible for the coal traffic, to estimate the number of trains required per week to supply coal to London. He was to give his report to Sturrock, who would consider the number of locomotives he had available and on order. Sturrock was to assume thirty wagons per train and indicate whether he needed extra locomotives.[11]

Sturrock and Middlemiss wasted no time in getting together. Three weeks later the traffic committee met again and agreed there was a need for thirty more goods engines over and above the thirty agreed by the Executive Committee in late October. The specification for the original engines had been approved by the Executive Committee on 4 February. The committee agreed to order an additional thirty goods engines on 11 February. A circular was sent to ten selected manufacturers asking them to quote for twenty engines each for delivery during 1851.[12]

Tenders were received from seven manufacturers a fortnight later. The prices varied from £1,790 to £2,250. Orders were given for twenty engines from Wilson's at £1,790 and twenty from Fairbairn's at £2,000 each. Orders had been placed for only forty new engines and not the sixty which Sturrock had been promised. These new engines were developed by Sturrock from the Class 116 engines built by Hawthorn and Wilson. The forty engines numbered 168–199 and 300–307 were delivered between October 1851 and December 1853. Due to strikes Fairbairn gave up part of their order in March 1852. The additional ten were built by Wilson at £1,945 for engine only. The tenders were to come from Sharp singles converted to tank engines.

The Class 168 goods engines had, in common with all Sturrock's 0-6-0s, outside sandwich frames and outside bearings. With six coupled 5ft wheels and an adhesive weight of 29½ tons in working order, the locomotives were powerful for the period. The external characteristics of the locomotives were subsequently adopted by other railway companies. Perhaps surprisingly if they were working off the same set of drawings, the Fairbairn's engines differed not just in appearance but also in significant dimensions from the Wilson locomotives. The 15ft 6in wheel base was equally divided on the Wilson engines, but unequal on the Fairbairns. The Fairbairn locomotive was heavier than the Wilson engine at 30 tons 11cwt in working order.[13]

Sturrock also struggled with a lack of adequate locomotive power for passenger traffic. Traffic had been very heavy in the run up to Christmas. Parliamentary trains had been particularly delayed and the absence of a telegraph made communication between stations impossible. Some trains were timed so tightly that delays could not be made up due to the heavy number of passengers and the wet and slippery road. Sturrock wrote:

> I regret very much that the Committee are dissatisfied with the duty performed by the locomotive stock and beg to inform the Committee the engines are in excellent working order and are taxed to their maximum power, indeed they could not have run the fast trains at all if I had not increased the pressure and altered the valves.

Sturrock drew the committee's attention to the need to replace some of the lighter engines by heavier machines.[14]

Whilst Sturrock was launching the coal and mineral trade to London and coping with the opening of the first branch lines, he was also designing and ordering more wagons for the mineral trade and obtaining carriages for the expected passengers to the 1851 Exhibition. It may have been as a result of this pressure that Sturrock turned to an old friend, Thomas Crampton, for help in designing his first new passenger locomotives. It was a decision he came to regret.

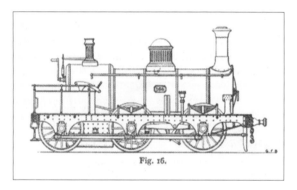

Fig. 16.

Above: No.70 was delivered in 1851 and was one of Sturrock's Class 168 0-6-0s; it is shown after modification by Stirling. (GNRS)

Left: The Class 168 0-6-0s were derived from the Class 116s and were the first goods locomotives wholly designed by Sturrock. (Bird)

By placing the driving wheels of his locomotive behind the firebox, Crampton was able to increase the size of the boiler and lower the centre of gravity. He considered stability would be increased if the centre of gravity was in line with the drawbar. The driving wheels had to be of substantial diameter to aid adhesion. A number of UK railways tried locomotives of the Crampton patent, including the South Eastern, the Eastern Counties and the LNWR. Crampton locomotives to this patent were widely adopted in France from 1850 and in Germany from 1852.[15]

Sturrock's new passenger locomotives used a subsequent Crampton patent, which retained the driving wheels behind the firebox but incorporated a dummy crankshaft. Power was transmitted to the driving wheels by an outside crank. The aim was to reduce crank axle fractures and improve valve timing. The design was claimed to be speedy, light on the rails and cheap to construct. At £1,600 including tender, the Cramptons were significantly cheaper than the 'small' Hawthorns bought by the GNR in 1848 for £1,875 plus £380 for the tender.

Sturrock had originally intended to acquire ten modified 'small' Hawthorns, before changing his mind in November and opting for the Cramptons. The parties tendering for the ten-passenger locomotives were advised of Sturrock's change of plan in late

November and told outline drawings were available at Boston. Sturrock advised the Executive Committee that a royalty of £50 per engine would have to be paid to Crampton.[16] R.B. Longridge, who offered the lowest price of ten tenders, was awarded the contract for delivery on 30 April 1851. In common with arrangements agreed for many subsequent orders, half the price was to be paid in cash after 2,000 satisfactory miles and half in mortgage deeds carrying interest at 4.5 per cent or cash, as the GNR preferred.

The GNR Cramptons had 6ft 6in driving wheels and a boiler pressure of 120lb. With the exception of some Cramptons built for the LBSC and the South Eastern, which had 6ft or 6ft 6in driving wheels, all other Cramptons built for British railways had 7ft or larger driving wheels to aid adhesion. The LNWR's two large Cramptons, Liverpool and London, had 8ft driving wheels. As Sturrock was to discover, his Cramptons would suffer from problems of adhesion.

While the Cramptons were being built, Sturrock obtained permission from the Board to visit France and see the French Cramptons in operation. Two Cramptons had been operating on the Chemin de Fer du Nord for two years when Sturrock picked up his train in Calais in late March 1851. His train to Paris may well have been headed by a Crampton. Sturrock was well received by Monsieur Petiet, the chief engineer, who showed him the French system of accounts and introduced him to the hot water footstools used in French first-class carriages. Sturrock reported that the French engines were designed on a 'somewhat similar principle though much inferior arrangement to those now being built by Messrs Longbridge' for the GNR. The French locomotives were designed to Crampton's original patent, had driving wheels 1in less than 7ft and did not have to cope with the GNR of England's undulations. Sturrock came back satisfied he had made the right choice, in particular because the Cramptons would cause less damage to the track than engines of similar weight of more usual construction.

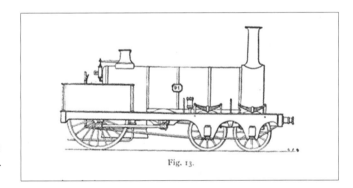

Fig. 13.

Sturrock took delivery of ten Crampton patent 4-2-0s built by Longridge during 1851-52. (Bird)

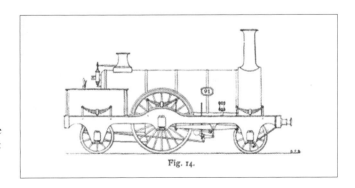

Fig. 14.

Sturrock altered all the Cramptons to 2-2-2s with the crank axle moved to the front of the firebox; in this form they ran well. (Bird)

It is not clear either from the minutes of the Executive Committee or Board, or from Sturrock's reports to those bodies, when he decided that the Cramptons were never going to perform as he had hoped. The Cramptons were delivered between April 1851 and March 1852. At least one, the final Crampton, was converted to a 2-4-0, with a second set of driving wheels attached to the 'dummy' axle, probably in Boston, almost as soon as it was delivered. This modification did not prove a success and a more comprehensive rebuilding of all the Cramptons as 2-2-2s proved necessary. To comply with custom at the time, costly double frames were adopted to give safe support in the event of a crank axle fracture. The remaining nine Cramptons appear to have been converted to 2-2-2s during 1853–54 probably at Doncaster. No information on the changes seems to have been supplied to the Board or Executive Committee at any time.

Sturrock did his best to confuse historians regarding the Cramptons. When G.F. Bird compiled his book on Great Northern engines, much of the information on the early engines was derived 'indirectly from that doyen of locomotive superintendents, Mr Archibald Sturrock himself'. Bird wrote of the Cramptons that 'it appears that they were actually ordered prior to Mr Sturrock's assumption of office on the line.' E.L. Ahrons, in his *British Steam Railway Locomotives*, mentions a letter he had from Sturrock, which stated there was only one Crampton acquired by the GNR. In a pencil note on his copy of Bird's book, Sturrock wrote 'not sure the number of Cramptons but altered several.' Sturrock never envisaged the full GNR Board and Executive Committee minutes would one day be available to railway historians.

As plans were being made for the Cramptons, Sturrock reminded the Board there were still twenty goods engines unordered for the next winter's coal trade. There were to be at least twelve coal trains per week, double the number run when the service opened the year before. Wilson was asked if he could supply engines at the same price as the last batch but refused and the Board decided to go out to tender.[17] Hawthorn's, which offered to build each engine and tender for £2,150, was the cheapest and Wilson came in with a price of £2,190. These offers were rejected in favour of tenders from Nasmyth and Stephenson, who agreed to supply at £2,220 and £2,300. Although the aim had been to get the twenty new engines delivered by October 1851, none were supplied till December 1851. The engines numbered 308-327 had circular boilers and a maximum boiler pressure of 140lb.

Sturrock's struggle to get adequate locomotive power for the coal trade was not eased by suggestions from the MSLR that GNR engines were inadequate. An accident had occurred to a GNR goods train at the Clarborough incline on the MSLR. The GNR maintained there was a need for sidings, so that a pilot engine could be provided, but Alford, the MSLR engineer, disagreed. He stated that the MSLR engines could cope with thirty-five wagons on the incline. The GNR, in his view, needed better engines. Sturrock suggested Alford's views should be treated with caution. If engines were built to cope with the incline safely in all circumstances, then they would be uneconomical for general working and too heavy for the GNR track. Sturrock convinced the GNR Board he knew what he was talking about, since he could draw on his experience with the Box tunnel incline on the GWR. The Board noted the problem would disappear once the 'Towns' line was opened.

To add to his diverse mix of engines, Sturrock acquired two *Jenny Linds* from Wilson in June 1851. These engines were a highly regarded stock design developed by David Joy and were lent to the GNR in hopes of a major order. Sturrock accepted they were good and powerful engines, particularly following his modifications to the blast pipe. They were used on the run from Doncaster to Boston, for heavy trains for the York races and for Newcastle expresses. The Board agreed to purchase the two engines at £2,000.[18]

Above: Class 308 0-6-0 goods
locomotive No.319 was delivered by
Nasmyth in October 1852, rebuilt
by Stirling and withdrawn in 1893.
(GNRS)

Right: A typical Jenny Lind 2-2-2, one
of the Leeds Foundry's most successful
class of locomotives; Sturrock
obtained two in 1850-51. (Bird)

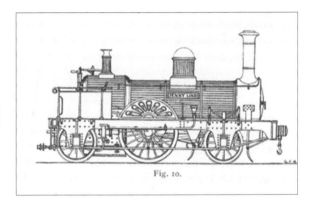

Fig. 10.

Sturrock's supply of passenger engines had been enhanced during the summer of 1851 with the delivery of the twenty Class 71 2-4-0s ordered on the day before his appointment and modified by Sturrock. Delivery commenced in April 1851 in time to help with traffic for the Great Exhibition, which ran from June to October 1851. Competition between the companies led to very low fares; but the volume of passengers ensured revenues were high. Sturrock and his team were challenged and found capable of coping with high passenger numbers. The capacity of the loop line via Boston was tested to the full.

Sturrock worked to improve the running of the service. In March 1851 he suggested to Seymour Clarke that it would be much more efficient to distribute coke to stations by attaching a few wagons to each goods train, a common practice on other lines. In April 1851 he explained the benefits of the Electric Telegraph, which the LNWR had already adopted. His concern for safety led him to recommend extending the distance between the distance and stop signals. 300 yards might be adequate on the level, but 1,000-1,200 yards was needed in wet weather on an incline of 1:200. He went down to inspect accident sites, in order to identify the cause and to ensure his men were not blamed unjustly. The GNR's signalling was above average for the time, but was less helpful than it could have been if the Electric Telegraph had been installed.[19]

The reputation of the GNR was enhanced by the decision of the Queen and Prince Albert to travel to Scotland on the East Coast route in August 1851. Arrangements had been put in hand with Walter Williams for a royal saloon to be built and a first-class carriage modified for Prince Albert's use.

> The Royal Saloon is 18 feet 1 inch long by 7 feet 4 inches broad, and is constructed entirely of East Indian Moulmein teak, unpainted but highly varnished… Over each doorway is a splendid gilt crown… The interior of each carriage is lined with the richest white brocaded Indian silk, and the pattern raised bouquets of flowers.[20]

The order for the saloon was approved retrospectively at a Board meeting on 5 August 1851, only three weeks before the Queen's journey. When the invoice arrived in December for £1,400, the Board was shocked. It was paid 'with reluctance' in January 1852, after Williams explained it would have been £1,531, if he had not applied a discount. A further £837 was paid for fitting out the interior, a charge which Sturrock thought extravagant.

In accordance with custom, the Royal Train of eight carriages was driven by Sturrock. It left Maiden Lane at about 2 p.m. on 27 August and stopped for six or seven minutes at Boston at 4.30 p.m. It reached Doncaster at 6.30 p.m., where the Queen and royal party made a triumphal progress through the town to the Angel Hotel 'which had been tastefully prepared by Mrs Pye with flowers and evergreens'. A banquet was given by the mayor in the evening. The Queen continued her journey to Scotland at 9 a.m. the following morning. At York the GNR engine was replaced by a York, Newcastle & Berwick engine. The train arrived at Edinburgh about 3.30 p.m.[21]

Interior of Queen Victoria's carriage for her journey north in August 1851. (*Illustrated London News*)

Queen Victoria and Prince Albert leaving Doncaster station for the Angel Hotel in August 1851.
(*Illustrated London News*)

As autumn was approaching, Sturrock became concerned as to whether the goods engines would be delivered on time. Nasmyth and Wilson appeared to be progressing well, but Fairbairns were running late and asked to attend a Board meeting on 25 August. Fairbairn himself attended and promised to start deliveries in October. The chairman advised Fairbairn that he would be held responsible for any damage done as a result of delays. In spite of his promise, Fairbairn did not deliver any engines till May 1852. Wilson started deliveries in October 1851 and had delivered nine by the year end and a further seven by the end of March. Nasmyth did not start deliveries till July 1852. Sturrock was to have another difficult winter.

Sturrock was also concerned about locomotive and rolling stock requirements when the 'Towns' line opened in the summer of 1852. With the agreement of the October Board, he prepared a paper in early November setting out his case for more passenger engines and for some tank engines. In April 1850 it had been estimated that there would be a requirement for thirty-four passenger engines and forty-four goods engines in steam daily and that these engines would run 55,680 miles per week. Sturrock reckoned that he needed a total of sixty-seven engines in order to have thirty-four always out on the line:

> Thus with 34 engines in steam and
> 7 or about one third in the shed
> Allowing 12 or one third of those in steam as spare engines
> Add 14 or about another one third in steam and in shed for repairs
> Would give a total of 67 engines required

Sturrock pointed out that the average mileage in the last three months had been upwards of 80,000 miles and reached 91,000 at the peak of the Exhibition traffic. In the last week of October, following the closure of the Exhibition, 83,076 miles were run. Such mileages required sixty-four passenger engines in steam per day and, using the same ratio as in April 1850, indicated a stock of 125 engines was necessary, against the current 101.

Sturrock supported his case for additional large passenger engines by reminding the Board that the Sharp 2-2-2s were regularly breaking crank axles before they had run the usual number of miles. Nine had broken in the last four months. Sturrock blamed the very high mileages and speeds as he had found no fault with the crank axles themselves. He also reminded the Board that the opening of the 'Towns' line would demand more engines for what would become the 'Loop' line branch. He assumed the number of through trains would not increase. He concluded thirty more engines costing about £2,200 each would be needed, of which twenty should be ordered now. He recommended ten singles and ten coupled.[22]

Clarke had advised Sturrock he needed two or three tank engines for shunting at Lincoln and Doncaster. Sturrock, therefore, asked the Board for permission to convert one Sharp 2-2-2 tender engine as an experiment at a cost of £200. This would save buying new and provide a more suitable locomotive for the sharp curves in the stations. Sturrock once again demonstrated his determination to keep costs down and capacity for innovation.

Sturrock made no progress with his request for twenty more passenger locomotives, so he came back to the next meeting of the committee with more modest proposals. He would like to order twelve new single passenger engines, unless the committee advised him that mileages would fall. To keep the costs down, he proposed to use the tenders from the converted Sharp 2-2-2s on the new passenger locomotives. The amount which would otherwise have been spent on tenders would meet the cost of the converting more Sharps. The Board authorised £4,800 to convert twelve Sharps to tank engines with the costs to be charged to capital.[23] It also agreed to obtain quotes from Sharp, Hawthorn, Wilson, Stephenson, Nasmyth and Kitson for twelve passenger locomotives. The twelve passenger locomotives without tenders were ordered by the Executive Committee on 13 January. Hawthorn came in with the cheapest price of £1,675 and promised delivery at a rate of one per week from 1 May 1852.[24]

These locomotives, which were to be known as 'large' Hawthorns, were the first 2-2-2s wholly designed and developed by Sturrock and were delivered from May 1852 onwards. Although the design had many characteristics of a Hawthorn engine of the period, Sturrock introduced a number of improved features. Cylinders were located between the inner iron frames, which extended the full length of engine, an uncommon feature at the time. The additional extra strength of the combined inner and outer frames made room for the expansion of the boiler. The firebox was 114sq ft with midfeather. Boiler pressure was capable of adjustment up to 150lb. The engines were good examples of locomotive practice of the time. With one exception, they were rebuilt by Stirling in 1867-69 and remained in service till 1880. The last was withdrawn in 1892.[25] Almost certainly it was the success of the 'large' Hawthorns which encouraged Sturrock to convert the Cramptons to 2-2-2s.

It was one of the 'large' Hawthorns, No.210, which was the subject of an incident recorded in Michael Reynold's book *Engine Driving Life*:

> The down Scotch express, driven by Oliver Hindley, was travelling down Retford bank when he saw a train going east from Sheffield to Lincoln, which would meet him on the level crossing at Retford station. Unable to stop, Hindley put on full steam and sent his train clean through the goods, scattering trucks like match splinters, but carrying all safe. No 210 carried the dents and scars like an old warrior.

I have been unable to trace any further details of the incident or the date when it occurred.

Sharp 2-2-2 tank engine conversion; this is probably No.33, which was converted in August 1852 and is shown running with a Stirling cab. (SLS)

Sharp single No.12 converted by Sturrock to an 0-4-2T and further modified by Stirling in 1871. (SLS)

Sharp single No.45 converted to an 0-2-2T in 1852 and again rebuilt in 1866; the photograph shows the engine with a Stirling cab roof and chimney in the late 1860s. (SLS)

Sharp single 2-2-2T conversion No.18 after an accident at Hitchin in July 1866. (GNRS)

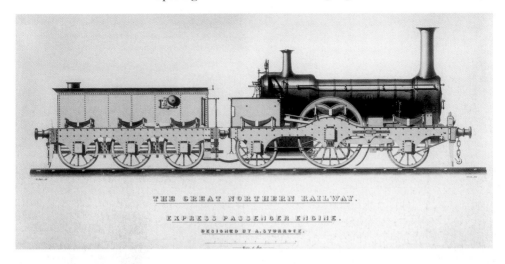

THE GREAT NORTHERN RAILWAY.

EXPRESS PASSENGER ENGINE.

DESIGNED BY A. STURROCK.

Large Hawthorn No.214 with a domeless boiler as built in September 1853 and a later large capacity tender. (GNRS)

Large Hawthorn No.212 following modifications to the boiler and cab by Stirling. (SLS)

Large Hawthorn No.208 with the manufacturer's typical steam dome used on all but three of the class. (GNRS)

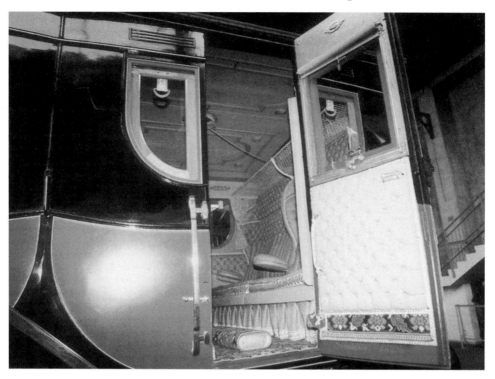

Coach of the type Sturrock may have used on his visit to France in March 1851 showing a French hot-water footstool, an idea Sturrock brought back to the UK. (Cité du Train, Mulhouse)

1851 ended with the Executive Committee discussing with Sturrock the provision of hot-water footstools to first-class passengers. Sturrock had a sample for the committee to look at and indicated that fifty had been made at a cost of 13*s* 6*d* each. Sturrock had brought a sample back from Petiet of the Chemin de Fer du Nord and had a number made up by the coppersmiths 'one half the length of the Frenchman'. Sturrock had them put into a carriage taking the directors to London. 'On presenting myself in the board room for my business, the Chairman pretended to scold me for having made those hot water cans without instructions.' The Board adopted the idea, which was soon copied by the LNWR and Midland. 'If there be any credit for getting the British public into hot water, I ought to have it.'[26] The apparatus used for supplying the hot water for the footstools was also used to prevent damp in the royal carriages. An example of a 'Frenchman' can still be seen in a Chemin de Fer du Nord first-class carriage of 1850 in the French National Railway Museum at Mulhouse, together with a surviving French Crampton.

The directors decided they needed to obtain more effective control of the cost of stores. Sturrock was asked how these matters had been handled at the GWR. A stores committee was formed and decisions made on which items should be obtained by public tender through advertisements and which by private tender. A fortnight's supply of coke should be kept where specified by Sturrock and Clarke. Seymour Clarke and Sturrock recommended systems based on GWR practice, which were endorsed by the Board on 3 January 1852. Sturrock had yet another committee to attend.

Sturrock continued to monitor deliveries of goods engines under order from Fairbairn and Nasmyth. Fairbairn, who had been troubled by strikes, agreed to give up half their order for twenty goods engines and promise to deliver the balance by 1 September, a delivery date which was not achieved. Sturrock obtained quotations from Wilson, Hawthorn and Nasmyth for the ten engines given up by Fairbairn. Wilson secured the order with a price of £1,945 and a penalty of £50 per week if he did not deliver by 1 September. Sturrock was given a credit of £4,000 in lieu of the tenders to meet the costs of further Sharp conversions.

Sturrock's costs were greatly influenced by the price of coal and coke. Fuel costs were considerably greater per mile than the footplate staff wages. At this time coke remained the dominant fuel for all locomotives, due to the requirement that engines should consume their own smoke. Seymour Clarke and Sturrock advised the Board in January 1852 that the coke manufacturers were getting together to hold up costs. They recommended setting up a nine- or twelve-month contract and this was agreed. Annual coke contracts became standard practice throughout Sturrock's time with the GNR. Tenders were obtained and Henry Stobart of York was given the contract at 11s per ton, the prevailing price. Although Elsecar coke might have been cheaper, the Board were mindful of the importance of quality. The Board also agreed to let Sturrock put up two coke ovens in Doncaster to experiment with the production of coke from South Yorkshire coal.

Sturrock's appointment by the Board to take charge of the rolling stock on 18 April 1850 was no minor additional task.[27] He was to be responsible for:

> the whole of the rolling stock, carriages, wagons etc. and all the machinery appertaining thereto; the same to be considered entirely under his management: and that he be requested to make an early report on the state of the rolling stock, particularly the coal and all wagons; and to make such suggestions as he may have to offer.

When Sturrock joined in April 1850, the GNR had 1,308 goods wagons and 326 passenger vehicles. The latter group included 246 carriages for the conveyance of passengers, thirty-three parcel and luggage vans, twenty-four trucks for taking horse drawn carriages, twenty-one horseboxes and two mail vans.

In May 1850 Sturrock reported that the rolling stock was generally 'built with great attention to the question of haulage and steady running.' He noted that the buffer stops were inadequate and recommended 'Mr Williams' registered draw gear'. His chief concern was for the axle boxes, which could be penetrated by sand. The grease holes were too far apart and he recommended modifications costing 16s per vehicle. He also asked to have built a coal wagon of a type used on the South Eastern. The Executive Committee agreed to his proposals.[28]

The Executive Committee liked to be involved in some detail with the development of rolling stock. In May 1850 the committee debated the problems caused by the absence of 'breaks' on coal wagons and agreed that the 200 wagons on order should be fitted with 'breaks'. This would mean one sixth of the fleet would have 'breaks', which was deemed sufficient for the present.[29] The same meeting also discussed a view expressed by one of the directors, Captain Laws, that the distance between the sets of wheels on wagons should be increased to aid stability. The subsequent meeting agreed to alter the distance on 240 low wagons to 8ft 8in at a cost of 20s per wagon. Booth's connection was to be adopted for all carriages in future. Patent disc wheels from the Vulcan Foundry were also to be tried.

When the GNR had wagons built, it took responsibility for choosing and obtaining wheel and axle sets. The decision on the choice of supplier was influenced by delivery dates and price. Penalties would be charged for late deliveries.[30] Wheel sets at July 1850 cost £27–£28. Twenty horse boxes were ordered from Finch & Willey at £62 10s each and thirty trucks to take carriages at £41 each. In the same month Sturrock asked for fifty iron coke wagons to meet the expansion of the trade. Wagons designed for the carriage of corn were also considered. More wagons were to be acquired for the cattle trade.

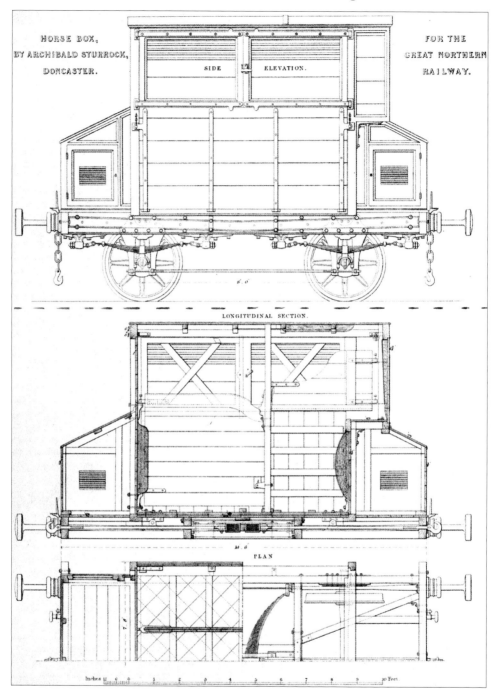

Above and opposite page: Horse Box and Carriage truck signed off by Sturrock in Boston in 1850. By the time Sturrock retired in 1866 the GNR had acquired 100 horse boxes and sixty-five trucks for conveying carriages. (D.K. Clark, *Railway Machinery*, 1855 Vol.2)

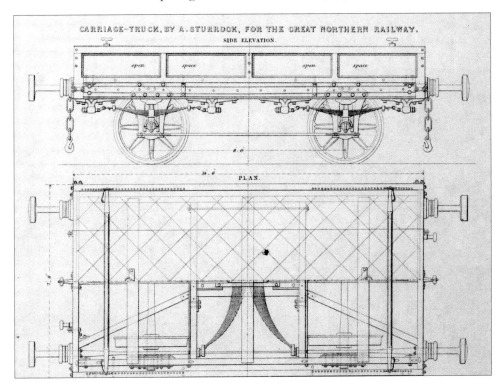

The Executive Committee agreed to the purchase of seventy goods and passenger luggage and 'break' vans at the end of October to designs prepared by Sturrock. The absence of sufficient break vans meant that heavy trains would take a very long time to stop. Initial orders for twelve passenger brakes and twelve goods brakes were to be given to Williams, provided he could deliver in three weeks. Sturrock could place the orders elsewhere if Williams could not match delivery dates.[31] Orders for fifty more brake vans were subsequently divided between Finch & Willey and Samuel Butcher in December 1850. Ashbury obtained an order for 100 iron coke wagons.

In November 1850 the traffic committee was concerning itself with the need for more carriages for the Great Exhibition. It was agreed that thirty-five first, thirty-four second, thirty-seven composite and thirty-four third-class carriages were required. Sturrock had pattern carriages built and orders were not to be placed till a judgement could be made on the pattern carriages. To ensure swift delivery, Sturrock asked to order the wheels, springs and axles for these carriages in early December, plus 500 sets for coal wagons and 500 for covered wagons. He reminded the committee that wheels were not always of a high standard and that if the GNR could not deliver wheels to the carriage and wagon builders on time, penalties were incurred.

When Sturrock had presented his specification and forms of tender for 500 goods and 500 coal wagons on 31 December 1850, the specification had been referred back to him as iron under-framing was not proposed. Sturrock explained that a wagon with an iron under-frame would weigh 1 ton more than a wagon with a wooden frame. This would add 30 tons to the weight of a 180-ton train and would be the equivalent of an extra 60 tons on a 1:200 gradient. The greater costs of running the iron-framed wagons would not be justified when compared with the saving in repair costs on wooden wagons. The committee accepted Sturrock's judgement.[32]

In early 1851 the committee debated the problem of broken wheels. An accident had occurred in February during the delivery of a new wagon from Adams. The spoke and tyre of the cast-iron wheel broke causing derailment. The GNR had 2,922 similar sets of wheels and Sturrock was asked to investigate the cost of replacing them all with wrought iron[33]. For the future, cast wheels would only be retained on coal wagons. The wisdom of the decision was confirmed when another wheel broke in March 1851. 1,379 trucks were to be changed gradually over a period. A further 2,034 coal and coke wagons would be left with cast wheels for the present. Because fish and meat trucks were attached to passenger trains, it was decided that these wagons should all be placed at the end of the train until such time as the cast wheels had been changed.

Sturrock also brought back to the committee the issue of sand in the axle boxes. To keep down construction costs, much of the permanent way had been covered in sand rather than shingle. As a consequence, wheels appeared to be solid when sand had filled the gaps between spokes and hot axle boxes were a regular occurrence. Sturrock had developed airtight axle boxes for carriages, which diminished the problem.[34] However the Executive Committee decided to spread gravel on the track to further reduce the problem.

Sturrock used the opportunity of his own visits to London to assess the extent to which axle boxes were being properly greased. He found it necessary to appoint men at York, Doncaster, Knottingley, Retford, Hitchin and London to grease axle boxes and check for overheating, since the job was not being done adequately by the traffic department.[35] Grease quality and cost were to be issues of some importance to Sturrock and the Executive Committee throughout much of Sturrock's career with the GNR.

As Sturrock's second year with the GNR drew to a close, his family was increased by the birth of his second daughter, Georgina Ramsay, in Peterborough. After her birth the family moved to Doncaster, where Sturrock had taken a house at 21 South Parade. However, before the family had settled in, Sturrock's wife Caroline Sophia died on 27 April 1852 leaving him with two daughters, aged four and two months, and a son aged two. Sturrock's challenging first two years with the GNR came to a sad conclusion.

EXPANSION AND EXPERIMENTATION 1852–55

Sturrock had started his role as locomotive superintendent in April 1850 with eighty-one locomotives, 1,308 goods wagons and 326 passenger carriages, including horse boxes, 'luggage' and carriage trucks. Less than two years later in December 1852, he was running a fleet of 228 locomotives, 4,812 goods wagons and 660 passenger carriages. This rapid expansion moderated over the subsequent three years, with twenty-two locomotives delivered in 1853, thirty-seven in 1854 and twenty-three in 1855. By the end of December 1855 Sturrock had acquired 243 locomotives and brought the total fleet up to 324.

The 'Towns' line from Peterborough to Retford, via Grantham and Newark, opened for goods traffic on 15 July 1852. Passenger traffic commenced on 1 August and King's Cross station opened on 14 October. For the new services Sturrock had available the Class 71 2-4-0s, which had proved very capable with the Exhibition traffic the previous year, the ten Cramptons and the first four 'large' Hawthorns. All but three of the twelve 'large' Hawthorns were delivered by the year end. As the 'large' Hawthorns became available for main line duties, the Class 71 2-4-0s could be used for secondary passenger working. One of the Cramptons in original form took the first 6 a.m. Parliamentary train out of King's Cross on 14 October.

Sturrock's confidence as a locomotive designer had been restored by the success of the 'large' Hawthorns. In July 1852 he asked the Board for permission to build an experimental locomotive, which would rival the power of the broad gauge and meet potential competition. The LNWR had announced their intention to introduce a service from London to Birmingham, which would cover the 112½ miles in two hours, an average speed of 56mph. McConnell, the locomotive superintendent for the southern section of the LNWR, had designed and built twelve locomotives to undertake the planned service. These 2-2-2 singles had 7ft 6in driving wheels, 18in by 24in cylinders and could operate up to a boiler pressure of 150lb. The track LNWR did not prove to be robust enough to cope with the planned speeds, but this was not apparent in July 1852.[1] The GNR were concerned that these engines might be used on the services to York and the north.

In the light of the potential threat, the GNR Board authorised Sturrock to build a locomotive. 'As an experiment and with a view to meeting competition he may be allowed to have an engine built to one of his designs which he believes would run easily at the rate of 60–65 miles per hour for 100 miles which he estimated would cost £2400 to £2500.[2] The contract was placed with Hawthorns. Many changes were made during construction and locomotive No.215 was not delivered till August 1853.

Sturrock recorded a version of the 215 story in his memoirs written in June 1892:

> On the closing of the Exhibition traffic the Directors of the London & North Western met the directors of the Great Northern at a joint committee. The London & North Western Board stated that they intended increasing the speeds to Yorkshire beyond what we could do on our inferior gradients of 1 in 200, and that they would thus deprive us of the Yorkshire traffic. My Board consulted me and I advised them there was no need for uneasiness on that score, and requested them to give me carte blanche to build a specimen engine, which I stated would be so constructed as to run a 100 miles without stopping, and that if the whole distance between London and Edinburgh was horsed by similar engines the train would reach Edinburgh from London in 8 hours. My proposal was to run from London to Grantham without stopping, Grantham to York ditto, York to Newcastle ditto, Newcastle to Berwick ditto and Berwick to Edinburgh ditto. Permission was given me and engine number 215 was built in Newcastle by Hawthorns and delivered to the Great Northern Railway in 1853. It succeeded in performing the promised task and became the type of Mr Stirling's Express engines which in 1892 are propelling the Great Northern trains from King's Cross to York at 50 miles per hour or to Edinburgh, if my proposal were carried out, in 8 hours. There is no difference in the principle of those engines and number 215.

By the time Sturrock came to give his final comments on 215 in his ninetieth year in 1907, he was even more positive about the success of 215.

> This engine successfully ran 100 mile lengths, obtaining a maximum speed of 75 miles per hour. At the time there was no demand for the high speeds of the present day, and no necessity for the long length traffic for which this engine was designed; the engine was therefore eventually used for the ordinary traffic of the line.[3]

Hamilton Ellis was of the view that 215 could have successfully taken a train to Edinburgh in eight hours with the relatively light coaches of the time.[4] Other commentators have been unwilling to commit themselves.

Sturrock's design for 215 was influenced by his experience of the GWR's Iron Duke Class 4-2-2 locomotives. Eighteen of these 8ft singles were built under Sturrock's management at Swindon between 1847 and 1850. Experience with the experimental Great Western 2-2-2 engine in 1846 had indicated to Gooch and Sturrock that there was too much weight on the leading axle, which broke when hauling a down train near Shrivenham. As a consequence Great Western was modified and the Iron Duke Class were built with two separate pairs of leading wheels. The total wheelbase was 18ft 8½in and the locomotive weighed 35 tons. The driving wheels were 8ft and flangeless. Boiler pressure was initially 100lb and subsequently increased to 115lb.

215 as originally built had two pairs of leading wheels and flangeless 7ft 6in driving wheels. Equalising levers connected the springs between the two sets of leading wheels and between the driving and trailing axles. The total wheelbase was 21ft 8½in, considerably longer than the GWR's Iron Dukes. Weight was 37 tons, about 9 tons heavier than the 'large' Hawthorns. The maximum recorded working boiler pressure was 120lb. With a total overall length, including tender, of 49ft 9½in over the buffers and a chimney rising 13ft 3in above rail level, it was an imposing locomotive. In line with GWR practice, the tender of 215 had a seat for a travelling porter, to keep a watch on the carriages behind. This uncomfortable arrangement was soon discontinued.

Sturrock's experimental 4-2-2 No.215 in its original form with a pair of fixed leading wheels was modelled on the GWR's Iron Duke class. (GNRS)

Unfortunately 215 did not initially perform as hoped. The blast pipe orifice proved to be too small and was increased from 3¾in to 4½in and then to 5in in diameter. The twin leading wheels were inclined to leave the rails. Sturrock had the leading four wheels converted to a bogie. The frame had to be cut away and iron plates inserted to ensure the necessary freedom of movement. The construction of a front bogie appears to have been something of an innovation at the time. Sturrock had built two engines with bogies for the GWR. On 215 he is reported to have used a damping out device developed by Fernihough in 1845 to reduce the potential for side to side oscillation[5]. The Birmingham & Gloucester had imported a number of 4-2-0s with a swivelling front bogie in 1839–41 for use on the Lickey incline, but such bogies do not appear to have been adopted on British express locomotives at the time 215 was built. With these significant modifications 215 proved to be a more satisfactory engine.[6]

Sturrock was reluctant to admit to the early problems with 215 and, in particular, to the conversion of the leading wheels to a bogie. In his report to the Board of 26 November 1853 he admitted to modifications to the bogie to reduce its weight and to costs of around £79. Bird's description of 215, which came from Sturrock and was published in 1903, gives the impression that the engine was originally built with a front bogie and Sturrock's later descriptions of the engine always mention a bogie. A different story had, however, been published by Clement Stretton in his *Development of the Locomotive Engine* in 1892. Stretton, who is not the most reliable of railway historians, stated:

This engine ran upon eight wheels, four in a group, but not in a bogie, a single pair of driving wheels 7 feet 6 inches diameter, and a pair of trailing wheels... When new this engine worked very unsatisfactorily, as it could not pass round curves easily; the four front wheels were taken out and placed in a 'bogie' and it ran till 1870.[7]

Unfortunately no drawings of 215 exist to enable the accuracy of the story to be checked.

The evidence available on 215's performance is limited. Sturrock's report to the Board in November 1853 covered the period 16–22 November, some three months after it entered service. Brief records for the twelve trips undertaken during the period still exist. The weather was not conducive to fast running, but some reasonable speeds were attained:[8]

A painting of No.215 after conversion of the four leading wheels to a bogie. (SLS)

17 November Fast train up from Hitchin to King's Cross:

> Average speed from Hitchin to London 50.5 miles per hour, if you allow 5 minutes for getting into speed and for stopping speed. The actual running speed was 58.1 miles per hour.

18 November King's Cross to Peterborough and return:

> The speed from Hitchin to Peterborough was 56.1 miles per hour, allowing 5 minutes for getting up speed and reducing it to stop. The actual running speed was 62.8 miles per hour.

> The distance from Hitchin to the ticket platform on the up journey was performed in 37 minutes starting to stopping, being an average speed of 51.8 miles per hour. The running speed is 60 miles per hour.

The morning was rather slippery.

Average speeds of about 60mph were not exceeded on subsequent runs. Delays often occurred due to other traffic on the line. Congestion and the absence of brakes on the locomotive made successful high-speed runs unlikely on a regular basis. Boiler pressure did not exceed 120lb on any of the runs.

Water consumption was monitored during the twelve runs. In spite of the tender holding 2,000 gallons, water supply for a non-stop run from King's Cross to Peterborough would have been a major problem. The tender had a depth of 35in and the consumption of water between Peterborough and King's Cross averaged 33½in for the 75 miles, with one trip using 37in of water. The tender was subsequently enlarged to 2,500 gallons. Perhaps with the enlarged tender, 215 might have run 100 miles without stopping for water, but it seems unlikely. Water troughs were not introduced to any UK railway till 1860, when John Ramsbottom of the LNWR introduced troughs between the rails at Mochdre in North Wales.

David Joy, a friend of Sturrock's from Joy's time as chief locomotive designer for Wilson, recalled in his diaries how Sturrock was fed-up with criticism from the directors that 215 'had never done anything'. One day Sturrock noted that 215 was on a train at

Hitchin with fourteen carriages and some of the directors onboard. He ordered the driver to do his best to Holloway Bridge, the ticket station for King's Cross. The 31-mile journey was undertaken in 28 minutes, an average speed of 66mph. It is possible the engine achieved 75mph at some point on this trip.

It is understandable that the directors were not much enamoured of the engine. When the invoice came to their attention on 9 August 1853, the costs exceeded the estimate by £1,000. Sturrock was required to write a letter of explanation to the accounts committee.[9] He stated the locomotive had been much altered in the course of construction and that the parts were more expensive than Hawthorns had contemplated.

> Being an experimental engine it was charged with a full set of drawings and plans and its construction took a much longer time than supposed. The price of materials increased very much during this period and so ran up the expense. The tender also cost more than contemplated in consequence of its capacity having been made up to 2,000 gallons and the wheels made 4ft 3in instead of 4ft. I regret that the charge has amounted to £3,500, but I believe it to be worth it and to have fully cost this sum and that I am to a great extent responsible for the excess cost, though at the same time I believe that Messrs. Hawthorn made a mistake in the original calculation.

It must be assumed that the extra £1,000 covered the cost of conversion to a bogie and a change to flanged driving wheels. Sturrock explained Hawthorns had agreed to waive any profit element and would only charge the actual cost. Sturrock's explanation was accepted and the bill paid.

With the benefit of hindsight the expenditure on 215 was hard to justify. Records show that the 'large' Hawthorns and Jenny Linds had averaged 280,000 miles in the period to December 1864. 215 averaged only 144,626 miles in the same period.[10] Repairs to a non-standard engine are likely to have been more costly and time-consuming than for a standard locomotive. 215 did not fit in with Sturrock's successor's rebuilding plans and was withdrawn in October 1869. Its wrought-iron driving wheel centres were found to be in good condition and were reused in Stirling's No.92, again the sole member of its Class.[11]

While 215 was under construction, Sturrock was much occupied with the design and development of new goods wagons. Sturrock and Seymour Clarke agreed on a design for a new covered wagon in June 1852. Two gunpowder vans and an invalid and family carriage were produced in the GNR's own shops. A number of road goods vans were also built at Boston for deliveries around London and the major cities. The drawings were signed off by Sturrock at Boston in August 1852.[12] The company made very few of its own carriages or wagons till the 1860s.

Sturrock managed to secure some holiday in 1852. At the 10 August Executive Committee he asked to be away until the second week in September as this time of year is 'least inconvenient to the service'. It also gave Sturrock the opportunity to return home to Scotland and shoot grouse and for his children to see their cousins and grandparents. Parker was left in charge of the locomotive department.

The first of Sturrock's reports from Doncaster is dated 13 September 1852 and concerned an accident to a tank engine on the MSLR main line. The mail train, consisting of two loose coupled goods vans, two coaches and a guards van, had left Sheffield at 9.10 p.m. for Retford. The tank engine No.29, a recently converted Sharp 2-2-2, was derailed as it descended the Dore House embankment at 30mph. The wagons and carriages went down the opposite side of the embankment to the locomotive. Five passengers were injured. The guard was killed and the driver subsequently died from his injuries.

The inquiry into the accident was conducted by Captain Galton, who noted that the position of the trailing wheels had remained unaltered when the locomotive was converted to a tank engine. This would have the effect of increasing the weight on the trailing wheels to more than the weight on the driving wheels. He argued that the engine would have a strong tendency to oscillation, particularly if the trucks were loose coupled. He believed that the trailing wheels had come off the rails first, since the fireman had seen sparks coming from these wheels.

Sturrock defended his tank engine conversions. He thought it unlikely that the trailing wheels came off first. He noted that many locomotives including the GNR's Cramptons and other designs built by Stephenson for the LNWR and the Newcastle & Berwick had greater weight on the trailing wheels.

> The evidence produced at the inquest did not lead to any satisfactory explanation of this accident, but on speculating on the cause, I came to the conclusion that, if the engine was to be blamed, it arose from its having been very improperly coupled to loose goods wagons and driven down a steep gradient at a most improper speed. The poor driver had neglected to see the engine screwed up to the wagon though a screw was fixed to all those engines for the purpose.

Sturrock accepted that the risk of oscillation would be reduced if the trailing wheels were further back, but the converted tank engines would not then be able to be turned on carriage turntables. Twenty converted Sharps had entered service between January and August 1852 and had completed 135,720 miles in the period without accident. Reluctantly he agreed to keep the inspector happy by moving the trailing wheels back; such changes would not be expensive.[13]

1853 opened with the placing of the final contracts for fitting out Doncaster. A larger engine-weighing machine was required, since the one on order could not cope with the new eight-wheeled express engines, and the cost would rise by £100. Gas fittings, heating and water pipes were also obtained. The committee accepted the lowest tender, where there was no doubt about quality and delivery. The highest tender for gas fittings was £936 16s 9d, very substantially more than the £610 18s 7d of the lowest tender from Knapton of York, who won the contract.

Sturrock and the Executive Committee were closely involved with decisions on the purchase of consumables used by the locomotive department. Two of the most important and costly items in the 1850s were coke and grease. Grease manufacture had ceased at Boston in August 1852 due to the fire risk; Sturrock advised the committee that his carriage and wagon staff liked Mr Cantrell's grease better than that produced by the company. Cantrell's grease continued to be bought for the next two years, until in June 1855 the Executive Committee asked why the company did not make its own grease. The storekeeper indicated he had suggested this to Sturrock and Cubitt many times, but they had taken no action. Estimates were then obtained for a grease factory for installation at King's Cross. Approval for the purchase was given in August 1855, a month before the Queen's 1855 journey to Scotland, a journey in which grease was to play a significant role.

Sturrock ensured that price alone did not determine the supplier of coke. A Board member, who asked why the company obtained their coke from Straker & Love since the coke was more costly than that from Pease, was told that the coke from Pease was of poor quality. Sturrock was prepared to stand his ground when it was in the interest of his department. By 1854 Straker & Love were supplying 600 tons per week at 12s 3d a ton. A request to increase the price by a shilling to take account of coal price increases was rejected by the Executive Committee. Sturrock was told to tell Straker & Love to stick to the contract price.

Six months later Sturrock was becoming concerned regarding coke supplies for 1855. He needed 2,000 tons of coke in the light of the expansion of the GNR's business and wrote to the Board in July 1854 suggesting he should get quotations. Only three of the four potential suppliers tendered and only two of the three could supply in the quantities required. Straker & Love offered 800 to 1,000 tons per week at 16s 3d per ton, Stobert & Co. 400 tons at 15s a ton and John Robinson of Merrifield Colliery 1,000 tons at 16s a ton. The prices were about one third up on the previous year. Sturrock was left to negotiate the best deal he could get and a new contract was agreed in August 1854 for supplies in 1855.

In his half-year report of August 1855 Sturrock noted that the main reason for an increase in his costs was the rise of 3s 1¾d per ton in coke costs. The chairman asked Sturrock to check out North Eastern Railway coke prices, since he had read in *The Times* that their coke was cheaper than GNR coke. Sturrock investigated and explained that much of the difference was accounted for by transport costs. The North Eastern Railway did have a proportion of its supply on a long-term contract to 1857, which was well below the going price. However, the other two suppliers would be more costly than GNR suppliers, when transport costs to York were added on. The figures were also distorted by the fact that the NER did not charge for the cost of its coke wagons. Coke was passed on to the traffic department at cost. Sturrock concluded the GNR coke costs were very reasonable.

In October 1855 Sturrock raised the question of supplies for 1856. He had written to potential suppliers and only one, a Mr Robson, could match the GNR's needs. Sturrock and three directors met Robson in York on 25 October and agreed a price of 13s a ton for 1,400 tons per week. A second contract was agreed with Sir John Kaye's Stockton Colliery near Barnsley for the supply of 100 tons per week also at 13s a ton. This contract proved unsatisfactory, since the tunnel access to the colliery was too small to permit the use of standard GNR wagons and the GNR had only a small number of wagons of a size to travel through Sir John Kaye's tunnel.

At the 18 October Board Sturrock suggested that coal might be used in passenger trains to reduce costs This practice had been banned in May 1854, when Seymour Clarke had accused drivers of taking coal from adjacent coal trucks to make their engines appear more economical than they really were. Sturrock had defended his drivers, who were still on a bonus related to fuel consumption, but the Board had sided with Seymour Clarke. Sturrock argued that 'a lump of coal could be most serviceable' and was much cheaper than coke. The Board agreed to the use of small amounts of coal provided smoke was prevented. Many engineers had started to experiment with the development of boilers suitable for burning coal in a way that would avoid smoke.

Sturrock also had to face the problem of insufficient accommodation for his workmen at Peterborough. Facilities for the overhaul of locomotives had been built at New England, some distance from the historic centre of the town. Sturrock advised the Board in February 1853 that he needed sixty cottages and suggested that, if the company donated some land, a builder might be happy to construct cottages for letting. The Board deferred a decision till May, when it agreed in principle to adopt Sturrock's suggestion, an approach which had been successful in Swindon.

Unfortunately the proposal made no progress, since builders could not be found to risk their capital. Sturrock came back to the Board in January 1854 with a letter from his foreman explaining that fifty cottages were essential. The men could never get a hot dinner unless they lived near the works and transport had to be provided to take them back and forth from Peterborough. This time the Board agreed to build the houses themselves. A contract for the construction of the houses was agreed in March 1854, more than a year after Sturrock made his first request.[14] More cottages were subsequently built in 1855, at the same time as an expansion of the repair facilities.

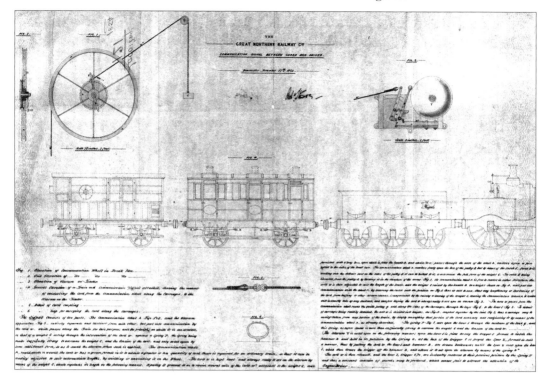

A drawing signed by Sturrock of the guard driver communication system adopted by the GNR; the cord connecting the pulley in the guard's van to the bell on the tender passed along the frame of the carriages just above the buffers. (National Archives)

Similar accommodation difficulties arose in London in June 1853, where there were insufficient houses for the skilled men Budge needed to staff his repair facilities. Men had to be given an advance of wages to meet rents, which had been pushed up by the opening of the GNR's line to King's Cross. Sturrock once again suggested making company land available for private builders to supply houses at fair rents. Sturrock believed this would help to keep wage rates down.

As train speeds increased, railways needed an arrangement which would help the traffic department identify where trains were on the system and, in addition, reduce the risk of accidents. The Electric Telegraph had been first installed at the main GNR stations in March 1852 and reached York by April of the same year. The system operated between the hours of 9 a.m. and 7 p.m. By October the Board had decided that the hours should be extended from 8 a.m. to 8 p.m., but Sturrock expressed the view that this was still inadequate. Winter was approaching and the goods traffic would be heavy. Without the Telegraph at night, there was no means of knowing where the trains were. He suggested appointing a duplicate set of clerks, so that twenty-four-hour cover could be provided at major stations. He commented that this would not be costly and 'will add to the safety and economy of the line'. The Board agreed, for additional clerks were cheap.[15] A year later in December 1853, the Board agreed to protect all tunnels with the Electric Telegraph.

Another problem which affected safety was the issue of communication between guard and driver and guard and passengers. Various possible systems had been patented and reviewed by Sturrock and Seymour Clarke, but the railways realised that this was an area where a common approach was desirable. The matter was debated between the general managers of the major railways, who agreed to adopt the bell and rope system, which did nothing to help a passenger in the event of an 'outrage' in a carriage. A rope passed along the carriages from the guard to the tender, where a bell could be rung in an emergency. Sturrock estimated the cost to the GNR would be about £1,500 if the system was fixed to all passenger trains. 116 passenger engines would require a bell on the tender and all the carriages and break vans would need to be adapted to carry the rope. The system was introduced from 1 February 1854.[16] By August 1855 the Board of Trade was pressing for the introduction of a similar system on goods trains. Sturrock and Seymour Clarke were asked to see if a cheaper system could be evolved for goods trains; they concluded in October that there was nothing simpler than the bell and rope.

The cost of introducing guard/driver communication was nothing in comparison with the costs of modifications that Sturrock proposed to coal wagons. He advised the Board that coal wagon axles were regularly breaking as a result of increased loads. Colliers were reluctant to fill the wagons to within 10cwt of a proper load. He proposed to change the axles, axle boxes and springs, so that all wagons could take modern loads. The cost would be £9 per wagon for those with adequate springs and £13 for those which needed new springs. The total cost was likely to be about £17,500. Sturrock made sure the Board knew the problems only related to wagons bought before he joined the GNR. The Board agreed to the expenditure provided it was phased. As a result accidents continued to arise from broken wheels or springs for a number of years.

Sturrock's standing in the railway world was recognised when he was called to give evidence to a select committee on Railway and Canal Bills and Amalgamations in April 1853. According to the select committee's report, the GNR was the third largest railway company when measured by number of engines. The GNR had 228 engines and was already larger than the GWR, which had 193 engines. Only the LNWR with 629 engines and the Midland with 331 engines were larger than the GNR.

One of the issues which concerned the committee was running powers over the lines of other railways. Some members of the committee and some witnesses, including Sir William Cubitt, believed it was desirable to create a single company or at least large regional companies, so that the risks associated with giving railways running powers over adjacent lines was reduced. In this debate the GNR and the MSLR were, at the time, in opposite camps. James Allport, then general manager of the MSLR, argued that GNR drivers were not sufficiently familiar with MSLR signalling and working methods, when the GNR trains used their running powers from Retford to Sheffield. Seymour Clarke dismissed the risk, using a letter from Sturrock which indicated that the GNR drivers all had MSLR Handbooks. Ultimately the committee was not convinced by the arguments of those in favour of running powers. However, current arrangements were not changed and, in subsequent years, Sturrock was to appear on behalf of other railway companies to explain how the GNR coped with many different railway companies running trains into GNR stations.

When Sturrock appeared before the committee on 18 April 1853, he was questioned on the potential impact of amalgamations on running costs and safety. Sturrock opposed amalgamations and said, 'I think that the probability is the working expenses would be increased … from the natural sluggishness which creeps into a large body governed by committees, who are dealing with technical subjects.' Sturrock argued that efficiency would be greatest if the officers had control over a railway of a manageable size. If that size was exceeded, engineers might have to carry out orders with which they disagreed as a result of being controlled by committees. With such a structure, 'I believe there would necessarily arise non-responsibility and less interest in the business and, consequently, increased expenditure'. Sturrock did not wish to be a 'big company' man.

The select committee debated an issue which remains relevant today. Should the officers be made criminally liable for their actions? Sturrock argued that this would lead officers to incur excessive expenditure to cover themselves. The committee asked if he did not think the public would be willing to pay for security and he replied, 'I certainly do not think so.' He noted that the cost of running trains – drivers, firemen, repairs, fuel, water and carriage repairs – ranged from about 8*d* to 1*s* 1½*d* per mile. If made criminally liable, Sturrock thought costs might rise by 3*d* to 4*d* per mile.

The select committee also discussed with him the interplay between accidents and punctuality. 89 million passengers had been carried in 1852. 381 passengers and fifty-one railway staff were killed. With trains running at defined time intervals, unpunctuality could lead to accidents and was often caused by detention at stations, when the train was held back for a passenger. 'I think we are not unwilling to see lost time made up occasionally, so as to bring the train punctual, because we believe it is safer to do so than to leave the train unpunctual.' Sturrock emphasised that drivers must not exceed a safe speed and had to take account of the dangers of oscillation and the state of the road. Sturrock did not favour dividing trains in two, since costs were increased and the more trains there were on a line the greater the potential for accidents.

With regard to limits on repair costs, Sturrock told the select committee he had none. However, if he was to be answerable for culpable negligence, he thought his expenditure would be much more lavish. He was asked what he would do if made to work without adequate engines or carriages. He indicated he would cover himself in his correspondence. He agreed it was a matter of opinion rather than demonstrable fact whether an engine was safe or not.

The issue of train speed and punctuality was a concern to both Sturrock and Seymour Clarke. Drivers were tempted to exceed acceptable speed limits in order to make up lost time. Seymour Clarke wrote to Sturrock in July 1853: 'On no account in the event of their being late to make up lost time by running faster than the maximum speed named in the authorised time bills for the fast express trains.' Sturrock was to ask drivers to try and save time when stopping and starting at stations.[17] The Board had had some discussions with the Lancashire & Yorkshire Railway in April 1853 about getting together to consider holding down speed, but nothing seems to have come of this. The public wanted fast and punctual trains.

Returning from his meeting with the select committee, Sturrock drafted another report to the Board asking for more goods locomotives. He had been told by Seymour Clarke that coal traffic was expected to rise by 50 per cent next winter. Sturrock pointed out that it was not just the volume of traffic which affected the demand for engines, but also the peaks in traffic in a particular week. Sturrock indicated he was awaiting delivery of nine goods locomotives from previous orders, including some Class 168 0-6-0s from Wilson and Fairbairn and Class 308s from Nasmyth. He asked for another ten engines to be ordered immediately, since they would take six to seven months to arrive. He recommended placing the orders with Stephenson, Hawthorn or Wilson, since they were more reliable than most with regard to delivery dates and two of the three were as cheap as any.

When he came before the Board on 3 May 1853, Sturrock asked to abandon his request back in November 1851 for ten more passenger engines and take an extra ten goods engines instead. He wanted to order a total of twenty goods engines. The Board agreed to obtain tenders from Hawthorn, Wilson, Stephenson and Sharp Stewart. In coming to a decision the committee took account of delivery dates as well as price. Hawthorn received an order for five engines at £3,025 and Kitson of Leeds an order for another five for £2,750. Sturrock had added Kitson to the list of those invited to tender. Both manufacturers had received their orders because they promised to deliver between September and the end of November. In practice only one engine was delivered by the end of October. Most were delivered during November and December, but the last Hawthorn did not arrive till February 1854. Wilson's tender had not arrived in time for the Executive Committee meeting, but permission was given subsequently to order five more engines from Wilson, not the ten Sturrock wanted.

Sturrock's responsibility for rolling stock was no sinecure. During the two years from March 1852 to March 1854 2,386 wagons and forty-four passenger carriages were added to the fleet. Specifications had to be prepared, tenders obtained and orders monitored. Rolling stock suppliers were no better at delivering on time than their locomotive manufacturing colleagues. Imposition of the penalties for late delivery could be difficult if the GNR had not supplied the wheels, axles or springs on time. The increase to the carriage stock included ten composite first-class coaches and ten composite second-class, plus twenty horse boxes. A shareholder at the August 1853 half-yearly meeting queried why the GNR had such a large fleet of rolling stock. Denison explained that GNR carriages were much preferred by the travelling public and often ran through to Edinburgh. It was the high standing of the GNR carriages, which was subsequently to lead to Sturrock and his team being asked in 1862 to design and build the joint stock to be used by all companies on the East Coast main line.

The popularity of the GNR stock was due in part to the poor quality of the carriages owned by the North British Railway (NBR). Sturrock and Seymour Clark had concerns about the safety of the NBR carriages and were reluctant to accept them on GNR lines. The NBR retaliated by saying GNR stock could not run north of Berwick, if NBR stock could not run south to London. Sturrock reported an incident when a tyre on a NBR coach had broken. An accident was only avoided by a passenger crawling along the carriage roof and warning the driver. The Board offered the passenger a £500 reward if he could be identified. The Board of Trade Inspector advised the GNR it was not absolved of responsibility for NBR stock when running on GNR lines. In January 1854 the Board asked the secretary to take the matter up again with the Board of Trade. Meanwhile Seymour Clarke was to use his discretion regarding the running of NBR stock on GNR lines.[18]

Relations between the GNR and the NBR had improved by the end of the year. Petre, the locomotive superintendent of the NBR, had approached Sturrock in October 1855 about the GNR providing help to the NBR with repairs or the loan of locomotives. Sturrock advised the December 1854 Board that the chairman had asked him to lend the NBR six goods locomotives and drivers for a period of two months from 4 December. The NBR would be responsible for maintenance and pay the GNR 6d per mile. GNR drivers were accompanying their engines.

Sturrock visited the NBR in Edinburgh over the Christmas period, by which time Petre had been dismissed. Sturrock established that the NBR was not exaggerating its problems. He found the NBR had only one engine capable of hauling main line expresses to London. If this broke down, the NBR could not fulfil its part in the East Coast service. The Board agreed to lend the NBR two passenger engines on the same basis as the first six goods engines. The NBR's problems were caused as much by a shortage of cash as by the poor quality of its locomotive engineers.[19] The NBR was not the only Scottish company to ask for help from the GNR. In November 1855 the Aberdeen & Scottish Midland requested a loan of three or four goods engines. The decision was left to Sturrock and Seymour Clarke.[20]

By August of 1853 it was already apparent that the facilities at Doncaster and Peterborough were inadequate for the growing railway. The Smithy was extended in Doncaster and new locomotive 'stables' and a fitting shop were to be erected at Peterborough. Two fire engines were also to be purchased for Doncaster and six special trucks were to be acquired with iron bottoms to move wheels around the works. The Board agreed regular small improvements and extensions to plant and machinery at Doncaster to enable the expanding fleet of rolling stock and locomotives to be maintained.

By November 1853 Sturrock was becoming concerned about his requirements for engines for the coal trade in the following year. He had been told that there would be twenty more coal trains in 1854, for which he would need twenty-five more engines.

Although there were still thirteen engines to come from the last order, these were needed for the existing trade. Engines had to be kept in fire and sent out on double trips. As a consequence, maintenance routines were not being followed and engines were deteriorating. The Board agreed with Sturrock and tenders were obtained for additional Class 308 goods engines with 5ft 3in driving wheels from ten manufacturers. Sharp Stewart received an order for fifteen at £2,980, Wilson for five at £2,980 and Vulcan for five at £2,925. At the same Executive Committee meeting orders were place for twenty composite carriages from Williams, one of only two manufacturers who tendered. 500 coal wagons were ordered from John Ashbury at £74 each.

By mid-February 1854 Seymour Clarke had again revised his forecasts for goods traffic the following year. He wanted to buy 500 coal wagons from Williams, who could supply at £75 each. Sturrock indicated that twenty-five more goods engines would now be needed over and above the twenty-five ordered a month earlier. Sturrock was aware that the York, Newcastle & Berwick Railway was about to buy engines and wished to get the GNR orders placed first. Sturrock obtained quotations for the Board meeting ten days later. Delivery dates had extended to twelve months or more. Wilson received an order for eleven engines to be delivered by January 1855 at a cost of £3,100 each for locomotive and tender. Sharp Stewart received an order for five at the same price for delivery in March and April 1855 and Kitson an order for five at £3,150 for January delivery. Sturrock met the three manufacturers and agreed the contract details for the twenty-one engines.

Sturrock was still short of four of the twenty-five engines he had been promised and the gap was to be filled by the purchase of four engines owned by C.C. Williams and manufactured by Wilsons. Williams had the contract to operate the Oxford, Worcester & Wolverhampton Railway (OWWR) and the engines were ordered for this railway, but appear never to have been used. Williams had originally offered the engines to the GNR in November 1854 and the offer had been rejected. Perhaps in the light of the long delivery dates for the latest orders, Sturrock changed his mind and in February persuaded the Board to negotiate with Williams. Two of the engines from Williams were 0-6-0s of very similar design to the Class 308s ordered at the previous Board. Sturrock noted that they were built to his own designs, with the same materials as specified for the GNR orders but with somewhat larger fireboxes. They were effectively treated as Class 308s for operational purposes and were delivered in March 1854, giving Sturrock some immediate relief at the end of the busiest period for the coal trade. The price was £3,100 for each engine and tender.

The second two engines acquired via Williams from the OWWR were 2-4-0 passenger locomotives costing £3,000. These two engines had also been built to Sturrock's specification by Wilson. Sturrock suggested the engines would be very suitable for the Bradford & Leeds[21] line for which he had no suitable locomotives due to the gradients. 'Having not had notice, I can not otherwise be prepared in time.' The engines were delivered in March 1854 and had 3ft 6in leading wheels and 5ft 9in coupled driving wheels. Their design appears to owe more to Sturrock than to Wilson's traditional Jenny Linds. The engines remained in regular use till 1886.

With the engine orders in place, Sturrock took the unusual step of asking for leave of absence 'for two to three weeks' in May 1854. On 9 May at the parish church of Steeple Ashton in Wiltshire, Archibald Sturrock and Helen Crawley were married by the bride's uncle, William Crawley. Helen was a first cousin to Sturrock's first wife Caroline Fullerton, their mothers being sisters. Helen had been a regular visitor to the Sturrock household when Caroline was alive and godmother to Sturrock's son Gordon. Her father, who had died in 1849, had left a substantial fortune of over £50,000, which Helen inherited. Helen died six months later on 9 November in Doncaster, leaving Sturrock a wealthy widower. He never married again. It was Helen's fortune which enabled him to retire at the age of fifty in 1866.

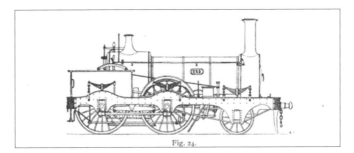

Developed from the Class 71 2-4-0s, the Class 223s were described by Bird as handsome. (Bird)

Fig. 24.

On his return from honeymoon, Sturrock had to give further thought to the locomotive requirements of the Leeds, Bradford & Halifax Railway. The acquisition of the two passenger engines from Williams was not sufficient to enable Sturrock to meet its needs. He had had to transfer engines from elsewhere to handle traffic on the opening in August 1854. He advised the Board he needed six more coupled passenger locomotives. The Board agreed and Sturrock came back to the Executive Committee in September with plans for his Class 223 2-4-0 passenger engines. He obtained the committee's consent to limit the manufacturers invited to tender to Sharp Stewart, Hawthorn, Wilson and Stephenson. Hawthorn received an order for six engines at £2,930 to be delivered at the rate of two per month from April to June 1855. They were delivered between June and September 1855.

The Class 223 2-4-0s were a development from the Class 71 2-4-0s, which had been ordered on the day before Sturrock was appointed and subject to significant modification by Sturrock before delivery. The new 2-4-0s were designed to cope with the heavy gradients around Leeds and Halifax. Their coupled wheels were 6ft 6in in diameter, an increase of 6in on the Class 71 2-4-0s. The cylinder diameter was also increased by ½in to 16½in and there were corresponding adjustments to boiler and wheelbase. They were considered handsome engines by Bird. Rebuilt by Stirling in 1866 and 1867, the engines continued in service till the 1880s.

As the GNR became more established, the Board started to give closer attention to costs. Sturrock's early half-yearly reports to the shareholders had a standardised form of wording, which suggested he could spend as he liked. In his report for the year ending December 1852, Sturrock wrote, 'I have not spared any expense in the maintenance of the rolling stock and that it is therefore in my opinion in full and efficient working condition.' In August 1853 he was even more confident: 'Engines and stock have been maintained in perfect working order'. Similar sentiments were expressed in 1854.

The increase in GNR locomotive running costs was questioned at the shareholders' meeting on 1 September 1854. Denison replied:

> I am told by Mr Sturrock, who stands behind me and who lives in the same town as I do and with whom I have frequent conversations on the subject of the current expenses, and perhaps more frequent than he likes, that everything he consumes has materially raised in price – coke is higher, wages are higher, wood is higher etc.

Sturrock and Denison had a close working relationship. They lived a few doors apart in Doncaster. Issues were reviewed with Denison before being discussed at Board or Executive Committees.

The Board requested more information on the work of Sturrock's department. The Board received a monthly report on the number of wagons under repair by type of wagon and examined the locomotive department's fortnightly pay sheets. Any increase in costs had to be explained by reference to increased mileage or, more rarely, increases in wage rates. In the half-yearly report to shareholders for the period to December 1854, Sturrock noted the mileage had risen from 2,587,258 to 2,834,107, a rise of 9.5 per cent. Costs had risen from 9.01*d* to 9.54*d* per mile, a rise of 5.9 per cent and there had been a greater proportion of goods and coal trains. The stock had still been maintained in 'perfect working order'.

Sturrock did not have an easy time with the Board in March 1855. His report on the locomotive pay sheets for the last two weeks of January 1855 had shown an increase from £4,198 in the corresponding period in the previous year to £4,467 in the current year, a rise of 6.4 per cent. The next fortnight's pay sheets were more troubling with a rise from £4,018 to £4,492, an uplift of nearly 12 per cent. Stating this was due to more coal trains did not get Sturrock off the hook. He was asked to 'furnish the Committee with an explanation of the items making up this large excess'.

Part of the problem was caused by the irregularity of the coal trains. Sturrock could not change the number of men employed on a daily basis to align with the number of coal trains, as the following table for January 1855 coal trains indicates.[22] Coal trains did not run on Sundays:

Date	No. of Coal Trains	Date	No. of Coal Trains	Date	No. of Coal Trains
Jan1	11	Jan 12	10	Jan 22	13
2	11	13	8	23	15
3	5			24	7
4	7	15	10	25	9
5	9	16	9	26	14
6	11	17	10	27	12
		18	10		
8	10	19	10	29	14
9	8	20	8	30	7
10	9			31	7
11	9				

Sturrock gave the committee a thorough and robust defence of his recent cost increases. He checked wage rates in Leeds, Manchester and Newcastle and in the workshops of the Midland, North Eastern and London North Western Railways. He advised the committee that GNR rates were below those in his comparator companies and as low as he considered appropriate if he was to obtain good workmen. He checked his department's costs against those of other railway companies and concluded: 'You will see my department has been worked much more cheaply than any of those railways … Expenditure is low because GNR stock is not of average age.'[23] By August, as a result of the opening of the LBHR, numbers employed in the locomotive department had risen from 1,787 in 1854 to 1,965 in 1855.

During 1855 Sturrock acquired nine locomotives and all the rolling stock from the Nottingham & Grantham Railway. Although the GNR had run services from London to Nottingham over the line from July 1852, the N&GR was not formally leased to the GNR till March 1855. The engines included three Wilson 0-4-0 tanks, which were immediately rebuilt by Sturrock as 0-4-2 saddle tanks, a Hawthorn and a Wilson 2-2-2, and three Wilson 0-6-0s. The Hawthorn was a copy of the GNR's 'large' Hawthorns and was a useful addition to the fleet. The three Wilson 0-6-0s were similar to those purchased by the GNR in 1861 and were later to be modified to draw steam tenders. The Wilson 2-2-2 was a Jenny Lind type, albeit somewhat smaller than the two already in the GNR fleet. The Wilson 2-4-0 was a goods engine, which was converted to a 0-6-0 saddle tank in 1867-8.

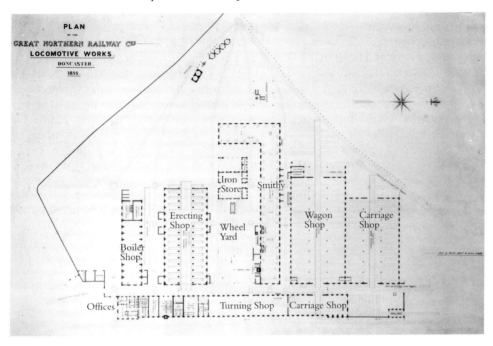

PLAN
GREAT NORTHERN RAILWAY CO
LOCOMOTIVE WORKS.
DONCASTER
1855

Iron Store · Smithy
Erecting Shop · Wheel Yard · Wagon Shop · Carriage Shop
Boiler Shop
Offices · Turning Shop · Carriage Shop

The Plant at Doncaster following the additions of 1855. (Wabtec Rail)

The white buildings on the left incorporate the buildings erected between 1852 and 1855 and continue to be used by Wabtec Rail for locomotive and rolling stock refurbishment in 2006. (Author)

In early 1855 Sturrock encouraged the Board to expand facilities in Doncaster and Peterborough. After some debate and a reference to Joseph Cubitt, the Board agreed to provide additional facilities at Doncaster at a cost of £4,350. These included roofing over the hooping furnace and hydraulic presses and roofing between the stables and repair shops. The coppersmiths and stores were to be moved to enable a new line to be installed so that traffic could work the station better. After a visit to Peterborough by a sub-committee of four directors, agreement was given to an enlarged engine shed for twelve more engines, a smiths' shop with twelve fires, a school room and fifty more cottages.[24]

Sturrock was confronted with a rather different problem at Peterborough. The committee asked why Sturrock's foreman, Owen, who was no longer performing his duties, had been included in the bonus list. Sturrock advised the committee that he had been ill off and on for several months between April and October 1854 and did not think he could ever resume his duties. 'It is far too responsible a post to entrust to any person who has, like Mr Owen, been in a state of lunacy'. Sturrock advised that Owen's employment should be terminated and that he should receive a gratuity of £50, as he was one of the company's oldest servants having joined in 1848.[25] Owen's departure gave Sturrock an opportunity to promote Charles Sacré from Boston to Peterborough. The Board agreed to spend £200 enlarging the Peterborough foreman's house to accommodate Charles Sacré's family.

In the light of a re-shuffle of responsibilities in the locomotive department, the Board agreed a new pay structure for Sturrock's team with effect from 1 July 1855:

Post	Location	Old Salary £	New Salary £	Benefits £
Coffin	Carriage Inspector Doncaster	250	315	15 housing allowance
Parker	Works Manager Doncaster	350	450	40 housing allowance
Budge	King's Cross	200	250	House
Sacré	Peterborough	200	250	House
Johnson	Doncaster	200	250	House
Froward	Boston	–	200*	–
Grinling	Accountant	200	250	–

*£200 on appointment and £250 on completion of his probationary period

Sturrock enjoyed his August holiday in 1855 and returned to work on 5 September, the day before the Queen was to make her usual visit to Balmoral. The GNR directors attached great importance to the Queens' patronage of the East Coast route and expected the senior officers to check personally that everything was in order. Seymour Clarke had written to Sturrock on 20 August to ask him to have the carriages ready in plenty of time and Sturrock had confirmed that 'all was perfectly arranged' before he went on holiday. However, the carriages only reached King's Cross from Doncaster on 4 September. Leith, the traffic superintendent, was unable to give them a long enough run the following day to test that all was in order. None of this would have mattered if the journey had proceeded without a problem.

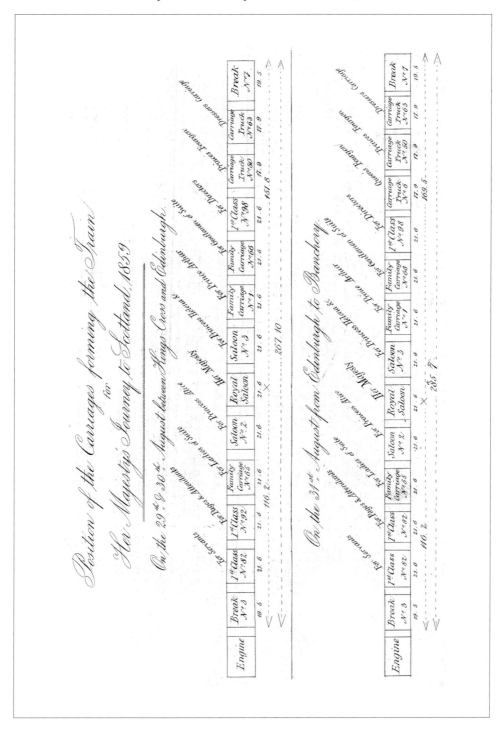

The plan shows the position of the carriages in the Royal Train to Scotland in August 1859. (National Archives)

Unfortunately for Sturrock, four of the carriages of the Royal Train suffered from overheated axle boxes. The Royal carriage itself was deemed to be unsafe to use when the train reached Darlington and the Queen had to move to one of the Saloon carriages. In addition two break vans and one first-class carriage suffered from overheated axle boxes. William Haigh, one of two men employed to grease the wheels whilst the train was in motion, was knocked from the train near Ferryhill and died. The Board and the Board of Trade conducted investigations. Sturrock was asked to explain the 'bad performance of the axles'.[2] The Queen awarded Mr Haigh's widow a pension of £30 per year.

Sturrock advised the Board that all the carriages had been carefully checked and tested in Doncaster before they were sent to London. He considered the problem arose solely from the use of too stiff grease.

> This grease would not run through the axle boxes till the journals had become so warm that they could not afterwards be cooled by lubricating matter. It was intended, as Mr Clarke had requested, that such might be the case for the grease to have been similar to that which answered so admirably last year, but I now believe was made with rather more tallow than previously and that therefore it failed.

Sturrock also considered that the addition of extra weights to make the Royal carriages run smoothly could have contributed to the problem and he advised removing the extra weights. Seymour Clarke suggested that Sturrock should find a way of making it impossible for an axle to overheat. Sturrock was not prepared to give such an undertaking, but argued that the risk would be much reduced if the train was stopped more frequently for a detailed examination.[27]

The Board reviewed Sturrock's report and those provided by Seymour Clarke and Leith, the traffic superintendent, on 18 September. They were of the 'opinion that the conduct of the locomotive engineer was negligent in the extreme.' His failure to give his personal attention to the Royal carriages was particularly reprehensible. Sturrock was called in by the chairman and asked to give some further explanation. Sturrock left the room and the Board continued its deliberations. It seems likely that his dismissal was considered. Sturrock was told that with due precaution some of the untoward events might have been prevented. The Board advised that any repeat of these events 'would incur their marked displeasure'.[28]

Sturrock's relationship with Seymour Clarke and Walter Leith can not have been improved by this incident. Seymour Clarke must have found it frustrating that Sturrock did not report to him. Any disputes over, for example, the disciplining of drivers out on the line had to be brought before the Board or Executive Committee, if Sturrock and Clarke could not agree. At the 20 November Board it was determined that any driver who disobeyed orders would be taken before the magistrate, if Clarke so decided. The traffic and locomotive departments fell out about responsibility for the cleanliness of carriages. Sturrock maintained that, once out on the line, it was up to traffic to check the carriages were clean and to decide when to send them to Sturrock for relining, a costly process. He wrote to the Board:

> My opinion is that the inspection fails on the part of the traffic department at small stations where it would be an improper expense for me to keep inspectors but where the traffic must have servants who should be perfectly competent to notice any defect in a carriage. The mode of inspection detailed above is the substance of what I arranged with Mr John Denniston, when he was superintendent of the line and I believe it is the only mode of conducting the coaching department of a railway with economy and I would therefore recommend its being carried out.[29]

In this instance, Sturrock's approach was followed.

As 1855 drew to a close, Sturrock must have looked to the future with some concern. He had disturbed the Board greatly as a result of the incident with the Queen's train. His relationship with the traffic department was less than wholly satisfactory. His personal life had been upset by the death of his second wife. The Board was giving increasingly close scrutiny to his departmental expenditure, which was bound to rise as engines, wagons and carriages aged.

On the plus side, his standing in the railway community was being recognised by requests for his advice from other railways. His 0-6-0s for the mineral and coal trades were proving to be satisfactory. The 'large' Hawthorns, the converted Cramptons and the new 2-4-0s were all meeting his passenger engine requirements. The converted Sharp tank engines were proving a sound investment. The GNR passenger carriages were recognised to be of high quality by the travelling public. He had a strong and supportive locomotive department management team.

7

CONSOLIDATION AND CHANGE ON THE GNR 1856–60

The five years from January 1856 to December 1860 were a period of consolidation and change for both the GNR and Sturrock. The dominance of the LNWR over the MSLR was ended. This enabled the GNR to forge links with the MSLR and introduce through express services from King's Cross to Manchester. From February 1858 Midland trains used the GNR line from Hitchin for access to London, a move which in due course led to congestion at King's Cross for both passenger and goods traffic. This was also a period of technical change. Grease was being supplanted by oil as an axle lubricant and coke was gradually being replaced by coal as the main locomotive fuel. As speeds increased, the debate on brake power intensified. Carriage and wagon building was greatly expanded at Doncaster.

Although some of the locomotives and rolling stock were starting to age, Sturrock was still expected to hold costs. No new locomotives were added to the fleet in the four years to May 1860, with the exception of the final three Class 308 0-6-0s delivered in January 1856. The number of wagons increased from 6,848 in December 1855 to 7,522 in December 1860, a rise of less than 10 per cent. Total train mileages and locomotive power costs also grew slowly and costs per mile were held down. Train miles run rose by 11.1 per cent and costs by 11.8 per cent in the five years to 1860.[1] The significant increase in mileage in 1858 arose largely from the introduction of the services to Manchester, where the hilly route on the MSLR pushed up running costs:

Year	Total Train Miles	Total Locomotive Costs £	Average Cost per Train Mile In Old Pence
1856	5,597,353	186,886	8.01d
1857	5,406,314	186,231	8.27d
1858	5,846,801	200,624	8.23d
1859	5,822,848	192,377	7.92d
1860	6,215,402	208,929	8.07d

Rolling stock repairs, although much more modest in overall terms than locomotive costs, climbed more rapidly as the rolling stock aged and improvements were introduced. The GNR preferred to write-off improvements, such as modifications to springs and axles and carriage upgrades, to revenue. Sturrock had difficulty persuading the Board to charge improvements to the capital account, which would have showed reduced costs per train mile. Accident repairs also had an impact on costs per mile.

Year	Average Number of Wagons in Year	Total Wagon Repair Costs £	Cost per Wagon per Year £ shillings & pence
1856	7222	35,172	£4 17s 6d
1857	7348	35,093	£4 15s 6d
1858	7388	40,006	£5 8s 4d
1859	7428	44,694	£6 0s 4d
1860	7475	50,452	£6 15 0d

At his first Board meeting in 1856 Sturrock had to handle a problem created by Charles Sacré, his Peterborough departmental head. Sacré had been in the habit of advising drivers to ignore the down distant signal at Peterborough and this led to an accident in November 1855, when a 'mixed express' ran into a goods train protected by the distant signal. Sacré made his position and that of Sturrock more difficult by telling the accident inspector before telling Sturrock. Sturrock defended Sacré by saying he had written to Sacré to tell him to do everything in his power to keep the trains to time and that he was supporting the general manager by doing this. The Board on 8 January 1856 heard full explanations from Clarke and Sturrock and allowed Sacré to keep his job, but emphasised any similar behaviour in future would not be tolerated.

During January 1856, 500 more coal wagons were ordered. Sturrock had made some late changes to the design of the buffer rod and shoe, which led to a marginal increase in price. The Board also debated the merits of Beattie's and Gibson's patent methods for fixing tyres. Sturrock thought Beattie's was the better of the two, but obtained Board approval to try Sandford & Owen's system. Beattie's patent was subsequently adopted by the GNR. As coal wagon buffers were regularly falling off and causing accidents, the Board also agreed to modify the whole fleet at a cost of £4,000.

The Executive Committee started 1856 with a close scrutiny of the locomotive department pay sheets. Costs for the fortnight ending 9 February 1856 had increased by £419 6s, 11d over 1855, the cost of which had in turn risen by more than £700 over 1854. Sturrock's justification was again the irregularity of the coal trade. Men were under notice and the locomotive department was very cheaply worked. He could make short-term savings but this would incur much greater expense later. He could not cope with the very heavy and fast traffic if he did not keep the stock in good repair.

Improvements and new machinery were ordered for Boston, Peterborough and Doncaster during the first half of 1856, including equipment for Doncaster to turn buffers round. The Board agreed to the construction of a new chimney at Doncaster after almost a year of debate, in order to reduce the complaints Sturrock received from local residents. Sturrock suggested the problem would never be entirely overcome, although some of the boilers could be made to consume their own smoke. Doncaster was changing from a pleasant market town to a manufacturing centre and the old established residents found it difficult to adjust.

Lubrication of axles remained an issue of concern to Sturrock. He had tried lubricating oil but 'the matter thrown over the works causes double the labour to keep them clean besides the liability to heat'. He had been using some of Cantrell's grease again, which he preferred to the grease made by the stores department at the GNR's plant. GNR grease was not, in Sturrock's opinion, of consistent quality and should be kept for two months, if it was to be suitable for express trains. The Board decided to transfer responsibility for the manufacture of grease to the locomotive department, who could then ensure sufficient stock of the required quality and maturity.[2]

In October 1856 the Board agreed to extend the grease factory and asked Sturrock to experiment with a new axle box offered by a Mr Curtis. An example using soap and water as the lubricant was demonstrated to the Board. The system was tried for two months in early 1857, using oil as the lubricant. Sturrock concluded the system was a waste of time as it was expensive to maintain and would not save money. Boxes could not be oiled on foreign lines. Curtis's axles were to be tried again in 1859, when oil was being more seriously considered as a lubricant for GNR axles.[3] In May 1860 the traffic department, with the consent of the Board, passed responsibility for greasing to the locomotive department, who recruited additional staff to ensure the job was done properly. Sturrock could now blame only himself if there were lubrication problems with the rolling stock.[4]

Sturrock managed to get his usual August break in Scotland to see family and to shoot. He was back in time for the GNR's AGM on the 23rd, well before the Queen's visit to Scotland on 28 August 1856. This year the journey itself went to plan, but Sturrock was embroiled in another row concerning the leak of information from Doncaster works. *The Times* reported on 27 August that a wheel on the Queen's carriage had had to be changed before the journey. This fact was known only to Doncaster employees and Seymour Clarke suggested someone working at the Plant had been paid by *The Times* to reveal the information. Sturrock was asked to find the guilty party. He failed to discover the source and advised the Board that he had given notice that anyone found leaking information to the press would be dismissed.[5]

In October 1856 the Board agreed to the coke contracts continuing with Robson and Sir John Kaye. Robson's price of 13s per ton was considered competitive and his quality was good. The contract with Sir John soon gave trouble. He complained his bills were not being paid on time, but Sturrock's investigations showed invoices were paid monthly in line with other suppliers. In December Sir John offered to reduce his price to 12s 6d, if an average of 100 tons a week was taken in 4- or 5-ton trucks. Sturrock had been under the impression that the tunnel to Sir John's plant was being enlarged to take standard size wagons. The GNR had only thirteen trucks of a size to fit Sir John's tunnel. They were not always available to take 100 tons per week. Meanwhile a Mr Braithwaite proposed to make coke much more cheaply from a mixture of small anthracite and shell bitumus coal. Sturrock experimented and reported the coke produced by Braithwaite's process was more costly than the coke from Robson's pit in Durham.

Coke supplies continued to be ordered from Robson in 1858. His contract was renewed in August 1857 at 13s per ton for the following year. This price looked very satisfactory, as the LNWR were paying 16s and 16s 9d per ton. Although Robson offered a three-year contract, the GNR opted for 1,600 to 1,800 tons per week for one year only. This suggests the annual coke bill for the GNR was about £70,000 a year. If LNWR prices had been paid, the cost would have been around £16,000 higher.

In May 1857 Sturrock approached the Board regarding a new repair shop at Peterborough. A portion of the engine sheds had to be used for repairs and many engines were kept outside. A new shop would eliminate the need for shunting engines. The Board visited Peterborough on 18 May and agreed to ask the engineer to look into plans for additional facilities expected to cost about £5,793. The engineer endorsed the plan and estimate, but indicated an additional £258 was needed for permanent way. The Board also considered 'the necessity for more water closets for ladies on the platform'. A contract was placed with a Peterborough firm in August 1857 for £4,343 for the new engine repair facilities.[6]

In the same month the Board's attention was drawn by Seymour Clarke to the high consumption of grease on the GNR. Sturrock used his usual excuses of high speeds and harsh gradients, but agreed to confer with his fellow engineers on the named railways.

Railway	Consumption of Grease per Mile
Eastern Counties	0.72
South Eastern	1.00
Midland	1.05
London & Brighton	1.15
London North Western	1,39
Great Western	1.60
North Eastern	2.72
Norht British	2.75
Great Northern	3.22

By the next Board at the end of May 1857 Clarke reported that the quantity of grease used in early 1857 had declined markedly by comparison with the same period in 1856. Consumption had fallen from 161 tons 13cwt to 82 tons 8cwt. GNR figures now looked reasonable and Sturrock might have thought he could relax. However, Clarke produced another report in early 1858 to show that GNR consumption in the second half of 1857 was again more than double the average for seven railways. The London & Brighton was the most economical, consuming 0.927 tons per train mile and the highest, apart from the GNR, was the North Eastern at 1.702 tons per mile in the half year. The GNR had consumed 4.070 tons per mile! Sturrock argued that the high consumption was due to high speeds and heat and the fact that the additional plant at Doncaster had been delivered late. The Board were reminded that there had been no carriages or trains taken off due to overheating. The issue was discussed at the accounts committee, which noted the GNR consumed 222 tons more than the LNWR, 218 tons more than the Midland and 248 tons more than the North Eastern. In March 1858 Sturrock obtained Board approval to try some grease from James Lawrie, who promised to save a third of current costs. In June black grease was tried from another supplier, but found inferior to GNR grease. The grease caught fire and burnt the man carrying out the experiment. Lawrie's grease did not achieve the savings promised.

During June 1857 Seymour Clarke identified a need for more carriages and suggested Sturrock's team should build twenty first-class carriages, including some with second-class compartments, plus six one-horse and twelve two-horse vans. The Doncaster shops had already built over twenty road goods vans, but had not previously built any first-class carriages. The only passenger vehicle constructed at Doncaster had been the composite invalid carriage completed in 1854 and eight passenger luggage vans. Sturrock noted at a subsequent Board that progress was slow as he was having difficulty getting supplies of timber from the stores department. Meanwhile Seymour Clarke had seen the quality of the carriages the LNWR was using for its Manchester service and suggested Sturrock had a look at some carriages that Williams had available. Sturrock mistook Clarke's message for an instruction to buy and arranged for GNR axles and lace to be installed in Williams' carriages. Clarke reported to the Board, 'No doubt Sturrock was activated by a desire to obtain stock when it was really wanted and that he no doubt thought he was justified in the steps he took.' At the Board on 17 October 1857, agreement was given to buy nine carriages from Williams. Six first-class carriages cost £325 each and three composites

£290 each. These replaced some of those to be built in Sturrock's carriage shops, which produced three first-class carriages between December 1857 and February 1858. Three more first-class and a composite were completed in Doncaster by 5 May 1858 to meet the requirements of the new Manchester services over the MSLR from Retford.[7]

The Queen's trip to Scotland took place again on 28 August 1857. Sturrock and Coffin were on the footplate and the line was cleared for thirty minutes either side of the Royal Train. The *Doncaster Gazette* reported that the train had to be stopped once to let an axle cool. The following month Sturrock was so busy at Doncaster for race week that he asked to be excused attendance at the 15 September Board.

September 1857 was marred by the GNR's first fatal accident on the main line between Tuxford and Carlton. Five passengers were killed and fourteen injured on the Manchester to London express, which had left Sheffield at 11.10 a.m. on 24 September. Sturrock and Coffin organised a train from Doncaster to take them and a party of men from the Plant to the scene of the accident. Neither the driver nor fireman could offer any explanation for the accident. Sturrock, who could not attend the Board on 29 September since he was present at the inquest, advised that the inspector did not consider the rolling stock to be faulty. A composite and a first-class coach had to be completely rebuilt and major repairs were needed to a luggage van. Repair costs totalled £540.[8]

The opening in November 1857 of a new route to Leeds via a junction at Gilderstone and Wakefield led to a requirement for more passenger engines capable of coping with steep gradients. Sturrock proposed converting eight of the remaining Sharp singles, which were inappropriate for the line in their current form, to 0-4-2s. Sturrock proposed to use some of his existing coupled passenger engines or even some six wheeled goods engines with their connecting rods removed until the Sharps had been converted. He believed converting the Sharps was the most cost effective approach, as they would otherwise be sitting idle. The Board endorsed the proposal. The cost was estimated at £300 per conversion, which would be charged to the capital account.[9]

A new year could seldom open without a Board review of the locomotive pay sheets and 1858 was no exception. This time Sturrock produced a detailed breakdown of his department's figures, which gives a fuller than usual picture of where the costs fell and of the relative expenditure of the GNR locomotive districts. Sturrock successfully demonstrated that costs per mile had fallen in all his departments.[10]

District	Pay to 7 Feb. 1857 £.s.d	Miles Run to To Feb. 1857	Costs Per Mile to Feb. 1857 d	Pay to 6 Feb. 1858 £.s.d	Miles Run to Feb. 1858	Costs Per Mile to Feb. 1858 d
London	693.16.8	29,556	5.634	812.0.1	35,007	5.567
Peterborough	1072.5.1	77,099	3.338	1,201.2.9	90.394	3.189
Boston	627.0.4	37,736	3.987	566.14.4	36,987	3.677
Doncaster	852.5.2	73,438	2.785	843.9.1	74,850	2.704
Doncaster Shops & Office	1547.15.1	217,829	1.705	1,666.12.10	237,238	1.686
Totals	4,793.2.4	217,829	5.281	5,089.19.1	237,238	5.149

Sturrock's difficulties were increased by a request from a director, Mr Faber, for the establishment of a Board Committee to look into the running costs of the company as a whole and of the locomotive department in particular.[11] The Expenditure Committee looked at costs item by item. In October 1858 their attention was focused on the rising costs of maintaining the road goods vans; in November their interest lay in great coats and trousers and a sample suit was examined; by January 1859 the committee was determining how stationery could be bought more cheaply. Sturrock had his main session with the committee in May 1859, when he looked back at costs over the previous three years and handed out tabular presentations to support his remarks and to explain variations. He obtained the committee's support for a number of clerical salary increases.[12]

On the morning of 18 February 1858 Sturrock attended a stores committee, where a long discussion took place on the method adopted by the locomotive department for ordering cloth. The storekeeper, Pulford, blamed the delay on the size of cloth required. Sturrock demonstrated the poor quality of the cloth with three examples. Pulford agreed to get the manufacturer to take the cloth back, but this further delayed the production of carriages.

In the afternoon of the same day, Sturrock and Seymour Clarke obtained agreement from the Board on carriage orders. Clarke asked the Board to instruct Sturrock to get on with the production of the ten new brake vans authorised in November 1857 and the twenty new carriages to be built by Sturrock's team. Sturrock argued that he could not get the materials in time from the stores and that his workshops were inadequate for the production of so many carriages. In the end the Board decided that only the eight carriages now under construction should be completed by Sturrock and the rest should be bought from outside suppliers. The meeting also considered the issue of brake power. An inspector had drawn the company's attention to the lack of brake power following an accident at St Neots. Seymour Clarke had looked at the patent brakes of Mr Newall and Mr Fay. The committee agreed to order four long carriages or two trains for local traffic using Fay's brakes.[13]

Sturrock continued to press for new carriage repair facilities at Doncaster. The men were often idle when it rained, for they were working on carriages in the open air. The expenditure review committee visited Doncaster and found forty carriages under repair in the open and all the shops full. They recognised that supervision was difficult and agreed the need for new facilities but worried about the cost. The Board asked the engineer to produce plans, which were approved in June. The work was let to a Mr Francis Rummens at 4.25 per cent below the estimate of £6,745 on 6 July 1858.[14]

During this busy period for the carriage and wagon section of the locomotive department, the carriage superintendent John Coffin died from jaundice at the age of fifty-two on 26 April 1858. He was an ex-GWR man and had joined the GNR at the same time as Seymour Clarke. Sturrock described him as a trustworthy and good man and asked for his widow to continue to receive his salary till 30 June. He was buried in Balby churchyard and a great crowd of men from the Plant attended his funeral. The Board agreed that Sturrock could look for a replacement at a salary of £200 per year. The successful applicant was John Griffiths, who came from the Lancashire & Yorkshire Railway. His starting salary is not recorded, but by February 1859 he was receiving £315 a year and was officially appointed assistant carriage and wagon superintendent.[15]

Sturrock raised the question of coke supplies for 1859 at a Board meeting at the end of June 1858. It was agreed that Robson should be asked to quote again and Seymour Clarke was asked to enquire of other railways for possible sources. Robson proposed 13s a ton or 12s 9d for two years. After negotiations agreement was reached at 12s 10½d for one year. The Board had been right to refuse the two-year contract at 13s offered the previous year. Sir John Kaye and Stansfield Colliery offered 300–400 tons per week. Sir John could still not cope with standard size trucks, so Sturrock was left to get additional coke from wherever he wished.

In July the GNR was criticised for the absence of brakes on some of its wagons. Thomas Aulden had been killed by a GNR truck at the Wentworth Colliery and the jury was of the view that all trucks should have brakes. Sturrock explained the circumstances to the Board, but the Board again declined to put brakes on all the wagons.

Brake power on passenger trains was the subject of another report in October 1858 from two inspectors. Sturrock remained convinced that more brake power was not the answer to the problem of accidents. He concluded in his paper to the Board that:

1. More brake power may not help prevent accidents, since what really matters is whether the brake power available is applied in good time.
2. If there is to be more power it should be controlled from the engine by the driver.
3. 'I disapprove of all breaks on carriages. They never can be successfully applied except for stopping trains. If used on fast trains, the wheels used will soon be unfit for fast running.'
4. 'I approve of break power at the rear of the train. This steadies the hind carriage.'
5. I approve of communication between guard and driver. The system ordered by the inspectors is used by most train companies.

Sturrock's relationship with the storekeeper Pulford and the stores committee seems to have remained difficult throughout 1858. In April Sturrock complained to the committee about the quality of cotton waste, palm oil and rivets. He had a long drawn-out dispute about the purchase of steam coal. The committee would not accept Sturrock's word that Seymour Clarke had agreed he could order steam coal from wherever he liked. Seymour Clarke confirmed what Sturrock had told the committee and queried whether the matter had really to go through the stores committee. The committee then wrote again to check whether Seymour Clarke was happy with a price of 5s. By the time all this correspondence had passed back and forth, a month had elapsed. It must have amused Sturrock when, in November, a tube supplier Sturrock had proposed was critical of Pulford. The supplier was told he could have the business if he withdrew his criticism of Pulford. In January 1859 cloth quality was again an issue and the stores department complained that the locomotive department did not give enough notice for exceptional orders. The stores committee records cease with a meeting on 23 March 1859, so maybe the committee was abandoned in its original form.

1858 ended with a resurrection of the debate on the GNR's consumption of grease and the problem of effective lubrication of carriages and wagons. A clerk at Hitchin suggested the GNR's consumption of grease was ten times that of the Midland, whose trains to London were now using the station. Sturrock thought the clerk had got his figures wrong, but the Board asked for a report from Seymour Clarke and Sturrock. Seymour Clarke encouraged Sturrock to look again at the use of oil as a lubricant. This time Curtis's patent axle boxes were tried with some success under four passenger carriages. Sturrock reported:

I find the journals have run cool and that the bearings as well as boxes are in good order.' Even after he had taken account of the higher consumption of lubricant in coal and goods trains, 'the difference in favour of oil would remain 3¼d per mile. Such would appear to be the result of the experiment, but how far that result would be borne out by a whole traffic worked by the system it is difficult to prognosticate [sic]. It is however a fact that the practical result of any mode of lubrication has never been as favourable as that shown by the experiment.[16]

To make a further assessment of the value of oil, Sturrock obtained permission in June 1859 to visit the Northern, Eastern and Orleans Railways in France, the Cologne & Minden Railway in Prussia and the Belgian State Railways. He reported to the Board on 2 July after what must have been a short and hardworking trip. 'All those railways except those in Belgium approve of and are using to a great extent oil as a lubricant. The Orleans railway has 3,500 and the Cologne & Minden 4,000 vehicles running regularly with oil.' The French and Prussian engineers told Sturrock that oil was a cheaper lubricant than grease and just as efficient. The Belgian railways were experimenting with oil. Sturrock told the Board that the application of oil to GNR carriages and wagons was simple and that most existing axle boxes could be adapted at little cost. He had given instructions for a number of axle boxes to be converted. He would not be convinced until he had tried oil on the GNR carriages and wagons, as the circumstances were so different on the GNR from those on the French railways.[17] Both oil and grease appear to have continued in use on the GNR for several years. In April 1863 Grinling advised the Executive Committee that GNR grease consumption was 50 per cent higher than that of the LNWR and another investigation was set in motion.[18]

Sturrock, while in France, had inspected the Imperial trains of the Eastern and Orleans Railways. Each train consisted of six to seven vehicles including reception rooms and a saloon for the *aide-de-camp*. They were fitted with elaborately carved furniture and tapestries and 'decorated in the highest style of French art … Each train has cost about £12,000.' By comparison the GNR's royal train had no interconnecting carriages and was composed largely of standard first-class and family carriages, trucks for carriages and brake vans at front and rear. The 1859 Royal Train between King's Cross and Edinburgh on 29 and 30 August included two brake vans, two first-class carriages, three family carriages, two carriage trucks and three saloons including the Royal Saloon. The GNR Board had debated replacing the Royal Saloon in May 1859, but concluded a clean and repair was sufficient.[19]

In February 1859 changes were made to the management team in the locomotive department. With some help from Sturrock, Charles Sacré had been appointed chief engineer and locomotive engineer to the MSLR in late 1858. Francis Cortazzi, who had been number two at Doncaster, was promoted to replace Sacré at Peterborough on £250 per year. Froward's salary at Boston was increased to £225 plus £25 for a house. Payne was appointed locomotive accountant on £250 a year to replace Grinling who had moved up to the position of company accountant for the whole of the GNR. At the same Board Griffith's position as assistant carriage and wagon superintendent was confirmed at £315 per year.[20]

In March 1859 Sturrock asked the Board's permission to convert another twelve of the remaining Sharp singles. The original eight conversions to 0-4-2 tender engines had provided sufficient power to work the traffic over the Leeds & Wakefield and the Leeds, Bradford & Halifax Railways. Sturrock advised the Board that the cost would be £400 per engine, an increase of £100 on the original conversions, as new cylinders would be needed. The conversions would cost £4,800 in total and would be undertaken over a period of years. They would save the Board buying new engines at a cost of about £2,000 each. The Board agreed to the conversions and to the cost being charged to capital. The converted 0-4-2 tender engines were used on the Boston & Sleaford line, which was about to open in early 1859, where they hauled mixed passenger and freight trains.

In October 1859 Sturrock obtained agreement from the Board to the purchase of twelve additional large passenger engines. These were Sturrock's first passenger engine designs for five years and his first 2-2-2 singles since the 'large' Hawthorns delivered between May 1852 and September 1853. The new designs took account of his experience with the experimental 4-2-2 No.215. As the weight of GNR passenger trains increased, Sturrock's existing engines could not cope with the loads in all circumstances 'though kept in first-class working order.' Tenders were reviewed at a Board meeting on 1 November 1859. All the manufacturers promised delivery in March and April 1860, but refused to accept a penalty clause for late delivery. They agreed the engines could be rejected if delivered late. Four engines were ordered from Kitson at £2,630, four from Stephenson at £2,800 and four from Sharp Stewart at £2,900. Hawthorn lost out with a price of £2,975.[21] They were all delivered late. Kitson's locomotives arrived between May and July 1860, Sharp's between June and July 1860, except one delivered in February 1861, and Stephenson's between July and September 1860. With the arrival of the new engines, the GNR planned to reduce the journey time from London to York from five hours to four.[22]

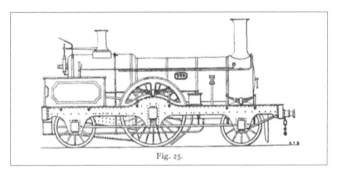

Above: Class 229 No.233 in final form as modified by Stirling; Bird described the class as a masterpiece of design. (SLS)

Right: The Class 229 2-2-2s were the first Sturrock express locomotives definitely built with boilers operating at 150lb per square inch. (Bird)

Fig. 25.

The delivery of the fourth Sharp 2-2-2 was delayed, as the engine originally intended for the GNR was sent to the Chemin de Fer du Nord. Petiet, the locomotive superintendent of the Nord, and some of his fellow engineers evaluated a number of British locomotives at this time. Other British locomotives tried out in France included designs by Kirtley of the Midland and McConnell of the LNWR. The principal dimensions of the 2-2-2 delivered to the Nord matched those of the GNR engines. The Nord engine was named *Sturrock* and appears to have given a good account of itself.

According to Byrd the twelve Class 229 2-2-2 singles 'might almost be regarded as Mr Sturrock's masterpiece in designing. These were single driving engines of generous dimensions and fine proportions, which must strike the observer as being well in the front rank of locomotives so far as grace of appearance is concerned, while their performance abundantly proved that in no way were workmanlike qualities of speed and power sacrificed to obtain a satisfactory outline.'[23] A significant feature was the greatly increased length of the firebox and a longitudinal midfeather. The firebox was 6ft 7¾in compared with 5ft 5in in 215 and 4ft 8in in the 2-4-0s of 1855. The leading wheels were placed directly under the smoke box, an unusual practice, which was continued by Stirling on his single and 2-4-0 passenger engines and increased the weight on the driving wheels. Another innovative feature was the use of iron hoops shrunk over the crank axle to reduce the risk of breakage. The 18ft wheelbase was unusually long for the time. The 150lb pressure was also exceptional, although McConnell of the LNWR was to use the same pressure on his express singles of 1861.

Sturrock may have intended to use coal in these new engines, but the Board remained reluctant in spite of the potential cost savings. Small amounts of coal had been used since October 1855 and it seems likely that both Seymour Clarke and Sturrock made sure coal was as widely used as possible without incurring the wrath of the Board. A simple method for burning coal effectively in locomotive boilers had been developed by Charles Markham under the direction of Matthew Kirtley, the locomotive engineer of the Midland Railway, between 1856 and 1860. The publication of Markham's paper by the Institute of Mechanical Engineers in 1860 led to the widespread adoption of his ideas on other railways. By March of that year Seymour Clarke considered the coal contract was a matter for discussion with the Executive Committee and Sturrock was told to identify suitable collieries to be invited to tender. In 1861 the GNR was using 1,800 tons of coal a week. The locomotive coal contract was now more important than the 800 tons per week contract for coke.[24]

The decision to protect the crank axles on the new passenger locomotives with iron hoops may have been instigated by Board fears of the potential danger from fractures. Sturrock had reported in April 1859 that some 300 crank axles had broken, mostly at speed and without accident. He advised the Board that there was no foolproof system to prevent breakages. Some axles broke at 30 miles and others at 135,000 miles. 'A breakage of a crank axle is only a question of expenditure.' He ran crank axles as long as possible to save money. They were always changed if there was any sign of failure.[25] In the light of an accident in September 1860 Sturrock decided to stamp all axles with a date.[26]

When it came to carriage standards, decisions were driven largely by the traffic department. In June 1859, Seymour Clarke asked Sturrock to design a more comfortable second-class carriage. Sturrock prepared an example, which was available for the Board to view at King's Cross on 5 July 1859. The carriage was an upgrade from a third-class carriage and had cost £45 to modify. Sturrock reckoned the cost would be about £4 to £6 less if several carriages were done at the same time. The Board agreed to convert 116 carriages at a total cost of about £4,600. The expenditure was to be charged to revenue over 4½ years and would therefore have an impact on Sturrock's costs. In his half-year report for the six months to July 1860 he noted: 'Considerable outlay beyond that due to ordinary repairs has been expended in improving the second-class carriages.'

The competence of Sturrock's carriage and wagon section and the abilities of his assistant carriage and wagon superintendent, John Griffiths, were recognised when the decision was made during 1860 to build all the carriages for the East Coast expresses at Doncaster. The companies operating the East Coast route from King's Cross to Edinburgh had agreed in 1855 to run united express trains composed of carriages from all the participating railways, but this created problems for the GNR because the carriages of the other railway companies were often not up to GNR standards. On 14 March 1860 Leith, the traffic superintendent of the GNR, met his opposite numbers in the NBR and the NER and raised again the possibility of building a common stock of East Coast carriages and brake vans. At the GNR Board meeting on 19 March 1860 Seymour Clarke was authorised to negotiate with the General Managers of the NER and NBR.

By late August 1860 Seymour Clarke had agreed with the NBR and NER that a common East Coast joint stock should be built. The carriages would be used only for through trains and there would be no mileage charges or demurrage. Revenues for traffic beyond Edinburgh would be shared on clearing house terms. Most significantly from the GNR's point of view, all the carriages were to be built and maintained at Doncaster. Captain O'Brien of the NER had spoken very favourably of GNR carriages and the NBR concurred. Seymour Clarke wrote, 'The stock will be built entirely in accordance with our views.'

The value of carriages to be owned by each railway was determined by reference to route miles. The GNR's mileage was 191, NER's 151 and NBR's 58. The GNR Board on 11 September 1860 agreed that fifty vehicles should be constructed at Doncaster and allocated between the railways on the basis shown in the next table.[27] The livery adopted for ECJS stock was varnished teak with gold lettering shaded red.

Initial ECJS Stock Allocations and Costs

	1st	2nd	3rd	Composite	Brake Van	Totals	Cost £
GNR	8	3	5	4	4	24	6425
NER	4	1	5	6	3	19	5080
NBR	4	2	0	0	1	7	1945
Totals	16	6	10	10	8	50	13,450

The initial estimate of the requirement for specific Classes of ECJS carriage proved to be flawed. Figures prepared by Seymour Clarke in February 1863 showed that even in summer, when the number of passengers was highest, only eight out of the sixteen first-class carriages were in use. It was agreed that four existing GNR composites, built about the same time as the ECJS, should be substituted for four first-class carriages from ECJS. Two break vans and two third-class carriages were added. The number of ECJS carriages rose to fifty-four and their value to £14,300. The GNR would take £406 of the extra cost of £850.

The ECJS was extended to Aberdeen in 1864 in order to compete with the West Coast route, which now ran through to Aberdeen. The number of carriages would be increased to sixty-three. Ten were to be built by Sturrock and his team at Doncaster and some transferred to and from the GNR with the approval of the other parties to reduce the number of first- and second-class carriages and increase the number of composites and third-class. The stock was divided into four sections for Aberdeen, Inverness, Glasgow and Edinburgh. In 1865 a decision was taken that all the carriages should be maintained as a single pool with the repair costs shared on a mileage basis.[28]

In the final months of 1860 Sturrock was troubled by staffing issues. Cortazzi, who had taken on the Peterborough foreman's role in February 1859, was appointed locomotive engineer on the Great Indian Peninsula Railway in September 1860. Brown was appointed in his place at £250 a year. Griffiths' contribution in the carriage and wagon section was recognised with a pay rise to £350.

An inspector suggested that footplate hours should be limited to ten per day and a Manchester-based trade union, which some of the footplate staff had joined, also pressed for a ten-hour day.[29] Sturrock argued that such a limit would 'completely overturn all the arrangements of your railway and cause great additional current and capital expenditure.' He advised that, where hours were exceptionally long, as on the Horncastle and Holbeach branches, he had authorised additional wages 'at rates agreed upon especially by me.' The minutes of 10 October 1860 stated, 'The board have consulted the Locomotive Engineer and are advised by him that it is not practice to fix a rigid limit to the hours of the engine drivers and firemen on the Great Northern.'

8

DONCASTER CITIZEN AND RAILWAY ADVISER 1852-60

Sturrock recognised the need to support the families of the men he employed at the Plant and was actively encouraged in this role by the example of his chairman, Edmund Denison. Through his work for the Doncaster community Sturrock achieved recognition and status in the town and district. During this same period he, in common with his peers on other leading lines, augmented his income by providing advice to other railways.

Sturrock established his family in Doncaster some time between the birth of his younger daughter Georgina in Peterborough on 13 February 1852 and the death of his first wife Caroline in Doncaster on 27 April 1852. He rented 21 South Parade, one of three pillared houses designed and built between 1795 and 1798 by William Lindley, a noted local architect. The pillared houses remain some of the most distinctive buildings in Doncaster and were fashionable at the time Sturrock arrived. Denison acquired a house in South Parade only fifty yards from the pillared houses in August 1855.

Doncaster was transformed by the arrival of the railway. Denison, who was MP for the West Riding till 1859 and had lived in Doncaster for many years, realised the railway was essential to the continuing prosperity of a town dependent on the coaching trade. What Denison may not have appreciated was the extent to which the railway and its associated works would change the character of the town. A market town and social centre for the aristocracy of the district would become a major industrial complex, polluted by smoke from the Plant and other factories supplying the Plant. The population of the town rose from 12,052 in 1851 to 18,133 in 1866, the year in which Sturrock retired. By 1891, shortly after Sturrock moved to London, the population had reached 25,933.

Denison, supported by Sturrock, had to bridge the gap between the old and the new inhabitants of the town. Many of the issues which arose in Doncaster in the 1850s were similar to those which Sturrock and Gooch had faced in Swindon ten years earlier, but the context was different. There was no existing population in Swindon. In Doncaster Denison and Sturrock had to maintain the goodwill of the local gentry to help fund the facilities needed by the new workforce brought in by the GNR. The provision of churches, schools, hospitals, technical education and recreational facilities were substantially dependent on subscriptions from wealthy local families.

The pillared houses in South Parade, Doncaster; Sturrock and his family lived in the right-hand house, No.21. (Images of England)

Denison's first concern was the lack of a church and school for the GNR workmen and their families. The Plant was in the ecclesiastical parish of Christchurch, the church where Denison and Sturrock and their families worshipped. Christchurch had a national and infants school and as a first step Denison, Robert Baxter, the solicitor to the GNR, and his brother Edmund involved themselves in March 1852 with a committee to fund an extension to Christchurch School. 'The school accommodation is already below what the population demands and the families of numerous mechanics which the Great Northern Plant will soon add.'[1] Edmund Baxter, who was a solicitor like his brother, and his family were to become life-long friends of the Sturrocks. The locomotive department accountant Grinling taught at Christchurch Sunday school.

It was plain to Denison and Sturrock that the expansion of Christchurch School was not going to be adequate for GNR families and a separate GNR school would be required. Christchurch parish would also need a second church more convenient for the GNR workers in the new houses being built close to the Plant. The problem of insufficient space for worship was made more acute by a fire on 27 February 1853, which totally destroyed Doncaster's main parish church of St George.

Denison estimated there was a population in Doncaster of about 2,900 without church or school and obtained GNR Board support for the provision of a church and school at a cost of around £8,000. He brought the proposal before the shareholders, who supported the provision of £1,000 for a school but objected to the company spending money on a church, for which expenditure Parliamentary consent was required. Denison reluctantly withdrew the Bill and asked individual shareholders to make a voluntary contribution of ½d per £1 of stock. Over £6,000 was raised from shareholders and the local gentry, including Earl Fitzwilliam, who gave £200. Denison gave £100.

A tender for the Great Northern School was accepted in June 1854. Designed by Henry Goddard, an architect who had undertaken a number of commissions for the GNR, the school opened in January 1855. Church services and a Sunday school, which had been conducted in the Plant reading room by the Revd J. Campion since 1853, were transferred to the school in December 1854. The GNR paid for the teachers at the school and a salary to Campion for his role as minister to the company and manager of the school. Sturrock was on the management committee of the school and worked with Campion for over thirty years to support the church and school.

Work on the GNR church proceeded more slowly. Gilbert Scott, who had designed St Mark's railway church in Swindon, was appointed architect for the church of St James. The foundation stone was laid on 24 September 1854 and the church was consecrated by the Archbishop of York on 15 October 1858. Sturrock was present together with his three most senior colleagues, Parker, the Plant superintendent, Griffiths, the carriage superintendent, and J. Grinling, the accountant. The two Denisons, father and son, led the team of GNR representatives. The church, built of Ancaster stone transported for free by the GNR, remains in regular use today and is still visible to travellers on the main line to the north.

Sturrock gave attention to the education of the Plant workforce. He recalled the benefit he had obtained from the Watt Institution in Dundee and the value of the Mechanics Institute in Swindon. The Great Northern Mechanics Club was established in 1853 'for the accommodation and intellectual improvement of the servants of the company employed in the Plant works, Doncaster'. The reading room was opened in October 1853 and a library established in 1854. Denison was the president, Sturrock vice-president and Parker chairman of the committee. In 1856 a GNR brass band was formed and Sturrock gave £30 towards the cost of instruments. The *Doncaster Gazette* commented: 'The servants of the GNR have opportunities such as few workmen possess.'[2]

St James's Church is still in use today but the school has been demolished. (Images of England)

Doncaster was one of the first towns to organise science and art classes at the GNR school in 1854. Government grants were available to pay half the fees and teachers obtained additional payments for exam successes. Sturrock supported the venture but felt the skills of the ordinary mechanics were underestimated. 'Almost any of them could, with a brick or a piece of chalk, mark up on a board or on the back of a shovel, what they meant to describe.'[3] Parker and Payne, who succeeded Grinling as locomotive department accountant, taught some of the classes in mechanical drawing, reading and writing.

A Locomotive Sick Society had been established by Sturrock in April 1853. Its aim was to provide relief to working men and their families in times of 'sickness and trouble'. To mark the fifth anniversary of the scheme and to publicise its activities, a *soirée* was held in Doncaster in December 1857. Once tea was concluded, Sturrock gave a talk on the growth of the society. In 1853 there had been 1,800 men in the locomotive department; now there were 2,400. Sixty-nine men had died and sixty-nine widows had been helped. Following speeches by the company doctor, Dr Dunn and by Parker and Johnson, the foreman of the locomotive running shed, the company of 350 were 'regaled with oranges and gingerbread' and the music of the Doncaster Harmonic Society.[4]

The formation of the Volunteer Rifle Corps helped Sturrock to achieve wider recognition in local society. In May 1859 the mayor issued a call for the creation of a Doncaster Corps. Similar corps were being formed throughout the country to defend Britain in the event of invasion from France. Denison and Sturrock were elected to a committee chaired by the mayor. The committee met several times during August and September 1859. Sixty men were needed to establish a corps. There was plenty of enthusiasm for the idea, but limited numbers came forward to register as the men were expected to provide their own uniforms.

Denison and Sturrock organised a meeting in the Plant to round up support for the volunteer corps. If sufficient numbers could not be found in Doncaster, a joint corps with Sheffield would have to be considered. Fifty recruits were obtained for a separate Plant corps by the end of September and a first meeting for drill took place in the Wagon Shop on Saturday 8 October. Sergeant Cooke took charge. Cooke was a former regular soldier, who was now landlord of the Thatched House Tavern and a member of the volunteer West Yorkshire Cavalry. Meanwhile the formation of the Town Corps proceeded more slowly but, by the end of the year, the Plant Corps had 116 recruits and the Town Corps fifty-five.

Officers were elected by the men and their recommendations passed to the Lord Lieutenant for approval. The GNR Corps met in December 1859 and elected Sturrock as captain, Payne as lieutenant and Richard Cortazzi Hardy as ensign. Sergeants and corporals were also appointed. The Plant Corps was officially the 20th West Yorkshire Rifles. In April 1860 Campion was appointed chaplain to the Corps.

Sturrock, a smart and careful dresser, and his opposite number, Captain Pilkington of the Town Corps, went to London in January 1860 to inspect the pattern of uniforms for the corps. Sturrock and Pilkington chose a short tunic of 'gray' material cut round at the corners and bound with two lines of black braid. A narrow strip of scarlet or green could be let into the cuffs. The trousers were peg shaped with a stripe down each side. Sturrock and Pilkington collected their uniforms from the tailor in London in early February and, according to the *Doncaster Chronicle*, 'very pretty they looked too' as they left the train at Doncaster station. Local tailors were selected to make the men's uniforms, which had to be ready for the Easter Parade, when both corps attended St George's for the first time.

Sturrock's role as captain of the Corps was time consuming. In July 1860 the Plant Corps and band attended St James's Church for the dedication of a memorial window to thank Edmund Denison for his work in organising the construction of the church. Sturrock and his fellow GNR officers were more assiduous in their duties than those of the Town Corps. When the two corps drilled in August the Town Corps had no officers present.

Sturrock in uniform; the date of the picture is
unknown. (Michael Brerton)

In September Captains Sturrock and Pilkington took their men by train to a volunteer
corps gathering on the Knavesmire at York. Sturrock took 100 men, but Pilkington only
mustered fifty. The men complained that they received very little beer with their meat
pies. They were disgruntled because they had no opportunity to meet their friends and
see the shows, as they were marched directly from and to the station.

When a foreman fitter, who was a volunteer and a regular at St James, was killed at the
Plant in October 1860, Sturrock ensured he was interred at St James's with full military
honours. Ten days later the Doncaster volunteers went to Rotherham to meet their
colleagues in the Rotherham Volunteers. The two corps in Doncaster plus those from
Rotherham and Pontefract had been formed into an administrative battalion in August
1860. Captain Bower, the officer responsible for the Rotherham corps and owner of
Tickhill Castle, was elected major. The Plant Corps became the 20th and the Town Corps
the 21st company of the West Riding Volunteers. To mark all that had been achieved by
the Plant Corps in 1860, Sturrock gave a supper for eighty men at the Thatched House
Tavern owned by Sergeant Cooke. The year ended less happily for the Town Corps.
Their unpopular officers had been pressed by the men to resign. A committee of enquiry
reinstated the officers and the men promptly resigned. The mayor agreed to form a new
town corps, but it was not to happen for many months.

Sturrock's role in the GNR and his responsibilities in the local community did not
prevent him from finding time to assist other railways. The most common requirement
was for an assessment of the condition and value of the rolling stock. The fee for such an
assignment might be £50 guineas, a useful supplement to Sturrock's salary.[5] More valuable
assignments were available with the right connections.

In May 1854 Sturrock was invited by Edward Watkin, the general manager of the
MSLR, to examine the MSLR's rolling stock. This was an assignment Sturrock undertook
for three years, reporting in the final year with J.E. McConnell of the LNWR.[6] Edward
Watkin had replaced James Allport as general manager of the MSLR in January 1854
and Richard Peacock, the locomotive engineer, had left to establish Beyer Peacock. His

replacement in April 1854 was W.G. Craig, formerly locomotive superintendent of the Monmouthshire Railway & Canal Co. With the arrival of Watkin, relations with the GNR improved to the mutual benefit of both companies and, as noted above, through passenger services were established from King's Cross to Manchester.

Sturrock first reported to the MSLR Board in September 1854 and carried out a second review in December 1855. In his third report in December 1856 Sturrock noted: 'whilst the Passenger Engines have been kept up, the Goods Engines are scarcely now in as good condition as when I examined them in December 1855.' Tender wheels were deficient and, due to the age of many locomotives, more tubing had been replaced than the average. The working parts of many of the goods engines were in poor order. As a consequence the engines were not working as economically as they should.

Sturrock was happy with the condition of the carriage stock bodies, but the wheels were below standard and the horse boxes, which he had criticised in 1854, still had not been replaced. Watkin had, however, adopted the stock-taking system used on the GNR. Sturrock concluded: 'the opinion above given will point to the necessity of expending in future an increased amount on repairs and renewals of your rolling stock.' McConnell supported Sturrock's conclusions.[7] Although the report might appear to reflect badly on the MSLR's locomotive engineer, Craig may have welcomed the pressure it put on the Board to allow him to spend more on repairs. Craig continued in post until May 1859, when he was replaced by Sturrock's most senior assistant, Charles Sacré.

Shortly after completing his first review for the MSLR, Sturrock was invited to advise the Newport, Abergavenny & Hereford Railway (NAHR) on issues normally handled by a company's own locomotive engineer. The NAHR was incorporated on 3 August 1846 to acquire three established tramways running between Hereford and Pontypool. Due to financial difficulties, the purchase of the Hereford Railway, the Llanfihangel Railway and the Grosmont Railway were not completed until November 1852. The old tramways were closed in April 1853 and the new line opened in January 1854, with motive power and rolling stock provided by the LNWR. The line ran from Hereford through Abergavenny to Pontypool, where it joined the Monmouthshire Railway at Coed-y-Gric junction for onward connection to Newport.[8]

Sturrock-designed carriages for the Newport, Abergavenny & Hereford Railway cross the Crumlin viaduct in South Wales. (MacDermot's *History of the GWR*)

Sturrock was brought in by Major Amsinck, a director of both the NAHR and the GNR, following a decision by the NAHR Board to terminate the arrangements with the LNWR, which refused to allow through traffic over the NAHR to the Mersey. The decision was taken in August 1854 and the contract with the LNWR ended on 1 October. Initially Brassey, who had supplied locomotive power to the LNWR, continued to provide power to the NAHR. The LNWR agreed to continue to provide rolling stock for an indefinite period.[9]

The precise date Sturrock started to act as an adviser on rolling stock and engine power is not evident from the records. However the NAHR traffic committee on 10 November 1854 noted that Sturrock was sending a 'trustworthy man' to drive engine No. 1, which was shortly to be delivered by Wilson to either Dudley or Wolverhampton. Wilson were to supply all but three of the company's engines.[10] At the 16 November 1854 Board, the secretary was instructed to ask Sturrock to produce plans and specifications for rolling stock and to give his views on the agreement with Brassey and the locomotive power requirements for the line.[11] Sturrock recommended three rolling stock suppliers, Joseph Wright, Charles Cave Williams and Marshalls & Co. and provided a set of drawings.[12] The Board agreed that the engineer and secretary should decide the pattern of the stock and Sturrock should ensure the manufacturers fulfilled their contracts. These events took place at a difficult time for Sturrock for his second wife Helen died on 14 November 1854.

By 14 December 1854 tenders for rolling stock had been received. Sturrock was in attendance and the NAHR Board debated with Sturrock's help whether to continue to rely on Brassey or to buy its own engines. A decision was taken to rely solely on its own locomotives and end the agreement with Brassey. During December Sturrock wrote to the Board regarding choice of wheel suppliers. The Board also asked him to find a foreman for the workshops at Hereford. Sturrock attended a further Board meeting on 25 January, when decisions were taken on wagon wheel suppliers and carriage stock. Orders were placed with Joseph Wright and Sturrock was asked to chase delivery of the company's rolling stock since the LNWR now wanted their stock back. By this time the NAHR had four goods and three passenger engines, which had powered all its trains from 1 January 1855.

Sturrock's terms of service do not seem to have been agreed until the NAHR Board meeting on 1 February 1855. No details are recorded in the minutes, but the Board authorised a payment of £500 to Sturrock on 8 November 1855, a not inconsiderable sum for a part-time role of much less than a year. Sturrock also received £35 11s 7d for tools. Sturrock's salary at the time from the GNR was £940 a year.[13]

By 14 February 1855 Morris, the NAHR general manager, was becoming increasingly concerned regarding delivery of rolling stock.[14] The NAHR traffic committee passed his letter on to Sturrock, who replied to the Board on 1 March on the position regarding stock deliveries. The secretary paid a visit to Sturrock in Doncaster to arrange to order trucks from Ashbury. The meeting debated whether to order fifty six-wheeled rail and timber trucks, but concluded such trucks would not cope with the tight curves of the NAHR. 100 smaller trucks, which could be used for a wider variety of loads, were ordered for delivery over the next six weeks. Unfortunately the LNWR withdrew its rolling stock at the end of March. In spite of Sturrock's efforts, the manufacturers had not delivered all the required rolling stock and the NAHR had to turn away business. Sturrock's initial involvement ended when all the rolling stock had been delivered. However, in November 1856 Sturrock was called back to be an expert witness at a fatal accident enquiry. He was asked to state a safe speed for a curve at Nantyderry and explain the GNR's policy on driver training. He was of the view that 50mph was safe on the particular section of line. Sturrock noted that the GNR always promoted drivers from the fireman role, typically after four years, but some served for a shorter period.[15] Two years later the NAHR adopted the GNR's bell, rope and pulley arrangement for communicating between guard and driver.[16]

J.E. McConnell of the LNWR and Sturrock worked together twice in 1856. The reports on the MSLR's rolling stock in December 1856 were preceded by an arbitration report in February 1856 in connection with the Oxford, Worcester & Wolverhampton's (OWWR) dispute with Charles Cave Williams. Sturrock was appointed to represent the interests of Williams and McConnell the interests of the GWR. The OWWR was a mixed gauge line from a junction with the GWR near Oxford to the Black Country. Due to a chronic shortage of money, the company had no funds to buy rolling stock and advertised for a contractor to run the railway and provide rolling stock, including locomotives. Such arrangements were not uncommon at the time. Williams had taken up the role without a formal contract. A dispute arose, which by mutual agreement was referred to arbitrators.[17] Sturrock and J.E. McConnell were appointed in Autumn 1855, but the issue was complex. They eventually concluded in February 1856 that the OWWR should pay Williams 'the sum of £60,880 4s for stock, stores and plant'.[18]

David Joy had been appointed by Williams as locomotive engineer for the OWWR. Sturrock knew Joy when he was Wilson's chief draughtsman at the Railway Foundry in Leeds. According to Joy's diary, the two arbitrators valued the locomotives, carriages and wagons at £183,205. Williams' invoice prices amounted to only £160,296. Joy's careful maintenance and Sturrock's persuasive powers led McConnell to agree to valuations which exceeded Williams' costs by £22,909. Joy and Sturrock are said to have joked about how they had been able to 'fog' McConnell.[19]

Two years after his 1855 visit to the Welsh borders, Sturrock was back to advise the Monmouthshire Railway, which interconnected with the NAHR near Pontypool. The Monmouthshire Railway developed from a canal and tramway company, which had been operating from Newport since 1792. A western valley line opened in 1850 and the eastern valley line from Newport to Pontypool in June 1852. Richard Laybourne had been appointed locomotive engineer in 1854 and was in post when Sturrock was invited to report on the 'construction of the Company's engines; the description and cost of repairs; the present money value of each engine and the description of the engine best suited to the Company's traffic.'[20] Sturrock was asked for a report by the company's half-yearly meeting in May but was unable to oblige. Sturrock eventually reported on 10 June 1857: 'I am pleased to say the value of the locomotive stock exceeds the expectations of Mr Laybourne.' Sturrock had personally and through his assistants examined the condition of the Monmouthshire's engines. The locomotives were in fair working order, but not as good as Sturrock would have thought advisable. The boilers were in generally good condition and equal to 80-100lb pressure. Sturrock recommended that, when refitted, the boilers should be modified to cope with 120-140lb, so as to obtain greater fuel economy. He commented on the engines being dirty and Laybourne explained the dirty engines were due to lack of 'stabling' and repair facilities. Sturrock accepted the explanation and expressed surprise at how well things were done bearing in mind the facilities available to Laybourne. Sturrock thought the thirty-two engines were worth £55,013 in their present state and would be worth £57,763 if refurbished as he suggested. He emphasised these values would not be achieved in a forced sale.[21] Laybourne obtained new workshops late in 1857, so he may well have seen Sturrock's report as helpful to his cause.

Sturrock was able to draw on the experience he had gained with the OWWR, the NAHR and the Monmouthshire in an action on behalf of the West Midland, which wished to secure running powers over the Monmouthshire Railway into Newport. The West Midland was constituted in 1860 by an amalgamation of the OWWR, the NAHR and the Worcester & Hereford Railway. The latter railway was incorporated in 1858, but was not fully open until after the merger with the West Midland, due to problems completing the Ledbury and Malvern tunnels. The lines totalled 198 miles.

The West Midland introduced a Bill to give it full running powers from Coed-y-Gric junction near Pontypool to Newport and Sturrock was invited to appear at the House of Lords in support of the West Midland. His knowledge of both the NAHR and the Monmouthshire enabled Sturrock to argue that there were no dangers in granting running powers to Newport. He had inspected the lines and he quoted many examples from the GNR where several companies used lines and stations safely. Peterborough had ninety trains a day from four companies; Doncaster coped with 123 trains a day from five companies. He gave more GNR examples from Knottingley, Low Moor, Halifax, Holbeck and Wakefield.[22] The West Midland obtained its running powers, but its independent existence was short. It was absorbed by the GWR in 1863. The Monmouthshire was taken over by the GWR in 1880.

Sturrock appears to have ceased to provide advice to other railways after 1860. It may have been that the income he received from the funds left to him by his second wife met his financial needs. His increasing involvement with the volunteers and with Doncaster society in general and the increasing demands of his 'day job' may have given him little time or inclination to take such assignments.

9

THE LATER GNR YEARS
1861–65

Sturrock's final years with the GNR were amongst his most innovative and busy. His experimental steam tender engines aimed to save capital and make more effective use of light rails and limited track space. The opening of suburban and underground services required the introduction of new tank engines. He designed two Classes of 2-4-0s for secondary and main line passenger operations. He rebuilt much of the wagon fleet and constructed new carriages. He expanded the facilities at Doncaster and elsewhere to provide for the construction of rolling stock and to maintain the expanding locomotive fleet. He completed the move to coal burning in passenger locomotives. Sturrock's engineering skills led investors to invite him to play a lead role in the formation of a new locomotive manufacturing company.

By early 1861 the major railways involved with the East and West Coast routes to Scotland realised that cooperation might in some areas be better than competition. Seymour Clarke raised the issue of speed with the general managers of the LNWR, NER and Caledonian. An agreement on passenger services was endorsed by the GNR Board on 5 February 1861 and relieved some of the pressure on Sturrock's limited fleet of new 2-2-2s. All but one of the twelve Class 229 2-2-2s had been delivered by September 1860. The twelfth locomotive was delivered in February 1861. The Class 229s comfortably hauled twelve four-wheeled passenger coaches weighing around 120 tons and met the needs of the heavy 1862 Exhibition trains.

The Executive Committee exerted more pressure on Sturrock to control costs, but Sturrock avoided explanations unless asked. In May 1861 the committee observed 'with surprise' an increase of £700 in locomotive wages, especially as mileage had fallen by 3,000. Two directors went to see Sturrock in Doncaster, who explained there was really no increase since the extra expenditure related to capital items. Sturrock's costs were again questioned in August 1861, when he was criticised for ordering a new coupling for high-sided wagons, which cost £2 more than the traditional coupling. Sturrock explained that the coupling increased safety for it enabled the porters to uncouple wagons without getting between them. He did not tell the committee about the new coupling because 'in eleven years I have served the GNR Company, I have never been instructed to trouble the Committee with purely mechanical details.'[1]

Much of the problem with Sturrock's accounts lay in the Board's reluctance to determine a consistent policy on the allocation of expenditure between income and capital. In January 1862 Sturrock noted that he had spent £2321 on improvements to rolling stock including £810 spent on converting eighteen third-class carriages to second-class. The Board decided to charge the whole sum to revenue, although similar costs for the conversion of the Sharps to tank engines had been charged to capital. With all railway companies adopting different accounting policies, inter-company comparisons were of limited validity, although this did not prevent the Board from asking for such comparisons from time to time.[2]

The pressure on Sturrock to hold costs resulted in him recommending to the Board in February 1862 that he should run engines through to Grantham from London and save about £200 a year. To achieve this he needed a new water crane at Peterborough, plus a new engine shed, carriage shed and turntable at Grantham.[3] It took the Board until October 1862 to agree with Sturrock a total of £1,650 of further expenditure.[4] The following year Sturrock obtained the Board's consent to the construction of a house for the Grantham foreman at £200. After all this capital expenditure the savings achieved by the move to Grantham must have taken time to show in the accounts.

A further innovation in May 1861 was the adoption of wooden-centred wheels on the new GNR carriages and on wagons to be used on passenger trains. Richard Mansell, carriage superintendent of the South Eastern Railway, had patented a design of wheel, which was to be widely adopted for new carriage stock for the next fifty years. A disc of sixteen teak segments was built up around a central iron or steel boss and forced onto the tyre by hydraulic pressure. Sturrock visited Mansell and noted the LNWR was also experimenting with his wheels. The wooden-centred wheels, Sturrock advised the Board, would be less noisy and dusty, more secure and cheaper than the existing wheels. Approval was given to fit the Mansell wheels to the 100 new carriages under construction and to twelve fish and ten ballast wagons now on order.[5] Beattie's patent wheels continued in use in parallel with the new Mansell wheels.

In August 1861 departmental responsibilities in the locomotive department were reshuffled. James Johnson moved from locomotive superintendent at Doncaster to Peterborough on a salary increased from £250 to £300. Froward moved on an unchanged salary of £225 from Boston to Doncaster and Hornby, the assistant at Boston, was promoted to take Froward's role at a salary of £200, an increase of £50.

In spite of the growth in the number of GNR employees, all requests for assistance to those who were injured in accidents came to the Board. Sturrock briefed the Board on each case and the Board tailored its response to the personal circumstances of the beneficiary and the extent to which the injured man could be held to blame. In January 1862 Sturrock asked the Board to meet the costs of building another room on to the house of a driver's widow, so she could take a lodger. The widow also asked for a mangle, so that she could take in washing. Sturrock noted the parish of Peterborough gave the same widow five shillings a week plus 'seven loaves being one for each child'. Around the same time the Board gave £20 to another widow whose husband had been killed in an accident at Newark. The driver had served seven years. The distribution of the £20 would be agreed between Sturrock and Seymour Clarke. A driver who was injured at Essendine had his medical and lodging bills of £117 13s 2d paid; the Board also met the cost of his artificial foot.

The exhibition of 1862 produced substantial additional revenue for the railways. The GNR allowed all its employees to attend at a flat fare of 3s for a husband and wife. Children went at half fare. As a result of the exhibition 280,943 passengers were carried and the Board declared a bonus pool of £4,000 for the traffic department. Fortunately Leith, who organised the distribution of the pool, noticed the locomotive department had been omitted. Leith advised the Board on 25 November that he had decided how to distribute £3,000 and had left £1,000 for the locomotive department. Sturrock came up with a scheme to give a bonus of eight days' pay to all staff on the line, plus foremen, clerks, examiners and greasers.[6]

In January 1862 Sturrock recommended the installation of gas lighting on the short trains from Hitchin to King's Cross. The idea had come from Leith, but Sturrock had been to see the lighting used on the Lancashire & Yorkshire Railway. He had noted that the costs exceeded those put out by the patentee in his pamphlet and seen how the gas holders were refilled. Appropriate boilers were installed in London, Hitchin and Hatfield at a cost of £156 each. Luggage space would be lost, but Leith was unconcerned.[7]

In the same week in 1862 Sturrock was again asked his views on brake power. He continued to oppose the adoption of continuous brakes, a not uncommon attitude amongst locomotive engineers at the time. Sturrock suggested there were four alternatives to achieve improved braking. In addition to continuous brakes, the Board could consider a brake on the engine, a brake on both the engine and tender and increasing the weight of the engine, tender and brake van. Sturrock believed the operation of continuous brakes on a railway running mixed traffic was impossible. 'It is a perfect delusion to suppose the public will derive any safety from such.' He told the Board the continuous brake would be expensive to maintain and 'a most efficient weapon to the passenger to obtain increased compensation.' He thought the Lancashire & Yorkshire used the continuous brake because the patentees were its officers. The North London had continuous brakes but they were out of action at the time of an accident. The MSLR had abandoned them and the West Midland also after a trial. He said the installation of a brake on the engine was possible, but it might rust through lack of use and linking a tender brake to an engine brake could be difficult. Sturrock favoured adding weight by increasing the number of wheels on the tender and enlarging the brake van or adding a second brake van. The Board made no decision.

Further changes took place to personnel in the locomotive department in early 1863. As a result of a loss of cash for wages, Payne was removed from his job as accountant for the locomotive department and replaced by Bonnett, who was promoted from within. Other accounting duties were reorganised and Sturrock saved £78 2s from his wages bill. Any savings were absorbed by increases for three senior posts. Parker was awarded a £50 rise to £500 a year; Budge's pay rose from £250 to £300 and Johnson received an extra £50, taking him to £350. Alfred Sacré was promoted to replace Johnson at Peterborough in January 1864 and received £250 a year plus a house.[8]

With his new team in place by March 1863, Sturrock was able to focus on the development of his auxiliary steam tender, an innovation which he expected to be cost effective for the company and financially beneficial to himself. Sturrock's steam tender was designed to provide additional power, whilst holding down capital and running costs. The steam tender would maximise the use of the main line to London by increasing the loads on each coal train and thereby reducing the number of trains run.[9]

The steam tender was not a new invention. The brothers Verpilleux took out a patent for a steam tender in September 1842 and their system was used for a period on the line from St Etienne to Lyons. Nearer home, Benjamin Conner of the Caledonian Railway had steam tenders built by Neilson in 1859. He experimented initially with attaching steam tenders to his Class 189 0-4-2s, but these provided insufficient steam. Steam tenders were then tried on numbers 201 to 209 of his Class 197 2-4-0s, but the problem of insufficient steam remained and the experiment was abandoned.[10]

Sturrock submitted his design to the patent office on 6 May 1863. The steam tender was a six-coupled locomotive with 4ft or 4ft 6in wheels and a pair of 12in by 17in inside cylinders, fed with steam from the boiler of the locomotive proper. The copper steam pipe was about 23ft in length and sufficiently flexible to operate without the use of compensating joints. The exhaust steam passed to separate condensers consisting of fifteen tubes in the base of the water tank. A vertical waste pipe took away the uncondensed steam from the two condensers. A baffle plate and inverted cone was inserted in each waste pipe to intercept any water, which was directed back to the tank. An enlarged firebox was needed to provide extra steam for the tender. The diagram demonstrates the length of the steam pipe and the requirement for two regulators.

By hauling 50 per cent more wagons than the norm, Sturrock envisaged two locomotives with steam tenders would do the work of three conventional locomotives. Sturrock had spare tenders at the Doncaster Plant, which could be converted to steam tenders. The fireboxes in existing 0-6-0 locomotives could be enlarged, so that each train would consist of about forty-five wagons or 320 tons as opposed to a conventional load of about thirty wagons or 210 tons.[11]

Sturrock anticipated significant capital cost saving on new locomotives. He estimated a new steam tender locomotive would cost £3,350 and a conventional 0-6-0 with tender about £2,900. For every two steam tender locomotives bought in place of three conventional locomotives, capital costs would be reduced from £8,700 (3 x £2,900) to £6700 (2 x £3,350), a saving of £2,000. A fleet of fifty steam tender locomotives would save £50,000.

Sturrock recognised that the cost per train mile would be higher for the steam tender locomotive. He estimated 57 pence per double mile for the steam tender engine and 47 pence per mile for a train hauled by a conventional engine. The steam tender engine would absorb only 19 per cent of receipts, whilst the conventional engine would absorb 25 per cent of receipts. Profits would therefore rise, since receipts per mile would rise faster than costs. Sturrock recognised that there would be presentation difficulties, for his departmental performance statistics were based on cost per train mile, irrespective of receipts or loads hauled.

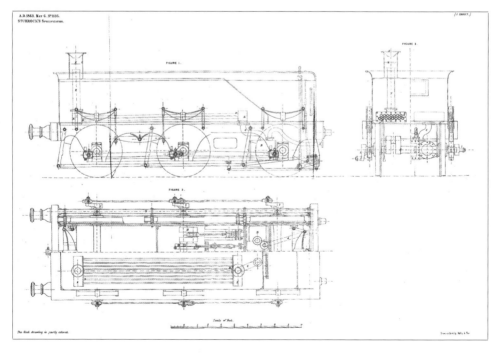

Section from the original drawing submitted with Sturrock's steam tender patent No.1135 of May 1863.

Sturrock could support the cost advantages with other benefits. The number of trains on the road would be reduced, if the total movement of goods remained unchanged. Alternatively the permanent way could handle more trains and more cargo. There would be fewer mineral trains to shunt into sidings to allow the passage of faster passenger trains. Fewer brake vans would be needed.

The first steam tender was made from a spare tender from Sharp single number 46, which had been converted to a tank engine in 1852. The cost of the conversion was £787 including £475 for materials, £250 for labour and £62 for general overheads. It was tried out behind number 391, an ex-Nottingham & Grantham 0-6-0 acquired by the GNR in 1855.

Sturrock recognised that the support of another locomotive engineer would make his invention more acceptable to his fellow officers and the GNR Board. He lent the experimental steam tender to Charles Sacré, locomotive superintendent of the MSLR, in the summer of 1863. Sacré wrote to his Board: 'Although I expected great results, my expectations have been far exceeded by its performance.' He indicated that the steam tender could take thirty-five to forty goods wagons up the MSLR's inclines. The norm for the Clarborough and Kirton banks was twenty-six wagons. Sacré had increased his loads by 50 per cent.[12]

In August 1863 Sacré followed up his successful use of the GNR's steam tender by obtaining permission from his Board to alter one MSLR tender at a cost of about £400 to £500 and stated 'it can not but be the most economical and best of adaptions which has come out for years'. Sacré reckoned the additional cost would be 2.5d per mile, but there would be a saving on the permanent way and a reduction in the number of trains. The MSLR Board approved the experiment. GNR records indicate the cost of converting the MSLR tender was £750.[13] In spite of his initial enthusiasm, Sacré did not persuade his Board to purchase more steam tender locomotives till October 1864. Six were acquired from Neilson, plus six conventional 0-6-0s.[14]

Sturrock did not raise the issue of steam tenders formally with the GNR Board until December 1863. Some discussion must, however, have taken place at a Board meeting in September 1863, when Sturrock received retrospective permission to convert the MSLR tender. Sturrock also needed to get his fellow officers on side before making specific proposal to acquire or convert more steam tenders and by December 1863 he had done this. No goods locomotives had been acquired by the GNR since January 1856, a period of nearly six years. In this period goods train mileage had grown from 1,780,446 miles in the six months to December 1856 to 2,125,269 miles in the six months to December 1863, an increase of 19 per cent. Sturrock's complaint that his locomotives were overworked was justified. The conversion of unused tenders to steam tenders could bring immediate relief in a very cost-effective manner.

The three most senior officers, Seymour Clarke, Archibald Sturrock and Walter Leith, wrote a joint letter to the Board over Christmas 1863.[15] The introduction of the steam tenders was one element in a seven-point plan to cope with the growth of the coal trade. The officers recommended:

1. Purchasing 500 open or coal wagons, 20 goods 'Breaks' and 1000 sheets;
2. Merging the locomotive department's fleet of 514 goods wagons with the general fleet under the Mineral Manager to achieve more efficient wagon operations;
3. Placing the 4 40 foot passenger carriages on 8 wheels to bring them up to the standard of the Metropolitan carriages;
4. Instructing Mr Sturrock to convert such tenders as he deems appropriate into auxiliary steam tenders and purchasing 20 new steam tender goods engines;
5. Altering 12 tank engines to make them suitable for shunting at King's Cross;
6. Extending the Doncaster repair shops by roofing the space between the Erecting and Boiler shops;
7. Erecting a new carriage and wagon shops at Doncaster.

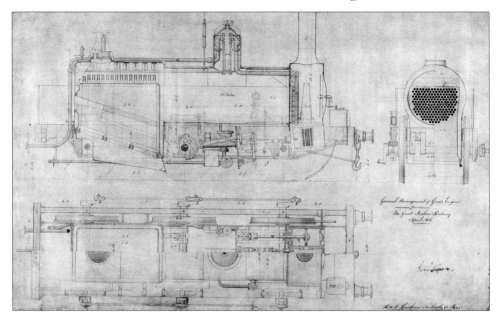

General arrangement drawing for the final batch of steam tender engines Nos 461–469 from
Hawthorns. (Tyne & Wear Museums)

The proposals received Board approval on 29 December 1863 and would cost £155,270.
Of this sum £66,000 would be spent on twenty new steam tender locomotives and a
further £15,000 on converting twenty-five old tenders to steam tenders.[16]

If Sturrock and his colleagues had opted for conventional engines instead of those with
steam tenders, an additional ten engines would have been required. The twenty-five steam
tenders should do the work of a further twelve locomotives. Ultimately Sturrock was to
convert thirty tenders to give a total of fifty, including those purchased with the new
0-6-0 goods locomotives. Earlier in the month the Board had agreed to expenditure of
£2,599 to lengthen sidings to accommodate longer coal trains, a prerequisite if the steam
tender engines were to be able to operate as intended.

Sturrock had a further reason to be satisfied. The Board increased his salary from 1 January
1864 to £1,500 a year.[17] What Sturrock may not have known was that Seymour Clarke's
deputy, Walter Leith, had been on a salary of £1,500 since August 1863. Leith's high salary
recognised his achievement in handling the 1862 Exhibition traffic.

Two days after the January 1864 Board, Sturrock wrote to his old friend, Daniel Gooch,
locomotive superintendent of the GWR, to promote the steam tender. 'My time has been
much occupied … with a report to the Board for the modest sum of £155,000 which I
want for new engines, trucks, shops. We are doing such a traffic that I am almost on my
beam ends. However I shall pull through this winter − by next I shall have 20 new engines
and 30 to 40 Tenders (Auxiliary) which will make me easy… I shall be most happy to call
upon you — have a crack re my scheme. I can assure you it is most successful - that we
are daily sending from Doncaster on to London forty-five wagons of coal or 50 per cent
more than the maximum load.'[18]

Sturrock wrote again to Gooch on 9 January 1864: 'Do you take care that your surfaces
be increased as much as possible? It will put you in a position to adopt the auxiliary tenders
whenever you choose. You will much oblige me by obtaining an order for one engine. I feel
some such will answer admirably on the South Wales line wherever there are heavy inclines.

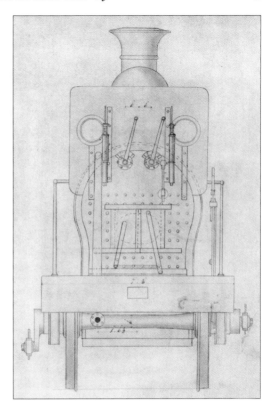

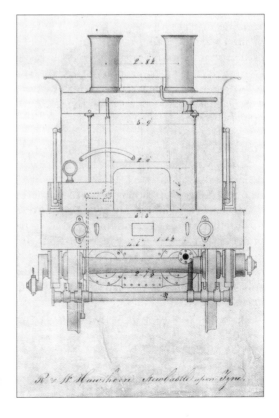

Above and right: Detailed drawings showing the footplate view of the cab and tender on the final batch of Class 400s from Hawthorn; a decision was taken before delivery to remove the steam tender equipment. (Tyne & Wear Museums)

The first Class 400 engine and steam tender delivered by Kitson in January 1865. (GNRS)

My engines with auxiliary tenders are earning £2,500 to £3,000 per annum more each than the other engines.' Sturrock did not persuade Gooch to buy.

The steam tender received favourable publicity in *Mechanics Magazine* in February 1864. It described the steam tender as perhaps the greatest improvement in locomotive design in the last twenty years. The steam tender engine would create a powerful engine for use on light track. Although heavy iron rails could be adopted, such improvements to the permanent way would be costly. All the adhesion benefits of a 60-ton engine could be achieved with a 35-ton engine with a powered 25-ton tender. By August 1864 *Mechanics Magazine* perceived the steam tender as the solution for light rural branch lines on the continent. Sturrock's was the only system which would permit the construction of branch lines at a cost which would 'render a good dividend certain.'[19]

On 1 February 1864 the GNR Board increased its commitment to Sturrock's new device. Eight manufacturers submitted tenders for the twenty new locomotives approved a month earlier. Hawthorn received an order for ten engines and steam tenders at £3,350. Their first engine was to arrive in August and the balance to be delivered by the end of December. A second order for ten locomotives went to Kitson, who reduced their price to Hawthorn's price and promised delivery between September and December 1864. With January to March being the peak months for the coal trade, the agreed delivery dates would meet the GNR's needs for the winter coal trade.[20] These engines were to be numbered 400–419 and were the final Class of Sturrock's 0-6-0 goods locomotives. They were built with 7ft 9in-length fireboxes to provide sufficient steam for both the engine proper and the steam tender. In spite of much chasing by Sturrock, Hawthorn and Kitson did not deliver the initial order for twenty Class 400 steam tender engines on time. Deliveries commenced in January 1865 and were completed by August.

In June 1864 Sturrock agreed with Colonel Packe, who was to succeed Denison as Chairman, the royalties the GNR would pay for the use of the steam tender patent.[21]

A works photograph of steam tender engine No.441 built by Neilson and delivered in March 1866. (Glasgow Mitchell Library)

Class 400 No.449 built by Neilson and shown after modifications to boiler and cab by Stirling. (GNRS)

Packe told the Board that Sturrock would charge one half of the amount charged to other companies not exceeding £50. It was agreed that, if Sturrock sold the patent, the GNR would be able to continue to use the patent on the same terms. Assuming Sturrock received £50 for each of the fifty tenders the GNR acquired, he would have made £2,500, somewhat less than two year's salary.

A Vulcan Foundry Class 400 No.453 with Stirling cab and boiler. (GNRS)

Sturrock's innovative steam tenders led to requests for his involvement in two new business ventures. Discussions about establishing a locomotive works in South Yorkshire had commenced in the summer of 1864. Local investors asked him to play a lead role in the foundation of the Yorkshire Engine Co. Sturrock was also approached by Daniel Gooch in July 1864 regarding another business venture. Sturrock wrote:

> It would have given me pleasure to have been engaged with you in a limited company...
> I can not now however for I am as deep in trading concerns as I think it prudent to be...
> I am pledged to embark in another manufacturing concern, similar to Tayleurs, on certain
> conditions, which are now under negotiation. Such renders it inappropriate for me to join
> any similar concern. I may mention to you that my late arrangement of auxiliary tenders
> has led to the said engagement on my part. I inform you of this to appraise you of the bona
> fides of my present interest.[22]

Charles Tayleur & Co. became The Vulcan Foundry Limited in 1864.

GNR goods traffic continued to increase. In October 1864 Sturrock asked for twenty more goods engines without tenders. He considered he would have sufficient power once the twenty new goods engines with steam tenders ordered in January were delivered, the thirty tenders converted to steam tenders were complete and twenty more engines without tenders added. Ten engines were ordered from Neilson at £2,295 and a second batch of ten from Kitson at £2,450 in December 1864. Kitson received the order, even though the Vulcan Foundry had come in with a lower price. These engines were numbered 420 to 439 and had marginally smaller fireboxes than the first twenty locomotives of Class 400. [23]

Ten passenger tank engines were also ordered from Avonside at the same meeting for £2,350 each. A penalty clause required Avonside to pay £75 per week if the engines were delivered more than six weeks late. These 0-4-2 tank engines were designed for the suburban and underground traffic, which the GNR intended to run from Hitchin over the Metropolitan line to Victoria and would have WB Adams patent radial axle boxes for the trailing wheels to assist stability on the tight curves of the new track. Their design was evolved from the Sharp 0-4-2 tank engine conversions. They were able to handle the heavy gradients in the tunnel from King's Cross down to the Metropolitan line. Numbered 241 to 250, the engines were delivered between October and January 1865. Rebuilt by Stirling between 1879 and 1881, most continued in service largely on branch line duties till the early years of the twentieth century.

At the officers' committee meeting during December 1864 the traffic department stated some locomotives were not fit for the work they had to do. The meeting agreed that Sturrock should work the Doncaster Plant day and night to complete repairs. Alterations to twelve of the oldest Class 116 0-6-0s to saddle tank engines, which had been agreed by the Board in December 1863, had not been completed, because they were always needed for traffic. Sturrock was told that at least four of the twelve conversions should be capable of handling a full trainload of goods wagons on the inclines at the junctions with the Metropolitan, North London and Ludgate Hill. Alternatively he should persuade the Board to buy suitable new engines. The committee agreed a number of measures to make more efficient use of the existing engine fleet and decided that twenty engines had to be borrowed from other lines. Clarke, Leith and Grinling left the meeting for Manchester, York and London to beg engines from the MSLR, the North Eastern and the Metropolitan.

Class 241 0-4-2T No.243 built by Avonside in 1865 as transferred to the duplicate list in 1879. (SLS)

Class 270 was a development of the Class 241 0-4-2T locomotives; No.272 was built by Neilson and delivered after Sturrock retired in March 1867. (SLS)

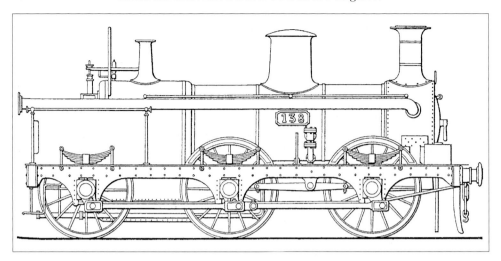

No.138 was one of several engines converted by Sturrock for use on the Metropolitan Railway when the GWR withdrew its services in August 1863; the drawings show the large pipe added to convey the exhaust steam to the condensing tank and the funnel lowered to the height of the dome. (*Railway Magazine* July 1964)

The Metropolitan Railway had every reason to be helpful and lent the GNR three engines on the same terms as the GNR had lent engines to the Metropolitan some fifteen months previously. In August 1863 the Metropolitan found itself without locomotives or rolling stock and the GNR agreed to meet its needs at very short notice. The Metropolitan had opened in January 1863 from a new station at Paddington to Farringdon Street, a length of about 4 miles. The track was laid to mixed gauge. The GWR had agreed to operate the line using the broad gauge track, for which Gooch had designed new condensing engines and eight wheeled carriages. Disputes soon arose between the GWR and the Metropolitan, particularly concerning the frequency of trains. As a result the GWR gave notice on 18 July 1863 that they intended to cease to work the railway from 1 October. The Metropolitan accepted the GWR's notice and then received a further letter from the GWR to say they would cease operations on 10 August. The Metropolitan had no carriages or locomotives of its own and approached the GNR for help.

The GNR Board of 3 August 1863 authorised Sturrock to help the Metropolitan. Sturrock was already in the process of converting a number of GNR engines to meet its own requirements for the planned services to the City along the Metropolitan's narrow gauge track. Sturrock hurriedly assembled sufficient engines and carriages to start a narrow gauge service over the Metropolitan on 10 August. Between ten and twelve either six- or four-coupled goods locomotives were fitted with condensing apparatus. The funnels were lowered to the height of the dome and a large pipe was run along the side of the engine past the footplate to the tender, where it terminated in a water tank above the level of the water. The connexion between the engine and the tender was made at the footplate by means of a flexible coupling. As a consequence of diverting so many engines to the Metropolitan, Sturrock had to come back to the GNR Board to get permission to convert more engines for the GNR's own services, which were to start on 1 September 1863. Meanwhile some problems were being experienced on the Metropolitan. The narrow gauge track had never been used and had to be re-ballasted to keep the GNR trains on the rails. The Metropolitan Board formally thanked Sturrock 'for his great energy and attention in providing engine power for working the traffic' at its Board meeting in December 1864 and sent £100 for Sturrock to distribute to his staff involved in the project.

As a result of a joint approach by Sturrock and Clarke in early 1865, the Board accepted that GNR locomotives were more heavily used than the norm. They were averaging 28,000 miles a year, whilst other railways averaged about 20,000 miles. The officers' meeting had gone fully into the operation of steam tenders, including the question as to whether they were more frequently in the shops than ordinary engines and the difficulty of running them out at stations. Clearly questions were being asked about the efficiency of the steam tenders, but Sturrock carried the officers and Board with him on this occasion. [24]

Sturrock's half-year report to December 1864 showed twenty-three steam tenders were operating in the period and had run 270,578 miles. They had completed 1,691 trips between Doncaster and Peterborough and dragged an average of forty-two wagons or an increased load of 90 tons. Sturrock estimated the net gain was £17,338. If the steam tenders had not been available, the railway would have run an extra 108,238 miles. In the subsequent six months to the end of June 1865 steam tender mileage had increased to 396,631.

Following discussion of Clarke's and Sturrock's paper, the Board meeting on 24 January 1865 agreed to acquire thirty goods and fifteen passenger engines. A fortnight later orders were placed for thirty 0-6-0s with steam tenders. Neilson was to supply ten at £2,900, Vulcan six at £2,975, Avonside five at £3,000 and Hawthorn nine at £3,250. The engines numbered 440 to 469 were delivered between January and May 1866. They were built with 7ft 2in-long fireboxes to permit the use of steam tenders; the outside length of the firebox was 6in smaller than the first twenty Class 400s, but the same length as the second batch of twenty. The steam tenders were replaced with ordinary tenders prior to delivery. The fireboxes were reduced to 5ft 6in by Stirling in 1868. Most of these locomotives served the GNR for over thirty-five years. [25]

In February 1865 the Board agreed to purchase ten passenger engines and not the fifteen discussed a fortnight previously. The ten 2-4-0 locomotives were a new Sturrock design and were ordered from Sharp Stewart at a price of £3,160 each for delivery in early 1866. They were to be used on secondary workings mainly in the West Riding of Yorkshire and replaced some of the 0-6-0s converted to tank engines for use on the suburban services. They were designed for the burning of coal as well as coke. In the light of his recent experience, Sturrock had both these engines and the latest Class 400s modified at a cost of £15 to £20 each to take account of some problems he had experienced with the use of coal. A cross partition was inserted on the top of the firebox to ease the strain from the expansion and contraction of the tube plate. Coal was now regularly used in GNR goods engines but still rarely used in passenger locomotives. The Class 251 2-4-0s were successful engines and were withdrawn between 1897 and 1900.

As a result of the delays to locomotive deliveries from UK manufacturers, the GNR Board considered buying locomotives from France. Cail & Co. were approached in April 1865. The French locomotives were priced at £3,500 and delivery promised in November or December 1865. The offer was rejected. The drawing in French and English of a Class 400 0-6-0 with steam tender dates from this period. [26]

Cost pressures eventually led the GNR Board to agree to use coal in passenger engines in April 1865, provided the coke already ordered was used up. [27] The Group Accountant Grinling had estimated that savings of £22,000 could be made if the GNR used coal. Clarke wrote to Ramsbottom of the LNWR to check his use of coal and found that the LNWR was using coal on all passenger trains, even the Royal train. The LNWR's use of coke was under 1 per cent of all fuel used. Sturrock was happy to make the change and admitted he had been experimenting with the use of coal on his express engines for some time. He was not, however, willing to accept Grinling's figures, which he described as 'all bosh'.

One of Sturrock's penultimate Class of 2-4-0s, No.251 as modified by Stirling standing alongside a Stirling 4-2-2. (GNRS)

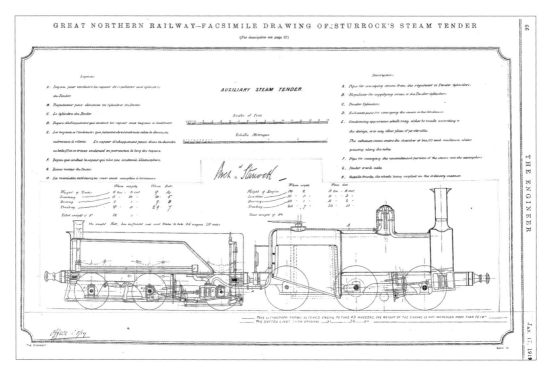

This drawing of the steam tender engine in French and English may have been used when the GNR invited tenders from French locomotive manufacturers. (*Engineer*, 1919)

One of two Avonside 0-8-0s modified by Sturrock for underground working in the King's Cross area and delivered in April 1866. (GNRS)

Grinling, Sturrock added, did not appreciate the significance of the steep gradients and heavier loads on the GNR. Sturrock wrote to Clarke: '*Vous me vantiez beaucoup les machines Ramsbottom.*' Clarke had suggested Ramsbottom's engines were much more fuel efficient than Sturrock's, but failed to appreciate that the GNR's more powerful engines pulled more wagons or tons per train. Costs per train mile were, therefore, misleading. Sturrock said he could easily reduce his costs per train mile by acquiring smaller engines and running more trains with fewer wagons.[28]

In January 1865 the Board agreed to buy six new tank engines of significant power to work the anticipated heavy goods traffic over the steep gradients on the North London, Metropolitan and London, Chatham and Dover lines. Sturrock mentioned his problem to Edward Slaughter of the Avonside works at Bristol, who described a 0-8-0 tank engine he had designed for the Vale of Neath Railway. Sturrock visited South Wales to see the locomotive and concluded that, with suitable adaptions for underground working, the engine would meet the GNR's needs. After much negotiation over his required modifications Sturrock received Board approval to purchase two 0-8-0 tank engines from Avonside on 21 March 1865. The final cost was expected to be about £3,600. Weighing 47 tons, the engines were numbered 472 to 473 and operated at a boiler pressure of 140lb. The engines were only used for a limited time on through goods and mineral workings to south London, for they damaged the permanent way. They were subsequently confined to marshalling goods trains at King's Cross and were scrapped in 1880.[29]

During 1865 Sturrock increased his involvement with the Yorkshire Engine Co. The inaugural meeting had taken place at the Victoria Hotel, Sheffield on 22 April 1865 with the Hon. W.G. Eden in the chair. Eden lived in Doncaster and knew Sturrock well through their charitable and philanthropic activities in the town. Sturrock had agreed to invest £5,000 and was invited to become a director and to take the Chair. He declined whilst still employed by the GNR, but agreed he would like to do so at some time in the future. Although not officially on the Yorkshire Engine Board, he nevertheless attended most Board meetings over the subsequent twelve months and played an active role in the selection of machinery for the new works. His district superintendent at Peterborough, Alfred Sacré, left the GNR in May 1865 to take up the post of managing director of the new company. Sturrock was preparing himself for a new role after fifteen years with the GNR.

During this period Sturrock extended the locomotive department's facilities at Doncaster, King's Cross and Peterborough. In-house construction of carriages had been expanded in 1860–61 with the building of stock for the ECJS and for the GNR's own use. A major reconstruction of coal wagons began in 1864 to increase capacity to 9 tons. As wagons and carriages aged, the maintenance workload increased. New locomotive and carriage sheds were constructed at King's Cross and new boiler shops, water supply and cottages provided at New England. A major expansion at Doncaster costing about £8,000 was approved in January 1864 in order to provide premises to alter engines and build steam tenders. The space between the boiler shop and the erecting shop was roofed over and the half of the turning shop used for carriage repairs was returned to its original planned use. To provide for carriage repairs, a new shop was built which, with fittings and rail access, cost £17,750. More foundry capacity was required and the number of steam hammers increased at Doncaster and Peterborough. As a result of a fire in December 1864, fire engines were bought and improved water supplies introduced at Doncaster. The construction of a gas works at Doncaster costing about £5,000 was approved in April 1865. These new buildings were to provide Stirling with the space to bring locomotive manufacture in-house in 1867.

Sturrock suffered from a shortage of labour as well as a shortage of space. In May 1864 Sturrock advised the Board that he needed to spend £4,093 on better tools, since he could not find sufficient mechanics. In July he obtained consent to the purchase of machinery to sharpen saws, a task till then done by hand. In January 1865 Sturrock asked the Board for sewing machines to improve efficiency in the trimming shop. Riveting machines were also purchased in the same month because boilermakers were difficult to get.

From 1861 onwards the Doncaster carriage and wagon shops manufactured a significant proportion of new carriages required for the expansion of the GNR, although priority was still given to repairs and enhancements to existing stock. In November 1861 a decision was made to spend £50 per wagon to lengthen sixty timber wagons. Ninety-six horse boxes were to be modified at £15 a box to provide a manger and a space for the groom. Thirty-five goods and seventy-two coal brake vans were altered to give the guard a better outlook. Some first-class carriages were converted to family or saloon carriages to meet changed passenger requirements. Weight was added to all brake vans weighing less than 10 tons to improve braking. To ensure his accounts looked favourable, Sturrock continued to encourage the Board to charge all improvements over and above normal refurbishments to capital account.

Seymour Clarke, Sturrock and Leith had come to realise that a joint appeal to the Board whether for locomotives, workshops or rolling stock was the best approach. In June 1864 they asked for eighty new carriages to be ordered for delivery by May 1865 for the summer traffic. The cost was expected to be about £48,000. The Board agreed and asked Sturrock how many he could make at Doncaster. He decided to make twenty composites, with the rest to be purchased from outside suppliers.

Between March 1861 and March 1866 the number of GNR passenger carriages rose from 826 to 1,195, an increase of 369 or 45 per cent. Twenty-eight first class, fifty-eight second class, fifty-seven third class and twenty-two composites were made in the company's shops for GNR passenger use, plus eight passenger luggage vans and fourteen wagons for the transport of carriages. In addition the shops made sixty-five goods brake vans, two covered wagons and one boiler truck. During the early months of 1861

Doncaster had also completed the balance of the fifty carriages ordered for the ECJS, of which twenty-four were allocated to the GNR.[30] During 1864 there was some reshuffling of the ECJS. Six first-class carriages were altered to second-class and one first and one second withdrawn from ECJS and added to the GNR's own stock. In December 1865 the Board instructed Sturrock to build twenty third-class carriages at a cost of £260–270 each.

In November 1864 Clarke, Leith and Sturrock recommended remodelling all the GNR's wagon stock. There were three choices; the present 6-ton wagons could be refurbished for £16 each, increased to 7 tons capacity at a cost of £22 or enlarged to 9-ton capacity by the expenditure of £32 per wagon. The Board agreed to the most expensive option. Unfortunately for Sturrock when reviewing progress the following April, the costs appeared to be nearer to £40 per wagon. Sturrock was disturbed to find that Griffiths had been massaging the figures to try and keep within the original estimate. The actual cost depended on how much ironwork could be reused, for all the woodwork was renewed and the springs strengthened. Sturrock found that six to seven new larger wagons could be made from ten old wagons. He believed that the cost would turn out to be about £29 when all factors had been taken into account. He argued that the costs should be charged to capital and not to revenue, where they had been charged.[31] New wagons, which would have been charged to capital, were bought for about £90–95 in 1864–65. To conserve cash the GNR decided in December 1864 to hire fifty wagons as an experiment. The cost to hire a £90 wagon was £13 per year for a three-year agreement.[32] Forty ballast wagons were hired on similar terms in October 1865.

The second half of 1865 was a difficult time for Sturrock. In spite of the delivery of new goods locomotives, there were still shortages due to a lack of shunting capacity and congestion due to the relaying of the main line with heavier iron rails. His coal engines could be out for eighteen hours a day instead of the standard twelve and a half hours. Delays at Holloway ranged between four and ten hours. Sturrock wrote to the Board in November 1865: 'A continuation of such working would not only run up my expenses very considerably, but would eventually prevent me working the railway with safety.' The goods trains could not be worked to the timetable and caused the express passenger trains to be delayed because of numerous caution signals.

Passenger train delays were exacerbated by the inadequate power of the current GNR main line locomotives for the increased length of trains. Bank engines had been provided in October 1865 at Grantham, Retford and Hitchin. Sturrock was convinced the good name of the GNR could only be maintained by dividing the heavier trains. Although the GNR engines were 8 tons heavier and had proportionately larger fireboxes than the LNWR engines, Sturrock's express locomotives could not cope, particularly in inclement weather. A decision was made to duplicate the principle main line services leaving King's Cross at 10 a.m. and 5 p.m. and their up equivalents. Sturrock advised the Board he needed six additional 7ft passenger engines if he was to undertake the work assigned to him. The Board approved the acquisition of six more engines from 'some of the best houses'.[33] The order for his final Class of express locomotives was to be placed on 9 January 1866.

By the end of 1865 Sturrock was ready to announce his intended departure from the GNR. The establishment of the Yorkshire Engine Co. in April 1865 and the invitation to take the Chair gave him a fresh challenge and a chance to continue to use his engineering and management skills in a new but less time-consuming way. In May 1865 he had secured the managing director role at Yorkshire Engine for his most senior subordinate, Alfred Sacré. The loss of his works manager, Fred Parker, to John Fowler & Co. of Leeds in October 1865 may have been encouraged by Sturrock, who saw the new role as an excellent opportunity for his most loyal lieutenant. Parker and Sturrock had worked together since Sturrock's arrival at the GNR fifteen years earlier. As works manager of John Fowler, Parker took the firm into the manufacture of locomotives. When tenders were accepted for Sturrock's last express locomotives, the orders went to Yorkshire Engine and John Fowler. They may have been 'some of the best houses' but they were not established locomotive manufacturers.

Sturrock did not need his salary to continue to live very comfortably. His second wife Helen had inherited in excess of £50,000 from her father and her assets had passed to Sturrock on their marriage in May 1854. Converting the value of pounds from 1854 to current values is not a precise art, but £50,000 is probably equivalent to £4 to 5 million today. Even Sturrock's investment of £5,000 in Yorkshire Engine was not significant in terms of the proportion of his wealth put at risk.

Other factors which may have influenced Sturrock's decision were the changes to the scale and management of the GNR. Sturrock had told the select committee on Railway and Canal Amalgamations in 1853 that he did not believe it was good for railways to be too big. Sturrock believed efficiency was maximised if officers had control of a railway of manageable size. As size increased, engineers might be dictated to by committees. He stated that, with such a structure, 'there would necessarily arise non-responsibility and less interest in the business and, consequently, increased expenditure.' The GNR's first locomotive committee was appointed in early 1866.

The top management team had also changed; he now had to deal with a new chairman, with whom it was no longer possible to explore ideas informally on the way to or from church or over a drink or meal in each other's houses, for Packe did not live in Doncaster. Walter Leith had moved on in February 1865 and Sturrock now had to work with Francis Cockshott, who had been recruited as traffic superintendent in Leith's place. James Grinling, the company accountant, had been replaced by his brother William.

Earlier commentators have argued that Sturrock resigned because of the failure of his steam tenders. This now seems improbable. The steam tenders were performing to plan during 1865 and had been instrumental in leading to his intended appointment with Yorkshire Engine. Although the enginemen and fireman may already have been unhappy about having to look after two engines for a negligible increase in pay, Sturrock was unlikely to have been moved by such pleas. He was always willing to help individual men in trouble and present a case to the Board, but took little interest in mass petitions from the men. When he was presented with a 'memorial' from his enginemen and fireman in July 1865 complaining about the way they were paid, he told the Board his only area of concern was the Horncastle branch where changes had been made to 'cut down improper earnings.'[34]

Sturrock was committed to leave the GNR once he had made the decision, in the spring of 1865, to accept the position of chairman of Yorkshire Engine, a role that was incompatible with his position at the GNR. His reasons for deferring an announcement may have been influenced by a wish to see the steam tenders successfully launched and sales of his patent extended to other railways. Sacré had taken till October 1864 to buy steam tender locomotives. Gooch was never persuaded. Sturrock may also have thought he might be in a better position to get an order for locomotives from the GNR for Yorkshire Engine while he was still GNR locomotive superintendent. Such arguments may have persuaded the Yorkshire Engine Board to agree to wait so long for his formal appointment to the Board. Even though Sturrock was not an official Board member during 1865, he provided Yorkshire Engine with as much help as any director at that time might have been expected to give.

10

FROM GNR TO THE YORKSHIRE ENGINE CO. 1866–71

Sturrock's final year with the GNR opened inauspiciously. The boiler of engine No.155, a Bury Class 116 goods locomotive, exploded at Nottingham on 1 January 1866. The pressure had been screwed down to 120lb, but the boiler had burst at 110lb. It had been inspected and found to be sound in December 1862. Its last full test had been to 140lb on 2 May 1865. As a precaution Sturrock had the boiler pressure of all other members of the Class reduced to 100lb, unless their boilers had already been replaced.

The first Board meeting of 1866 considered the purchase of the six new passenger locomotives approved on 14 November 1865. John Fowler's offer to deliver three engines at £2,890 each by 31 August 1865 was accepted. The second lowest tender was £2,950 from the Yorkshire Engine Co. Alfred Sacré was called into the meeting and agreed to reduce his price to £2,850 and to deliver one engine in October and two more in November 1865. Originally designed as 2-2-2s, Sturrock had second thoughts a month later and suggested to the Board that four-wheeled coupled engines might cope better with the banks between London and Potters Bar and between Peterborough and the 100 mile post. Sturrock estimated the change would cost about £100 to £150 per engine if the Board would 'decide to try the experiment'; the cost was eventually agreed at £175 per engine. A large coupled express engine for main line work was unusual at the time. The John Fowler engines numbered 264–266 arrived in November and December 1866 and the Yorkshire Engine locomotives 267–269 between December 1866 and February 1867. The Class 264s had occasional problems with bent coupling rods, but Stirling found the engines useful, for they ran in coupled form till the mid-1870s, when they were converted to 2-2-2s to conform to Stirling's standard policy. They were retained on fast main line duties till the late 1890s.

After agreeing the orders for the new express engines, Colonel Packe, the chairman, opened a discussion about the replacement for Fred Parker, the works manager at Doncaster, who now managed John Fowler's works. The post was advertised in November 1865 and seven of the fifteen applicants were interviewed by the Executive Committee on 1 December including Patrick Stirling, locomotive engineer of the Glasgow & South Western Railway. He was not one of two candidates short-listed for second interviews, which never took place.

One of Sturrock's final Class 264 2-4-0s No.266 was built by John Fowler and delivered in December 1866. (GNRS)

Class 264 2-4-0 No.269 following rebuilding by Stirling as a 2-2-2. (SLS)

Drawing of Class 264 2-4-0 Nos 264–266 built by John Fowler; Nos 267–269 were built by Yorkshire Engine Co. (*Engineer*, March 1867)

When the Board returned to the subject of Parker's replacement on 9 January 1866, it was apparent Colonel Packe had had conversations with Sturrock and with his fellow directors. Packe stated that neither of the short-listed candidates for Parker's job matched the requirements. 'Further enquiries had been made with a view to finding a competent successor to Mr Parker and, if possible one qualified after having experience in the service, to succeed Mr Sturrock who has announced his retirement within a limited period.' It seems likely that Sturrock decided he needed to tell Packe about his discussions with Yorkshire Engine after the first set of interviews and suggested to Packe that the Board should seek someone who would have the skills to succeed him. Sturrock probably recommended Stirling, for their apprenticeships at the Dundee Foundry had overlapped and they both worked on locomotives for the Arbroath & Forfar Railway. After a period with R.&W. Hawthorn, Stirling had joined the Glasgow & South Western Railway as locomotive engineer in 1853.

Packe believed Stirling was qualified by his attainments and references to fill the role of assistant locomotive engineer and to succeed Sturrock on his retirement. He would report to Sturrock and run the workshops. Stirling had already met some of the directors and described his duties, including his locomotive building experience and his methods for controlling costs. He was called in to meet the other directors and to answer questions. After his interview, the Board offered Stirling £1,000 a year on joining and £2,000 a year as soon as he succeeded Sturrock. This was £500 a year more than Sturrock's current salary of £1,500. The Board then called in Sturrock who indicated he would be content to retire at the end of the year, if that would suit the directors. Sturrock left the meeting; Stirling was recalled, told that Sturrock would retire in twelve to fifteen months and advised of his status, duties and salary. Stirling joined the GNR two months later.

At the 23 January Board, Sturrock reported encouraging results for his steam tenders. Forty-eight steam tenders had completed 526,559 miles in the six months to December 1865. The tenders 'dragged the loads originally determined upon with regularity and at the estimated additional cost.' By the year end all fifty tenders were at work and, on an annualised basis, were doing 21,940 miles per year, more than the standard 20,000 miles a year for a goods engine, and suggesting availability was not a significant problem.

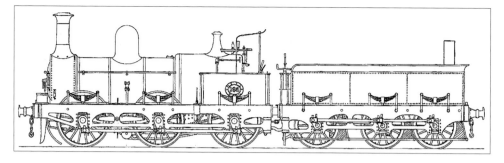

A steam tender locomotive No.198 built by Neilson for the Manchester, Sheffield & Lincolnshire Railway.

However, this brief report to the Board did not reveal the difficulties Sturrock was encountering with Seymour Clarke and his traffic department colleagues. Sturrock had to call in his friend Charles Sacré of the MSLR to help.

Sacré remained an enthusiastic supporter of the steam tender. He reported in glowing terms to the MSLR Board on 17 January 1866. Sacré's locomotive foreman had asked for more engines with steam tenders. Sacré said many people were against and many were for the steam tender, but he persisted with his original view that the steam tender was one of the most economical things a company can resort to 'where the traffic will warrant such mechanical combinations. Our South Yorkshire, Mexborough & Keadby traffic is one of the best experiments and the result is of such a nature that it will solve the destiny of the steam tender.' Sacré reminded his Board that the MSLR had seven steam tenders, the six ordered from Neilsons and the one converted at Doncaster. Underdown, the MSLR general manager at the time, concurred with Sacré's views. More orders were never placed. [1]

Sturrock was dissatisfied with the way the GNR traffic department were using the steam tender engines. Sacré and Underdown met Seymour Clarke in Sheffield in early 1866. Sacré criticised the way the GNR's traffic department loaded the steam tender engines. Sacré told Clarke that the MSLR had achieved 50 per cent uplift in loads for 12.5 per cent uplift in costs and that one less brake van costing £200 was needed as the tender with its side rods and extra weight gave the necessary braking power.

The support Sturrock received from Sacré and the MSLR was countered by unfavourable press speculation. In the 19 January 1866 edition of *Engineering*, Sturrock was accused of promoting the steam tender by making statements that were not attributable concerning the ability of the steam tender engines to pull forty-five wagons rather than the normal twenty-eight. 'The steam tender is not new. It was long since employed and abandoned in France, and various proposals upon the same plan have been from time to time advanced without gaining adoption. We believe the steam tender to be a mistake.' The article argued: 'It is the want of proper knowledge of the value and application of sand that has led to steam tenders.' Sturrock was well aware of the value of the application of sand.

Sturrock had one last opportunity to promote the steam tender. As locomotive superintendent of the GNR, he appeared before the Royal Commission on Railway Charges in May 1866.[2] During his interview Sturrock drew the commission's attention to the benefits of the steam tender. He indicated loads could be increased from 210–220 tons to 320 tons at an additional cost of 1d per mile for repairs and ½d per mile for fuel for the locomotive. Sturrock admitted to the committee that the use of the steam tender 'is to some extent still an experiment'. The Commission's final report singled out the steam tender as one of the innovatory ideas adopted by railway companies to hold down costs and included Sturrock's figures in its report.

MINUTES OF EVIDENCE.   889

CALCULATIONS showing the Cost of hauling a Train of Coals with an Ordinary Engine compared with an Engine fitted with an Auxiliary Tender.

Mr. A. Sturrock,

31 May 1866,

Load with an Ordinary Engine, 30 Trucks or 210 Tons.	Load with Engine and Auxiliary Tender, 45 Trucks or 320 Tons.
Engine (including interest) - 10·0d. per mile Waggons do. - 3·5 „ Permanent way - 5·0 „ Guards and greasing - 1·5 „ Lighting and other charges - 3·5 „ 23·5 × 2 = 47·0d., or 3s. 11d. per double mile.	Engine (including interest) - 11·5d. per mile Waggons do. - 5·0 „ Permanent way - 6·5 „ Guards and greasing - 2·0 „ Lighting and other charges - 3·5 „ 28·5 × 2 = 57·0d., or 4s. 9d. per double mile.

PER-CENTAGE of Cost of Engine-power on Receipts in hauling the above loads :—

Receipts { 210 tons at ¾d. per ton per mile = 6s. 6½d. per double mile.
Expenses { 210 „ 20d. per double mile run, or 25 per cent. of receipts.
Receipts { 320 tons at ¾d. per ton per mile = 10s. per double mile.
Expenses { 320 „ 23d. per double mile run, or 19 per cent. of receipts.

RELATIVE Cost of Engine with Ordinary and with Auxiliary Steam Tender.

Engine with steam tender costs - - - - - £3,350
Do. without do. - - - - - £2,900
Two engines with steam tenders drag the load of three engines with ordinary tenders.
£2,900 × 3 = £8,700
3,350 × 2 = 6,700
──────
£2,000 less cost, or £2,000 = 23 per cent. less capital for a similar amount of traffic.

Adjourned sine die.

Extract of figures Sturrock provided to the Royal Commission in May 1866.

On 23 January 1866 Sturrock had once again to try and convince the Board that he needed more engines. Sturrock reckoned he needed another twenty-two engines just to bring his mileage down to the accepted standard of 20,000 a year before taking account of traffic growth. The Board established a committee under Packe which concluded that fifteen new passenger tank engines and five new gas-lit trains were needed for the Metropolitan and suburban traffic and twenty-two goods engines. The Board approved the proposals. [3]

Winter weather was not making Sturrock's life easy. Trains were being delayed due to gales and, on 13 February, three engines had broken down. Sturrock told Clarke: 'For years I have told you we have no margin. We have to have favourable conditions to keep time.' Sturrock argued that the permanent way could not carry an engine of sufficient power to cope with the long GNR trains in bad weather and maintain the good name the GNR had once enjoyed for timekeeping. The only solution was to split the longer trains. The effect of this would be to increase overall costs, but, somewhat perversely, reduce costs per train mile, one of the Board's favourite measures of Sturrock's performance. [4]

Sturrock had always realised that, as the GNR grew, more committees were likely to be created. He must have been thankful that he had decided to go, when the Board of the 6 March 1866 established a permanent locomotive committee. The first meeting took place at Doncaster on 9 and 10 March and drew Sturrock's attention to the waste iron lying about the shops. Although the committee agreed to the enlargement of the boiler and erecting shops at Doncaster and to the purchase of more tools in the light of the difficulty in getting labour, it also asked Sturrock to look again at his engine requirements. 'The chairman explained to Mr Sturrock that it was necessary the committee should be furnished from time to time with returns showing the locality of the engines, the cost of their running, wages and materials, the cost of repairs to engines and carriages and wagons separately and also the cost of accidents.' Sturrock was asked to make suggestions regarding the form of the returns.[5] Sturrock's initial proposals were laid before the committee on 9 April and, perhaps not surprisingly in the light of his reluctance to provide information in earlier years, found wanting. In particular prior year comparisons were required in all instances and more detail was requested on engine, carriage and wagon conditions.

Sturrock persisted with his efforts to get more goods engines, but had to content himself initially with an order for ten more tank engines for passenger duties. On 16 March he reminded the Board that no goods engines had been purchased between 1856 and 1865. In this period goods train mileage had increased by 30 per cent from 3.6 million to 4.7 million miles per year. The typical goods engine was running nearly 27,000 miles a year and even when the engines on order had been delivered, the mileage would still be 20,557 miles per engine per year. The Board of 20 March took no notice of his plea for more goods engines, but agreed to order fifteen more tank engines for the suburban passenger services. Twelve manufacturers tendered and orders were placed with the two cheapest suppliers. Avonside were to supply five at £2,480 and Neilson five at £2,380. The locomotive committee decided to withhold the orders for the final five locomotives. The ten 0-4-2 tank engines numbered 270-279 were delivered in February and March 1867 after Sturrock retired. They had a long life and the last three of the Class were withdrawn in 1905.

Tenders were received for more goods engines at the 10 April Board, but once again a decision was deferred. The position was reviewed by the locomotive committee, where Sturrock again reminded the Board that he required twenty-two more goods engines and that they would not be available to the GNR for at least twelve months even if ordered that day. The locomotive committee decided to order no more engines and the Board endorsed the committee's decision the next day. Only the order for carriages for the five new gas-lit trains proceeded.[6]

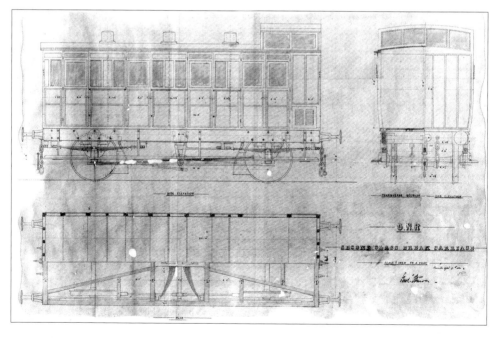

A second-class brake van signed off by Sturrock in April 1866, five months before he handed over to Stirling. (National Archives)

All the extra information Sturrock was now assembling for the locomotive committee led to more questions about cost increases. Sturrock told the committee that he felt it imperative to spend as much as possible on engine repairs as the engines were 'under par' as a result of the excessive mileage run. He kept the workshops open at night and wished to keep to the current level of repairs. Sturrock agreed to look for cost savings and the store keeper was asked to see if he could reduce stocks in the locomotive department.

The question of cost comparisons between railways was a matter of interest to the Royal Commission on Railway Charges. Although the commission produced figures to show that the GNR's overall costs per mile were lower than those on the GWR, the South Eastern and the Northern of France, Sturrock argued that such comparisons were flawed. The clearing house had looked to find a satisfactory method for comparison, but concluded this was not practical due to variations in mix of traffic, age of rolling stock, speed of trains, method used to calculate mileage, nature of the line and variations in accounting practice.

By early July it would seem that Sturrock was falling out of favour and Stirling's qualities recognised. Packe announced on 10 July that he had arranged for Stirling to visit all stations and that he would take over from Sturrock on 1 October, with Sturrock remaining as a consultant to the end of the year. Stirling quickly set about finding someone to take his place at Doncaster and appointed John Shotton from Stephenson on 7 August at a salary of £400 a year.

Sturrock continued to run the locomotive department between July and the end of September. He submitted his final Board report in July for the six months to the end of June 1866. The steam tender mileage had been 585,704 against 396,631 for the same period in the previous year, indicating each tender was averaging 23,428 miles a year and confirming the steam tenders were fully used. The report makes no mention of the average number of wagons hauled, which might suggest the tenders were not being operated as originally intended. The discussions between Sacré and Clarke in Sheffield some six months earlier had not led to the changes in GNR operating practice, which Sturrock and Sacré thought were needed to maximise the benefits of the steam tenders.

In September Sturrock renewed his campaign to get more engines for both general and suburban work and enlisted the help of Budge, his foreman at King's Cross, and the new traffic superintendent, Cockshott. Even with support from Clarke, Sturrock's final appeal was in vain. The subject was discussed at the locomotive committee meeting on 1 October 1866, when both Sturrock and Stirling were present and Packe confirmed the handover to Stirling. Sturrock attended no more committees during the final three months of 1866.[7]

Stirling made the steam tender the subject of his first report to the Board 'not from any wish to find fault with the invention of my predecessor but simply to give the Board a picture of its value.' Stirling considered the steam tender first due to its novelty and 'comparatively exceptional use' on the GNR.[8] Stirling had difficulty, he admits, in finding reliable data, since the tenders were exchanged between engines. As a first step he compared the overall cost of the new engines with steam tenders against the costs of engines with ordinary tenders in their first seven months of working. This showed a balance in favour of the steam tender of 1.65d per mile.

Stirling then examined repair costs. Steam tender engines cost about 3.53d per mile and ordinary engines about 3.27d per mile to run. The initial repair cost for the steam tenders in the first seven months was only 0.61d per mile. The oldest steam tenders, which had been operating for three years at most, were costing 1.75d per mile in repairs. Stirling expected this figure to rise and that any initial saving would be balanced by higher repair costs in later life. He concludes,. 'This seems to bring the two systems practically to an equality, showing no advantage got by the use of steam tenders except a trifling reduction in the number of trains.'

Twelve engines with steam tenders were required daily to handle the work of sixteen ordinary engines and tenders from Doncaster to Peterborough and a similar number between Peterborough and London. Overall he reckoned the additional cost of using steam tenders would be £14 14s per day. He listed a number of other reasons for discontinuing steam tenders:

- Engines can not get out because steam tenders are under repair in the shops
- Wagon stock is injured by long and heavy trains
- Casualties increase through the use of so much heavy machinery in motion
- Drivers can not give adequate attention to two engines
- Fireboxes and tubes are subject to excessive wear. This, in Stirling's view, was the fatal flaw in the system. The extra volume and intensity of heat can not be taken up by the water with sufficient rapidity and is lost. Smoke boxes get red hot. The high pressure of 140lbs per square inch or more puts too much of a load on the copper box and tube plates.

Stirling was influenced by the locomotive men, who hated the steam 'roasting' machines from the start. Their dislike of the steam tender engines was understandable. Their pay was only uplifted by 6d per day for looking after two engines. After running for some time, the water in the tender became so hot that it would not condense and was blown out of the two tender waste pipes. As a consequence the crew could not see the wagons behind. Deliberate lack of care by the footplate crews contributed to high repair bills and sheared crank pins. The locomotive committee decided in December 1866 not to repair the steam tenders when in need of extensive work. The mechanism should be removed and, at the same time, engine boilers reduced in size. The steam tender was on the way out even before Sturrock had ceased to draw his salary.[9]

Some steam tenders continued in use during 1867 and 1868. In a report of January 1869 Stirling compared his new goods locomotives with the performance of Sturrock's steam tender engines. He concluded the steam tender engines were costing 5s 19d per mile and his new engines 2s 91d per mile. If the steam tender engines had been hauling to their capacity of forty-five wagons, the differential would have been less significant than first appears. Unfortunately the steam tender trains were hauling thirty-four wagons, only two more than the conventional engines.

The old steam tender gear was put up for sale at £45 a set. Purchasers included Davy Brothers of Sheffield, W.J. Walker of Rotherham and I.W. Boulton of Ashton under Lyme. Boulton used two sets of steam tender gear as a basis for two locomotives. One of the locomotives *Stamford*, a 0-6-0 saddle tank, was used to determine the efficiency of cross-water tubes.[10]

Sturrock recorded he sold the steam tender patent to Belgium and America. Two 0-6-0 goods engines with steam tenders were built in 1867 at Garfenstaden for heavy work in Alsace and the Vosges mountains. Similar troubles were experienced to those on the GNR and, in 1873 the tenders were converted by placing boilers on the frames to make shunting engines.[11]

Sturrock believed the steam tender would have been a success if it had been persistently pursued. Writing in the memoir for his children in 1892, he recognised the steam tender 'forms another of the schemes which was supposed likely to make a great fortune, but which historically will be described as a failure.' He might have been right, for the Fairlie locomotive, which was patented a year after the steam tender, adopted many of the same principles. In spite of the need for the driver and fireman of the Fairlie to handle two boilers, the design proved to be a success in certain situations. Perhaps somewhat ironically, the Yorkshire Engine Co. was to be one of a handful of UK locomotive manufacturers who were to build Fairlie locomotives. They were also to build a steam tender locomotive for the Ravenglass and Eskdale Railway to a design by E.C. Poultney in 1927.[12]

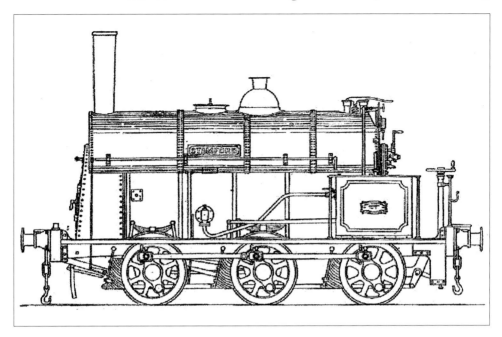

Stamford was built by I.W. Boulton from old steam tender gear sold off by the GNR. (Chronicles of Boulton's Sidings)

Sturrock played a significant role in establishing the Yorkshire Engine Co. during his final eighteen months with the GNR. Following the preliminary meeting of the company in April 1865, Alfred Sacré was recruited from the GNR as managing director on an initial salary of £500 a year, to be increased to £1,000 plus a bonus of 1 per cent of profits above 10 per cent. He was given a five-year service agreement and had the power to enter into contracts conjointly with any two directors; he could set wages. Charles Sacré was appointed consultant engineer for the project and received a fee of £300. Sturrock, Charles Sacré and another director, George Wilson, formed a committee to advise on the construction of the works, which Alfred Sacré had estimated to cost £126,427, about 63 per cent of the funds raised. Sturrock visited machinery manufacturers with Alfred to select equipment. The works was constructed by Craven Brothers, a Sheffield firm on a twenty-two-acre site at Meadowhall in open country 3 miles from Sheffield and 2 from Rotherham.

Sturrock finally joined the Yorkshire Engine Board on 10 May 1866, four months after agreeing his retirement arrangements with the GNR Board. He still deferred taking the chairman position. Sturrock, Alfred Sacré and Barker, the deputy chairman of the company, formed a stores committee to oversee purchases. Hunt & Sacré were appointed London agents to develop contacts with customers. The agents would receive between 0.5 per cent and 2 per cent of the value of each order. Edward Sacré, joint managing partner of Hunt & Sacré and brother of Charles and Alfred, thus became involved[13].

Once freed from his involvement with the GNR, Sturrock was elected chairman on 10 January 1867. Eden, the founding chairman and a resident of Doncaster, took over the deputy chairman role from Barker. Board days were busy. The stores committee met at 10.30 a.m., the finance committee at 12 noon and the Board proper immediately after lunch. The Sheffield and Rotherham Bank managed the firm's accounts and agreed an overdraft facility of £30,000, subject to appropriate security.[14]

An undated exterior view of the Yorkshire Engine Works at Meadowhall; the buildings still stand in 2006. (Sheffield Archives)

An interior view of the Yorkshire Engine Works in early days. (Sheffield Archives)

The East Indian Railway placed an order for thirty 0-6-0s in May 1866 for delivery in 1867. (Sheffield Archives)

Sturrock took up the chairman role as the last two of his Class 264 2-4-0 express locomotives were delivered to Doncaster. This first Yorkshire Engine order for the GNR was not profitable, as the locomotives were constructed in a partially built works. However, the quality of the workmanship must have satisfied Stirling, for the GNR Board placed a further order for ten of Stirling's first four wheeled coupled passenger engines with Yorkshire Engine in March 1867. The order was shared with Avonside and won in open competition with thirty manufacturers. The twenty engines of Stirling's 280 series had 6ft 7in driving wheels and 4ft 1in leading wheels.[15] Yorkshire Engine had to reduce its price to match to the £2,370 proposed by Avonside.

When Sturrock took up the chairmanship, he must have been cautiously hopeful for the future. As well as Alfred Sacré in the managing director post, he could call on Charles Sacré as consulting engineer. Edward Sacré in London brought commercial expertise to the management team. Hampson, who had monitored the construction of GNR engines at Neilsons, was works manager. Work-in-hand in January 1867 included an order for thirty 0-6-0s from the East Indian Railway (EIR) and an order for twenty 0-6-0s from the Great Indian Peninsula Railway (GIPR). The EIR operated over 1,000 miles of 5ft 6in gauge line from Calcutta to Delhi. The GIPR ran for 700 miles from Bombay towards the Ganges plain. Both lines were British-owned companies, with shareholders receiving a government-guaranteed 5 per cent return.

As 1867 progressed, the market fell away and Yorkshire Engine became desperate for orders. Some shareholders were already disgruntled. W.W. Hulse, an early investor and partner with his cousin James Whitworth in the Manchester firm of tool makers, sold out in January 1867. Others objected to calls being made earlier than promised. Only twenty-four locomotives were ordered in 1867. The GNR order for ten 2-4-0s in February was followed by an order in June from Fairbairns for four 0-6-0s. The year ended with an encouraging order for ten 0-6-0s from the Midland. In spite of hard work involving both Edward and Alfred Sacré and Sturrock to agree payment terms, a tender for fifty locomotives for the Grand Trunk of Canada was lost due to price.

The order for 0-6-0 tender engines from the Moscow Riazan Railway in July 1869 was one of several Russian orders which created problems for Yorkshire Engine. (Sheffield Archives)

Sturrock and Alfred Sacré made every effort to keep the workforce in place. Cast steel tyres were turned; locomotive crank axles were planed and drilled; twenty armour-plated shields were produced for the government. Fifty lamp posts and fifty lamp tops were made for the chief constable of Sheffield. An order for 10,000 safes was taken to keep the boiler shop busy. In January 1868 wages were reduced and in March the shareholders were advised there would be no dividend, as Yorkshire Engine had incurred a loss of £1,054 16s. By June Hampson, the works manager, and the secretary had been given notice, although the former never left.

Alfred Sacré knew that many leading UK locomotive manufacturers were supplying Russian railways, including Beyer Peacock, Dubs, Kitson, Neilson, Sharp Stewart and Robert Stephenson. With Sturrock's support he looked to Russia for orders. Between June 1868 and June 1870 Yorkshire Engine obtained eighty-three orders for locomotives. Of these, fifty-eight, or almost 70 per cent of the company's orders, were placed by three Russian railways. The first Russian customer in August 1868 was the Tambov-Koslov, which was to open in 1869 and subsequently became part of the Ryazan-Uralsk Railway. An order was placed for eight 0-6-0s and four 2-4-0s for delivery in early 1869. The order was dispatched in April 1869 and part payment received. Although the engines performed well, £11,709 10s was still outstanding in January 1870 and the company's overdraft was uncomfortably high.

Yorkshire Engine's largest Russian customer was the Poti-Tiflis Railway. Built initially for strategic reasons, the railway was to run from the small port of Poti on the Black Sea to Baku on the Caspian Sea. The first 169-mile section of 5ft gauge line ran from Poti to Tiflis, now Tbilisi, the present capital of Georgia. It was constructed by a French/British-owned firm of contractors using soldiers from a Russian railway battalion. A total of thirty-eight locomotives were supplied over a two-year period and orders were received for spares in subsequent years. The third Russian customer was the Moscow-Ryazan Railway. Largely financed by a railway speculator using German money, the line was one of the few to prosper in the 1860s. Eight 0-6-0s were ordered in July 1869.

To develop its Russian business, the company appointed George Payne Kitson and John Arthur Wright as agents in St Petersburg. To facilitate the signing of contracts, Wright was given power of attorney.[16] Using this power Wright signed the Moscow-Ryazan contract in July 1869 with a penalty clause of £3,500 if the engines were not delivered by 31 December 1869. Even worse, the engines could be rejected if not delivered on time.

The Poti-Tiflis (Tiblisi) Railway was Yorkshire Engine's largest Russian customer; the 0-6-4Ts were designed by Yorkshire Engine and the drawings signed off by Sturrock's son Gordon. (Finnish Railway Museum)

Wright defended his action to the Yorkshire Engine Board by stating Kitson had accepted an order on worse terms and that the order would not have been obtained if Wright had not agreed to the penalties. By November it was clear the order would not be delivered on time. The issue was discussed with Sturrock and the Board declined to dispatch the engines in case they were rejected for late delivery. The locomotives were eventually dispatched in February, when Kitson & Wright assured the Board the locomotives would be accepted or they would find other buyers.

The first two contracts for supplying twenty locomotives to the Poti-Tiflis Railway were signed in Paris in December 1868 and were also to prove less than satisfactory. Yorkshire Engine was required to accept a second order the following year for a further eighteen locomotives at a lower price. The locomotives were to be designed by Yorkshire Engine. The initial order was for ten 0-6-4Ts for goods traffic and ten 0-4-4Ts for passenger work, an unusual choice in both instances. The Poti-Tiflis locomotives were at the forefront of new design.[17] It is not clear whether this was inspired by the contractors or by Sturrock's liking for innovation. The drawings are signed off by Sturrock's son Gordon, suggesting Sturrock himself may have been involved in the design.

The first eight engines were loaded on ship for delivery to Poti in August 1869. The second order for fifteen more 0-6-4Ts and three more 0-4-4Ts was received the following month. Sturrock had been in discussion with the contractors and advised the Board they wanted some modifications to the design. The Board agreed, provided Crawley & Meynier, the contractors, paid the extra cost. When the first shipment reached Poti, there was no pier to unload the engines, one fell into the sea and the ship took the rest of the consignment back to Constantinople. Sturrock advised the shareholders that the company should not ultimately be out of pocket, but there looked to be scope for a long drawn-out lawsuit. Yorkshire Engine's claim for extra costs of £7,412 for modifications to all thirty-eight engines and the dispute with the shipper was still being pursued three years later.

The company was now showing a profit, but running out of cash. The accounts recorded a profit of £3,455 after depreciation in the year to March 1869. A profit of £3,179 was shown in the following year, but there was no cash to pay the promised dividend of 2.5 per cent. Due to the failure of its Russian customers to pay up and the extra costs of shipping and erecting locomotives in Russia, the overdraft limit of £30,000 had been reached. Sturrock went to the Sheffield & Rotherham Bank in May 1870 to ask

The provision of 0-4-0 saddle tank engines to industrial users such as collieries and steel works was a regular element of the Yorkshire Engine order book; three of these saddle tanks were ordered by Earl Fitzwilliam in June 1869. (Sheffield Archives)

Yorkshire Engine supplied a number of Fairlie locomotives to both UK and overseas railways, including five 0-6-6-0s to Mexican Railway in 1872. (Sheffield Archives)

for an extension to the overdraft. The bank agreed £35,000 for six weeks, but required the overdraft to be reduced to £20,000 in six months. The Board would have either to call for an additional £5 per share from shareholders or raise a mortgage, if it was to continue in business.

Sturrock decided the responsibilities of the chairman position were not enjoyable. He tendered his resignation to the Board on 27 May 1870, but agreed to stay on as a director. The cash position continued to deteriorate. £22,000 was owed on Russian contracts in July and the overdraft was still above £28,000. To maintain confidence between the Board and the shareholders, the Board agreed to ask for an independent report on the company from W. W. Hulse, a former shareholder and at one time managing partner of Whitworths the tool makers. Hulse accused the Board of 'mismanagement and waste of economy'. He wanted to abolish the post of managing director and suggested all work not directly concerned with locomotive manufacture and repair should cease. He stated the buildings were overvalued in the balance sheet and recommended the Board should be replaced. He suggested raising funds through preference shares with 5 per cent interest.

Barker refuted the recommendations one by one. Hulse's credibility was not helped by erroneous profit figures in his report. Barker thought ordinary shares would be cheaper than preference shares. He did not agree with abandoning other engineering work which could enable the machinery to be used profitably. Sturrock supported Barker and suggested the total loss of £1,628 in four years was hardly mismanagement. Avonside had lost £8,000 in one year and £4,000 in another. Material costs were low and prices kept down by competition. Barker, Eden (who had been the first chairman of the company), Sturrock and the other directors resigned. Alfred Sacré told the Board he was joining Avonside at the end of March, since his five-year contract had not been renewed

By the following month the new Board realised they could not cope without the experience of the former directors. Barker, Eden (now Lord Auckland) and Sturrock were reappointed. Hampson was promoted to manager on £400 per year plus a bonus. Charles Sacré continued as a shareholder representative. The accounts to March 1871 showed a loss of £11,621 13s and £17,200 was still owed on the Russian contracts.

In May 1871 Sturrock sold his shares and resigned his directorship. The chairman advised the AGM that Sturrock wished 'to be relieved of any further trouble' and 'to leave himself leisure for more congenial pursuits'. Lord Auckland also resigned. The new Board concluded that the business could not justify a general manager or managing director. Edward Sacré and his firm of Hunt & Sacré were employed to run the business on a commission of 1 per cent of turnover plus 5 per cent of profits after payment of dividend. This arrangement continued till October 1879, when Edward Sacré had to give up the role due to ill-health. He died of kidney failure on 26 October 1881 at the age of forty-three.

The original Yorkshire Engine Co. continued in existence till 1880, when it was put into voluntary liquidation. The shareholders of the company set up by Sturrock and his friends were offered £10 cash or £15 credit if they took shares in the new Yorkshire Engine Co. The typical investment in the old company had been fifty £100 shares or £5,000, equivalent to perhaps £250,000 today. If these investors took shares in the new company in 1883 worth £15 each, they would have lost £4,250 on their original investment, equivalent to £215,000 in today's money.[18]

Sturrock's six-year involvement with the Yorkshire Engine Co. from April 1865 to May 1871 was not mentioned in his memoir. He maintained he had given up business of every description when he retired from the GNR in 1866. For Sturrock it was the business failure rather than the loss of money which was probably most hurtful. Fortunately he had developed many interests apart from his career in business, which provided scope for a long and active retirement.

11

AN ACTIVE RETIREMENT IN
DONCASTER AND LONDON

In common with many wealthy men of the period, Sturrock accepted he had a duty to serve the community in which he lived and to contribute financially to its well-being. His captaincy of the Volunteer Rifle Corps kept him in touch with life in the Plant after his retirement. His involvement with local church, political, educational and charitable activities was combined with an ability to enjoy himself hunting, shooting and racing. Little happened in Doncaster between about 1860 and Sturrock's departure for London in 1889 without Sturrock and his family playing some part.

Sturrock's retirement from the GNR was marked in style by the officers and men of the locomotive department. On the afternoon of Saturday 16 February 1867 between 1,500 and 2,000 men assembled in the erecting shop at the Plant to make a presentation to Sturrock. A table had been set up on the locomotive platform and covered with black velvet 'in order to set off to best advantage the several articles intended for presentation'. A collection had been organised by Richard Bonnett, the locomotive department accountant, and around £200 received.

The principle gift was a substantial silver salver engraved with the inscription: 'Presented to Archibald Sturrock Esq. on the occasion of his resigning the appointment of locomotive engineer to the Company after nearly 17 years' service to the great regret of those who have had the happiness to serve under him; Doncaster 31 December 1866.' He also received a 'richly chased' silver tankard, a gold watch and chain and 'a small travelling time-piece of exquisite movement and workmanship.'[1]

Sturrock stepped onto the platform a few minutes after 2 p.m. to rousing cheers. Budge, the London locomotive department head, made the presentation. He noted that when Sturrock arrived in 1850 there had been 340 employees in the locomotive department and the total GNR mileage in the year had been 609,092. When Sturrock retired at the end of 1866, there were 3,834 people employed in the locomotive department and the total mileage was 4,873,113. After several further speeches, an illuminated scroll was presented to Sturrock, who made a suitable speech of thanks and the volunteer band struck up 'Should auld acquaintance be forgot'. Distinguished guests then sat down to a hot lunch prepared by Miss Pye of the Royal Hotel with Stirling in the chair and Sturrock on his right.

Sturrock at retirement in 1866.
(NRM)

There is no evidence that Sturrock received a formal vote of thanks from the Board. In the light of the costs the GNR faced in replacing the steam tenders with more conventional engines, this may not be surprising. Reports of the Board's concern had reached shareholders, for a Mr Marriott stated at the half-yearly meeting in February 1867. 'I have heard very remarkable rumours on that subject and I can only say that if those rumours are correct I cannot understand the presence of Mr Stirling, his successor, at a meeting the other day at Doncaster to endorse Mr Sturrock's conduct and offer him a testimonial in the presence of the officials of the company.' The chairman replied:

> I can only say that twelve months ago Mr Sturrock intimated to me that he, having had a long period of years of active work in the company, wished to retire to his *otium cum dignitate*. I asked him if he would give me time to look out for another gentleman; and he said, Oh I am not in a particular hurry; and I said Well let us name ten months hence – 1st January 1867 – for the day of your retirement. After the useful services of Mr Sturrock for a number of years, we have parted the best of friends … I am a little surprised at this insinuation and I hope I have contradicted it.

No further questions were asked about Sturrock's retirement.

For his last six years with the GNR, Sturrock's life was much occupied with his role as captain of the 20th or Plant Volunteer Rifle Corps. He enjoyed its day-to-day activities and regularly took part in rifle practice at a butt on the common. 60 members met for a competition in April 1861. The highest score was ten and the average five, with Sturrock scoring seven. In August 1862 a major review of volunteers from the North East and Yorkshire took place on Doncaster Racecourse. Between 30,000 and 40,000 people were brought by train to Doncaster to watch the review, which included a mock battle. Lord Scarborough and Edmund Denison were present and the Plant Corps was highly commended by the local press. Profits from selling seats in the grandstands at the review were used to cover the costs of the rifle contest organised by the Mayor of Doncaster and Sturrock. The corporation had given £25, Denison £5 and Sturrock 2gns to the £200 prize fund.

The Volunteer Rifle Corps were largely responsible for finding their own funds to clothe the men and arm the rifles. Denison and Sturrock had to interest the local gentry in supporting the cause. The first ball in aid of the two volunteer corps was held in the Guildhall in January 1863. In August of the same year a bazaar was held to fund the cost of new uniforms. Sturrock as captain of the Plant Corps and his opposite number from the Town Corps were ex-officio members of the organising committees of many fund-raising events. Patronage was sought from the local aristocratic families and the first ball was supported by the Countess Fitzwilliam, the Countess of Effingham and the Countess of Scarborough. Sturrock would often give a personal donation of £10.

Entertainments and musical evenings were also organised at the Theatre Royal to raise funds for the volunteers. 'The Gentlemen Niggers' performed a concert party in March 1865 under the patronage of Sturrock and Egremont, the captain of the Town Corps. Parker, the Plant works manager, was a leading member of the concert party. In 1868, when new uniforms were again introduced, Captain Sturrock was noted to 'have done everything for our local corps, which personal interest and good example could suggest.'[2] At a November 1871 dinner for men of the Plant Corps at the Reindeer Inn, Sturrock was referred to as 'the popular commandant of the company'.[3]

Sturrock was promoted to major in 1873 and took responsibility for both Doncaster corps. Sturrock would lead the men, accompanied by the volunteer band, on their monthly church parades to either St James's or St George's Church and for the annual volunteer inspection. Annual dinners were a regular feature of corps life in the 1870s with Sturrock in the chair. The mayor would preside at the annual volunteer prize-giving. Most prizes combined cash with a gift. In December 1877 Lance Corporal Scholes received 13s, a leg of mutton and twelve bottles of Mrs Huddle's sauce. At the prize-giving Sturrock appealed for more officers for the two corps and gave a witty speech alluding to Darwin's theory of evolution, a topic of serious debate in the 1870s.[4]

In 1878 Sturrock took the Plant Corps with the rest of the battalion of West Yorkshire Rifle Volunteers to camp at Bridlington for the first time. Such camps were to become a regular feature of the volunteer year. Sturrock believed in the value to Britain of the volunteer force. 'If ever the dominions need defending, the whole of the service would be ready ... to give freedom and promote the civilization of the world.'[5] By the early 1880s there were around 200,000 active volunteers and over 500,000 men had been trained to use a rifle and could be called up in the event of an invasion. Sturrock maintained involvement with the Doncaster volunteers until he left the town in 1889.

Sturrock and his family moved from 21 South Parade to Elmfield, a substantial house set in twenty-eight acres on the outskirts of Doncaster in 1872–73. It had been built by the Walbanke Childers of Cantley Hall in 1803 and acquired by the trustees of John Jarratt, who leased the property to Sturrock. The property still stands today with the grounds converted into a public park. The new property gave Sturrock more scope for entertaining and enabled him to keep additional horses for hunting. When Sturrock moved to London in 1889, the property was occupied by Ellen Jarratt, who sold the house and grounds to Doncaster Corporation in 1928.[6]

Elmfield, Sturrock's second house, in Doncaster in 2003; the grounds are now a public park. (Douglas Brown)

Sturrock and Georgina hunted with the Badsworth, one of several hunts in the area. 'Mr Sturrock in "pink" and well mounted was more immaculate than ever – at least the ladies used to say so.'[7] Founded in about 1700, the Badsworth country extended 16 miles north to south and about 23 miles east to west. In the 1870s the Badsworth was deemed one of the hardest hunts under its new Master, Mr J. Hope Barton. Hope Barton died in 1876 when a blood vessel burst as he blew his horn. He was succeeded by a Mr C.B. Wright, who was master till Sturrock ceased to hunt in 1889.[8]

In retirement Sturrock regularly rented the shooting at the Retreat in Glen Esk, close to Brechin in his Scottish home county of Angus. The shooting lodge had been built by Captain Weymess in the 1840s and is now a folk museum. Sturrock went with friends from Doncaster and was the best shot. On 12 August 1871, the party obtained eighty-four brace of grouse, six hares and one rabbit. Sturrock shot fifty-four, Baxter, his solicitor friend from Doncaster twenty-two and Percival, the third member of the party, only eight brace. The following year on the best day Sturrock shot eighty-three brace, Baxter twenty-nine and a half and Percival fifteen and a half.[9]

The major sporting event in the Doncaster year was (and remains) the St Leger in September. The twenty great houses in the vicinity organised house parties and it was the busiest period of the year for Doncaster station, with every siding filled with special trains. It was the custom for the local papers to list the distinguished guests at the Leger and Sturrock's name first appears on the list in 1862. In retirement and without the worry of the traffic at Doncaster station, Captain Sturrock often went to the Leger with his own party. In 1869 in addition to his two daughters Captain Sturrock was joined by his brother Dr David Sturrock. When Sturrock came to leave Doncaster, a friend, John Richard Haig, presented him with a silver hip flask engraved with his initials 'in memory of many pleasant Legers'.

Sturrock's interest in country matters was not confined to shooting, hunting and racing. In the 1880s he was a vice-president and a member of the planning committee of the Doncaster Agricultural Society, which organised an annual show at Nether Hall Park.

Sturrock gave donations each year of between 2 guineas and £10, as well as a cup for the best four-year-old gelding or filly up to thirteen hands. Lord Auckland, who had brought Sturrock into the Yorkshire Engine Co., was the president of the society and involved with Sturrock on a committee established under the Contagious Diseases (Animals) Act of 1869. Sturrock chaired the local committee for several years in the 1880s. Foot and Mouth had been first identified in 1839. The committee had to decide which premises should be added to or deleted from the list of restricted premises and what compensation should be paid.

One of Sturrock's first acts following retirement was to help with the establishment of the Great Northern Permanent Building Society (GNPBS) in November 1867. The first Doncaster Building Society had gone into liquidation following a fraud by one of the Society's officials. Although called the GNPBS, the Society was intended to benefit all inhabitants of the town and not just Great Northern employees. It operated from the GN schools and Sturrock was one of three trustees whose main duty was to sign the mortgage deeds on behalf of the society. Records in the Wakefield archive show that the borrowers included not only engine drivers, clerks, wagon builders, cabinet makers, signal men and others who might have worked on the GNR, but also grocers, lawyers, builders and labourers. When Sturrock retired at the AGM of the Society in March 1889, his former accountant and old friend of thirty-five years' standing, Richard Bonnett, expressed regret that Sturrock was ceasing to be a trustee after twenty-one years. He proposed a resolution thanking Sturrock and reminded the meeting of Sturrock's many acts of kindness. Bonnett knew of a man who had had to give up work. Sturrock had promised the man a monthly allowance for the rest of his days.[10]

Until the latter part of the nineteenth century the magistrates' bench had been the preserve of the local landed gentry. By the 1870s it was becoming more common to invite industrialists to join.[11] Sturrock was appointed a West Riding magistrate in July 1876 at the age of sixty. He sat for the first time at the Michaelmas Quarter Sessions in October 1876. Thereafter he sat regularly once a week whenever the courts were sitting. In 1878, by which date he was often chairman of the bench, he sat for at least twenty-five days. In 1880 he sat on over thirty-three occasions. Sentences could seem harsh by today's standards. A defendant found sleeping in an outhouse near Mexborough the previous night was sentenced to ten days' prison with hard labour.[12] A labourer charged with begging was committed to prison for fourteen days. Sturrock served as a magistrate until 1888, only giving up the role because he could no longer hear the witnesses.

Sturrock played his part in politics. The *Doncaster Chronicle* recalled in his obituary 'a general election day when engines ran out of the sheds at Doncaster station with yellow rosettes and streamers.' During the early 1880s Sturrock played an active role in the local Liberal Association. In 1885 Sturrock chaired what the *Doncaster Chronicle* described as an uproarious meeting to choose the Liberal candidate. Walter Shirley, who had shown radical leanings, won the nomination over Bacon Franks, a scion of a distinguished local family and the preferred choice of the Executive Committee. Shirley favoured the disestablishment of the Church of England, a cause which found no favour with Sturrock. However, it was not the threat to disestablish the Church of England but the issue of home rule for Ireland which ultimately drove Sturrock and many other Liberals nationwide to support Conservative or Liberal Unionist candidates. In February 1888 Sturrock urged all local Liberals to support the Tory candidate, H.W. Fitzwilliam, who would uphold the union with Ireland. Sturrock argued that it was money from Irish Americans who supported Parnell and the advocates of home rule for Ireland. He did not think there was a man in Yorkshire who would like to be under the control of Parnell and the Irish Americans. Fitzwilliam won the election by 200 votes, Sturrock and others of the local gentry having provided carriages to take the voters to the poll.[13]

Sturrock also enjoyed the active social life in Doncaster, where the local aristocracy still mixed with the professionals brought in as a result of the railway. The construction of the infirmary in 1864-5 was dependent on donations from local families. Sturrock gave ten guineas and a total of over £3,427 was raised. Sturrock served for many years on a committee established to run an annual ball for infirmary funds. Lord Auckland was the chairman and county families gave dinner parties in their houses. Sturrock would hold a party at Elmfield and attend with his three children and bring one of his brothers or a nephew and other friends. Dancing started at 9.30 p.m. and supper was served at midnight. Dancing continued till 3.30 or 4 a.m. and finished with the gallop. Sturrock was still a steward in 1888, when he and Georgina attended their last ball before leaving for London. Lady Mary Fitzwilliam was the patron that year and the volunteer band provided the music. Tickets cost 12s 6d for men and 10s for ladies. In a typical year the ball made a profit of £70 to £80 for infirmary funds.

The aristocracy and gentry of Doncaster and its surroundings enjoyed balls, dinners and social events throughout the year at the Mansion House or Guildhall. Sturrock and his family attended and Sturrock frequently had to make a speech or propose a toast. As captain of the Volunteers Rifle Corps, Sturrock was invited to the annual ball held by the First West Yorkshire Yeoman Cavalry, the local volunteer cavalry regiment with Earl Fitzwilliam as patron. The menus were elaborate as the example for January 1879 mayor's inaugural dinner indicates:

> *Soup* – Oxtail and thick turtle
> *Entrées* – Lamb's fry, sweetbreads, lobster patties, mushrooms, stewed oysters, lamb cutlets
> *Removes* – Boiled and roast turkeys, fowls, ham, tongue, venison, mutton, beef
> *Second Service* – Lamb, pheasant, woodcock, wild duck, champagne ham, salad
> *Entremets* – Orange & mandarin, crème à l'italienne, jellies, fig & lemon pudding, mince pies, iced puddings, macaroni, devilled sardines
> *Wines* – punch, Madeira, sherry, Chablis, Steinberg hock, champagne, claret, port

Royal events were celebrated by subscription balls at the Mansion House. In March 1853 Sturrock attended a ball with 250 others to mark the Prince of Wales's marriage. For the Queen's jubilee in 1887 a fancy dress ball was arranged. Sturrock went as a huntsman and Georgina as 'Cherry Ripe'. Dances included the waltz, lancers, quadrille, Schottische and gallop. Musical evenings were popular with full dress concerts at the Corn Exchange, of which Sturrock was a patron. A 'large and fashionable audience' enjoyed a visit from the Royal Hand Bell Ringers in April 1878 under the patronage of Lord Halifax, Lord Auckland, the vicar and Major Sturrock.

In the summer months the Doncaster and Barnsdale Archery & Croquet Club provided an opportunity for young and old to enjoy some sport and end the day with dinner and dancing. The club met usually at the grandstand on the race course or at the Belle Vue ground for five or six meetings a year in the summer months. About sixty to eighty adults and young people attended, including Lord and Lady Auckland, Mr and Mrs Edmund Baxter and the vicar of Christchurch and his family. Sturrock sometimes took his brother David as well as his son and daughters. Archery and croquet were supplemented by the new sport of Lawn Tennis. In 1877 Sturrock's elder daughter took the ladies' lawn tennis prize. Gordon lost out to a Mr Mahon for the gentleman's prize. The club was wound up in July 1887, but by then a lawn tennis club had been established. Mrs Beckett Denison was president and Sturrock was one of several vice presidents.

The summer months were also occasions for Sunday school outings. Caroline and Georgina Sturrock both helped at the Sunday schools at Christchurch and St James's churches from 1867 onwards. 500 to 600 children would be taken to a local country house, such as Nether Hall or Carlton Park for cricket, football and other games. Tea was provided and the GNR would arrange a train for the longer journeys. Bonnett and Griffiths were often involved with the St James's outings as well as the Sturrock daughters. Caroline Sturrock continued to teach at St James's Sunday School until she married in 1880. Georgina taught there for seventeen years till she left Doncaster with her father in April 1889.

In addition to concerts and balls, the winter months were occupied by talks and lectures at the YMCA and the Great Northern recreation meetings, as well as parish church teas and bazaars. Sturrock continued to preside at GN recreation meetings after he had left the company. The YMCA aimed to promote religious and general knowledge in a non-denominational context and was supported by Sturrock and his daughters. Donations in cash or kind were provided for fund-raising events. Lectures covered a wide range of topics including Stanley's journeys in Africa, the Island of Ceylon (Sri Lanka), Charles Dickens and the Aurora and Star Showers. Both Christchurch and St James's Church organised parish teas in December or January, when the work of the church and schools could be reviewed by the parishioners. Sturrock, as a manager of the GN schools, had to speak each year about the work of the GN schools. He also used it as an opportunity to comment on the worship at St James. In 1868 he found the services satisfactory but considered the music might be taken a little faster. Sturrock's elder daughter played the organ in the church.

As the town population grew, more churches were required. Christchurch decided to build a new 'free' church in its parish. Opened in April 1872 St John the Evangelist's had to provide services according to the rites of the Church of England with ritual and ceremonial as used in Christchurch. It is difficult for us today to appreciate the concern stirred up by changes in ceremony and ritual in church services in the nineteenth century. It was deemed a 'free' church, for parishioners were not required to rent a pew as was the custom at Christchurch. Sturrock was one of three trustees for the land on which the church was built.[14] Sturrock's daughters played a major role in organising fund-raising for St John's. In 1874 Sturrock was one of the most generous subscribers when he gave £25 towards the construction costs of a new Church of England chapel at Hexthorpe.

As the parish of St James's expanded with the growth in population to between 6-7,000, Vicar Campion needed not only more churches but also more clerical help. Amongst his curates was a young Oxford graduate, Henry Robinson. Robinson was born in York in 1849, the son of Mark Robinson, a chemist, and his wife Sophia. His first and only curacy was at St James's Church, where he arrived as a deacon in 1875. He and Caroline Sturrock became friends. Following Robinson's appointment as vicar of the parish of Grosmont, near Whitby, in 1879, he and Caroline married at St Marylebone Church in London on 18 June 1880, the church where Archibald Sturrock and Caroline Fullerton had married thirty-five years before. Caroline produced two grandchildren for Sturrock, Gladys who was born in May 1881 and Everil, the author's grandmother, who was born in November 1882.

In addition to encouraging the art and science evening classes at the schools, Sturrock supported the establishment of a girl's high school in the town in 1881. Sturrock was trustee of the Doncaster Ragged School, part of a nationwide movement to help disadvantaged children obtain an education. Founded in 1858, the school was designed to meet the needs of those who could not afford school fees. By 1881 it had 175 pupils, who were taught reading, writing and arithmetic, plus a daily non-denominational service. The school cost £150 to £200 a year to run and relied on private donations.[15] In 1886 Councillor Clarke spoke warmly of Sturrock's support. 'On many occasions Major Sturrock has most kindly and without solicitation sent a cheque in aid of the funds of the school. When there was no deficit, he sent a cheque at any rate for a special feature such as an outside trip.'[16]

Caroline Robinson, Sturrock's eldest daughter and the author's great-grandmother. (Author)

Sturrock's daughter Georgina, who never married and lived with her father till he died. (Author)

Sturrock was always willing to help with local needs. When floods struck Doncaster in December 1878, Sturrock joined a storm relief committee under the chairmanship of the mayor to raise and distribute funds. The committee were concerned to distinguish between careless fathers and the mothers and children. When the first distribution was made seventy applicants received coal, tea and bread. Children's tickets were given out to be exchanged for a free cup of tea and a bun at the Cocoa House or free soup at the Ragged School. The Doncaster corporation found work for some of the able-bodied men at 1s 6d per hour sweeping the streets.[17] In February 1879 the committee were supporting 500 families. The Doncaster charities were re-organised in 1880 and Sturrock attended regular meetings of the committee which managed the charities.

Sturrock maintained his contacts with those he had worked with at the Plant. When the Plant workmen were granted a nine-hour day on Friday 9 November 1871, the workmen marched through the streets of Doncaster the next afternoon. They went first to Stirling's house, then to Denison's and on to Sturrock's before marching down the Thorne road. When Mrs Denison (Lady Beckett) died in April 1874, Sturrock was one of the chief mourners in the procession. He was also present at the funeral of his former chairman the following year. He and Stirling attended the funeral of Griffiths, the carriage superintendent, in January 1877.

Almost thirty years after his retirement Sturrock continued to defend his reputation in the railway press. In August 1888 he commented that locomotives of today were not very different from their predecessors even a few years ago. 'I write to inform you that the GWR possessed engines with 8 foot driving wheels in 1848 that could run the highest present speeds and that an express from Paddington to Bristol did 77 miles in 90 minutes.' Sturrock reminded readers of his own engine (No.215) which had been delivered on 6 August 1853 and repeated his view that the engine could have run for London to Edinburgh in eight hours with stops only at Grantham, York, Newcastle and Berwick.[18]

In spite of increasing age and deafness, Sturrock remained active in Doncaster till his departure in April 1889. At Christmas 1885 he went with the mayor and Georgina to the Girls' Reformatory for their Christmas celebrations. He was elected chairman of the local branch of the Church Defence Association in Doncaster. He supported the traditional role of the Church of England and argued to great applause that the Church of England was especially valuable to the poor, even if they were not worshippers in a Church of England church.[19]

In December 1888 Sturrock attended the St James's Annual Tea for the last time. He explained that circumstances had forced him to leave Doncaster. He liked the tea, but not the speech that went with it. He spoke of the great happiness he had experienced in Doncaster and wished the parish every blessing the world could afford. His son-in-law, Henry Robinson, was present and also spoke. He said that the vicar had complained that when Robinson left to take up the post of Vicar of Grosmont, he had taken 'their best friend, best school teacher, organist and district visitor' to be his wife.[20]

The reason for Sturrock's move to London is not clear. It seems likely that the lease of Elmfield was up and the Jarratts wanted the house back. Sturrock was rising seventy-three and was suffering from deafness, so that he could no longer act as a magistrate and must have found his role on many committees difficult. He was also ready to give up hunting, although he continued to shoot and fish. Georgina was thirty-seven and may have felt life would be more interesting in London. She is said to have had many proposals of marriage, but turned them all down.

Sturrock does not appear to have considered moving to Dundee. However, his continuing love of the area was expressed in the gift of a stained-glass window to Forfar Episcopal Church in 1884. The inscription on the window reads: 'In memory of John Sturrock of Pitreuchie who gave the site on which the Episcopal Church in Forfar was erected after the '45. This window is the gift of his great grandson Archibald Sturrock AD 1884.'

Left: A window in the Episcopal
Church in Forfar presented by
Sturrock in memory of his great-
grandfather who provided the land
for the first Episcopal chapel after
1745. (Douglas Brown)

Below: The Sturrock carriage outside
57 Cadogan Place in 1903. Were Bob
and Phil, who are named on the back
of the photograph, the horses or the
coachmen? (Author)

Opposite: A family picnic at the
Rufus Stone near Lyndhurst in 1906;
Sturrock is seated in the centre of his
family with the author's grandmother
Everil Leatham standing behind him.
(Author)

Georgina and her father rented 57 Cadogan Place, Chelsea and employed an appropriate staff for the time. Ann Lister, who had had been Sturrock's cook in Doncaster, came with him to London. In addition to a ladies' maid for Georgina, the resident staff included the butler, William White aged thirty-seven from Derbyshire, two housemaids, a kitchen maid and a footman. Sturrock had not lived in London since the 1840s, but he had been a member of the Reform Club in Pall Mall since 1862. One of his sponsors at the Reform was Thomas Fairbairn, a connection developed from his six months with Fairbairns in Manchester in 1838-9.

Sturrock lived in London for nearly twenty years and worshipped at Holy Trinity in Sloane Street, where a memorial plaque to him and to his son Gordon can be seen on the north aisle wall. Sturrock and Georgina took holidays with Caroline and Henry Robinson and their children. He was still fit enough in 1906 at the age of ninety to stay at the Grand Hotel in Lyndhurst with the family. He welcomed friends and relations from Scotland and Doncaster at his new home. At the time of the 1901 census he had staying Robert Don and his wife Lucy. Robert was a descendant of Sturrock's Aunt Isabella and worked in the family linen and jute business in Dundee. With his first cousin John Bogle Don, he was to be one of Sturrock's executors.

In the 1890s Sturrock was invited to join an association under the presidency of Charles Rous-Marten, the New Zealander who wrote extensively on railway matters for the *Engineer*. The aim of the association was to establish a museum of transport. The idea foundered through lack of interest on the part of the railway companies and was not revived till 1908, by which time Sturrock was not fit to take part.

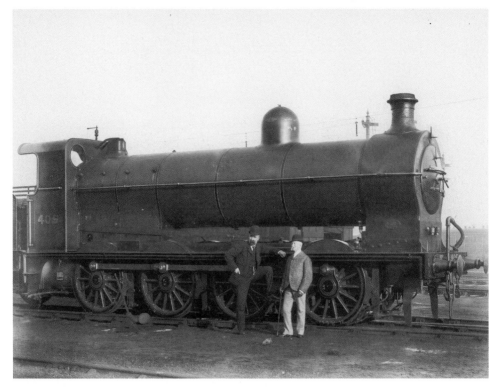

Above: Sturrock and Ivatt, Stirling's successor, in front of Ivatt 0–8–0 No.405 at the Plant's fiftieth anniversary in 1903. (NRM)

Left: Sturrock shortly before his death and still smartly dressed. (Geoffrey Hughes)

When British Rail named their A1 Pacific No.60018 Archibald Sturrock on 13 July 1950, they did not realise that Sturrock's youngest daughter Georgina was still alive. H.G. Ivatt performed the ceremony. (Author)

The only remnant of a Sturrock locomotive is a tender originally supplied with a Hawthorn 0-4-2 No.112 and rebuilt by Sturrock; the tender is now attached to the Stirling 4-2-2 No.1 at the National Railway Museum.

The 150th anniversary of the Plant at Doncaster was marked by celebrations in July 2003; the author (fourth from the left), his wife, the Mayor of Doncaster and other guests are being shown round by the managing director of Wabtec Rail. During the day a plaque was unveiled by the Duke of Kent to commemorate the achievements of Sturrock and Stirling. (Fastline Photographic)

In 1896 Sturrock visited Doncaster to mark his eightieth birthday. He spoke at an Association of Railway Locomotive Engineers' dinner in November 1898 and participated in the fiftieth anniversary celebration at the Plant in December 1903, when he was shown round by Stirling's successor, Ivatt. They posed for a photograph in front of an Ivatt K1 0-8-0 goods locomotive No.405, perhaps as a reminder that Sturrock had ordered the first two 0-8-0s in the Great Northern fleet from Avonside in 1865. Sturrock's final letter to *Railway Magazine* was written in February 1908 asking the editor to advise him whether the contest between the narrow and the broad gauge engines was held in 1847 or 1848.

His contribution to the volunteer movement was recognised by the award of the Volunteer Decoration. When the volunteer movement was reorganised in April 1908, the Doncaster Infantry Volunteers were absorbed into the 5th Battalion of the King's Own Yorkshire Light Infantry and Sturrock was appointed Honorary Colonel. As a consequence many of his obituaries referred to him as Colonel Archibald Sturrock V.D.

Sturrock died at his home in Cadogan Square on New Year's Day 1909 in his ninety-third year. He had wanted to be buried with his wives in Christchurch Doncaster, but this proved to be impossible. His funeral service at Holy Trinity, Sloane Street was conducted by his son-in-law Henry Robinson and the curate-in-charge the Revd C.H. Mylne. Senior representatives attended from the Kings Own Yorkshire Light Infantry, as well as his immediate family, his nephews, several members of the Don family and many friends. The only GNR connection present was the widow of Walter Leith. Sturrock had outlived his engineering contemporaries of forty years ago and many of their children as well. He was buried in the Brompton cemetery. His daughter Caroline and her husband Henry lie in the adjacent grave.

Sturrock summarised his achievements in his memorandum to his children:

> It is a source of pleasure to every man to believe that his life has been of some use and that he has done something for the progress of the world. I do not say that I have ever had an enthusiasm for my profession or loved it for itself. I, however, worked very hard and honestly during my career and I consider I can claim:-
>
> The introduction and use of very high pressure steam by locomotives, hence economy and power...
>
> That I constructed in 1853 the first (No.215) engine for the narrow (4 foot 8 ½ inch) gauge which ran 100 miles without stopping, and did occasional miles at the rate of 75 miles per hour, being the highest speed the Great Northern Railway had ever obtained by their 8 foot wheel engines, thus giving the narrow gauge as high speeds as the wide.
>
> That I gave the high speeds of the Great Western Railway, which is a level line, to the Great Northern Railway, the ruling gradient of which is 1 in 200 and rises 360 in the first 13 miles from King's Cross and I did this by doubling the area of the usual firebox of the narrow gauge and using 150 lbs. steam. In this I was followed by the whole of the narrow gauge of England.
>
> That I gave the comfort of hot water cans to the British public.
>
> That I schemed the mode now in use on the Metropolitan Railway by their engines.'
>
> He concluded: 'I think, therefore, that my life has been useful in a moderate way to the world, and I thank God that he inspired me with the desire and gave me the health to work hard at a profession which I honestly confess I do not know why I ever entered; and <u>I did work as hard and honestly for the two railways I served as if they had been my own property.</u> [Sturrock's underline]

Sturrock failed to mention the special skills he required to manage a new and expanding locomotive department. Under Denison's chairmanship he and Seymour Clarke took the GNR from a byway in Lincolnshire to become one of the premier lines in the UK. Hamilton Ellis said of Sturrock: 'His ability, activity and originality were outstanding.' F.A.S. Brown said: 'His work as a designing engineer was undeniably good and progressive, considering the financial difficulties under which he so often had to operate.' Sturrock would have been content with such compliments.[21] Sturrock accepted that a man in his position and with his wealth should contribute to the well-being of others and to the service of his country. He made a significant difference to Doncaster and its people over more than fifty years, but he was no dull 'do-gooder'. He also knew how to enjoy himself and amuse others.

APPENDIX:
SUMMARY OF LOCOMOTIVES OPERATED BY STURROCK

Locomotives Received before Sturrock's Arrival

When Sturrock joined in April 1850 the GNR had a fleet of eighty-one locomotives, of which forty were Sharp 2-2-2s. A total of fifty 'Sharpies' were acquired with the final ten numbered 41–50 delivered after Sturrock arrived. As the 'Sharpies' became unsuitable for heavier trains, Sturrock converted many to tank engines principally for use on branch lines. Others were rebuilt as 0-4-2 tender engines in 1858 for use largely in the London area.

Twelve of an order for twenty Hawthorn 2-2-2 singles had also been delivered when Sturrock joined. These were subsequently known as 'small' Hawthorns to distinguish them from a later Sturrock designed 2-2-2 built by Hawthorn. The GNR had also acquired fifteen 0-4-2 goods engines from Hawthorn and twelve Bury designed 0-4-0 goods engines. Six were built by Bury Curtis and six by Fairbairn. They proved inadequate as goods services developed and were converted to saddle tanks.

Other engines delivered prior to Sturrock's arrival included the Bury prototype 2-4-0 originally numbered sixty-six, but renumbered as 100 in 1850 and intended as a suitable design for the opening to London. Following an accident in 1855 due to a broken crank axle, Sturrock modified this locomotive with an extra set of outside plate frames and springs connected by compensating levers. A 2-4-0 Peto and Betts contractor's locomotive numbered 133 had also been acquired.

March–December 1850

During Sturrock's first nine months to December 1850 forty-seven more locomotives were delivered in the following Classes:

Class	Numbers In Year	Maker	Nos	Designer
Sharp 2-2-2 Tender	41–50	Sharp	10	Firm's standard
'Small' Hawthorn 2-2-2	63–70	Hawthorn	8	Firm's standard
Class 116 5ft 0-6-0 Goods	116–120 134–138 144–153	Hawthorn Hawthorn E.B. Wilson	20	Bury modified by Sturrock
Contractors' 2-4-0	159–161	Tayleur and Hick	3	Purchased second hand, later 0-4-2
Special Purchase Goods 0-6-0 Tender	163–166	E.B. Wilson, Hawthorn C. Todd	4	Firm's standard
Jenny Lind 2-2-2 Single	201–202	E.B. Wilson	2	Firm's standard modified by Sturrock

During 1850 Sturrock took delivery of the first locomotives for which he made a design input. The Class 116 Goods locomotives from Hawthorn and E.B. Wilson had been ordered the day before Sturrock was appointed, but Sturrock took immediate steps to have the fireboxes enlarged, cylinders increased to 15in diameter and the boiler pressure increased to 110lb for an additional cost of £100.

In late 1850 Sturrock was offered the loan of two Jenny Lind-type locomotives from E.B. Wilson. After modifications to the blast pipe and the opportunity to use the engines for more than six months, Sturrock found they ran well and obtained the agreement of the Board to purchase the two locomotives numbered 201–202 in July 1851.

In addition during his first nine months Sturrock acquired the remaining three Peto and Betts Contractors locomotives numbered 159–161 and purchased four 0-6-0 goods locomotives. Two were from E.B. Wilson and one each from Hawthorns and C. Todd.

January–December 1851

During 1851 forty-nine locomotives were delivered, of which twenty-one were goods engines and twenty-eight for passenger use.

Class	Numbers In Year	Maker	No.	Designer
Class 71 2-4-0	71–75 76–90	Hawthorn E.B. Wilson	5 15	Bury prototype modified by Sturrock
Crampton 4-2-0	91–98	Longridge	8	Sturrock using Crampton patent
Class 116 5ft 0-6-0 Goods	139–143 154–158 & 167	Hawthorn E.B. Wilson	5 6	Bury modified by Sturrock
Class 168 5ft 0-6-0 Goods	168–174	E.B. Wilson	9	Sturrock
Class 308 5ft3in 0-6-0 Goods	308	Stephenson	1	Sturrock

Twenty of the Class 71 2-4-0 passenger engines were ordered the day before Sturrock was appointed. The modifications were more significant and costly than those required on the Class 116 goods locomotives. They were to have outside plate frames; the boilers were enlarged, tube design changed and boiler pressure increased to 120lb. As a consequence delivery was delayed.

Sturrock also took delivery during 1851 of the first express passenger locomotives for which he had full accountability. Perhaps as a result of his friendship with Crampton, he developed a design incorporating Crampton's second patent. The design was said to be speedy, light on the permanent way and cheap to build.

Like other Crampton's the locomotives suffered a lack of adhesion. Sturrock experimented with a conversion of the last of the ten engines No.200 to 2-4-0 but this proved unsatisfactory. As a consequence all were converted to 2-2-2 singles.

Sturrock also took delivery during 1851 of the first nine of his Class 168 goods locomotives and a single Class 308 goods locomotive. Developed from the successful Class 116 goods locomotives, these were the first goods engines wholly designed by Sturrock. The majority of the Class 168s were manufactured by E.B. Wilson. Ten of the Class were made by Fairbairn, who lost part of their original order due to a strike. The Fairbairn engines differed not only in appearance but also in boiler dmensions, weight and in the way the wheel base was divided.

The Class 308 locomotives were similar in design to the Class 168 but with generally larger dimensions. The wheels were, for example, 5ft 3in as opposed to 5ft on the Class 168. A total of eighty-three locomotives of this Class were made by seven different manufacturers between 1851 and 1856.

January–December 1852

During 1852 numbers delivered rose slightly to fifty-one, with goods engines predominating. Of the fifty-one locomotives delivered, only eleven were passenger engines, including the last two Cramptons and nine 'large' Hawthorns.

Class	Numbers In Year	Maker	No.	Designer
Crampton 4-2-0	99 & 200	Longridge	2	Sturrock using Crampton patent
Class 168 5ft 0-6-0 Goods	177–195 198–199 & 300–303	E.B. Wilson W. Fairbairn	19 6	Sturrock
'Large' Hawthorn 2-2-2	203–211	Hawthorn	9	Sturrock's First Express Passenger locomotives
Class 308 5ft3in 0-6-0 Goods	309–317 318–323	Stephenson Nasmyth	9 6	Sturrock

The 'large' Hawthorns were the only new Class of locomotive delivered in 1852. They were good examples of locomotive practice of the period and of effective cooperation between Sturrock and Hawthorns. Innovatory ideas included locating the cylinders between the inner iron frames, which extended the full length of the engine. It was the success of the 'large' Hawthorns which led Sturrock to convert the Cramptons to 2-2-2s.

January–December 1853

Deliveries declined to twenty-two and were again predominantly goods locomotives. 1853 was also the year in which Sturrock took delivery of his express prototype No.215.

Class	Numbers In Year	Maker	No.	Designer
Class 168 5ft 0-6-0 Goods	196–197 304–307	E.B. Wilson W. Fairbairn	2 4	Sturrock
'Large' Hawthorn 222	212–214	Hawthorn	3	Sturrock's First Express Passenger locomotives
Experimental 4-2-2	215	Hawthorn	1	Sturrock
Class 308 5ft3in 0-6-0 Goods	324–327 328–330 333–337	Nasmyth Hawthorn Kitson	4 3 5	Sturrock

The only new Class of engine in 1853 was Sturrock's experimental 4-2-2. The order was placed with Hawthorns in August 1852, but the engine was not delivered until 31 July 1853. Modelled on the GWR's Iron Duke Class, which had been built at Swindon under Sturrock's management, it was intended to counter a potential threat to the East Coast passenger traffic from the LNWR. Sturrock wrote on the drawing 'Type of Stirling's express engine'.

The purchase price of the locomotive exceeded the estimate by £1,000 and amounted to £3,500. As neither the correspondence nor drawings survive, it must be assumed that much of the extra cost arose from modifications to the blast pipe and from changes to the front pair of leading wheels. These four wheels were initially constructed as two pairs of fixed leading wheels, like the Iron Dukes. Due to problems with derailment, the front four wheels were subsequently placed on a bogie, an innovatory approach at the time, although Sturrock had built two goods engines with bogies at Swindon. The bogie caused some problems due to tight clearances and Sturrock had to incur further costs to get the bogie to move freely.

January–December 1854

Of the thirty-seven locomotives delivered during 1854, only two were passenger engines and these were ex-Oxford, Worcester & Wolverhampton Railway (OWWR) engines, which had been made by Wilson with some design input from Sturrock.

Class	Numbers In Year	Maker	No.	Designer
2-4-0 Pass ex OWWR	216–217	E.B. Wilson	2	Wilsons with Sturrock input

Class 308 5ft 3in 0-60 Goods	331–332 338–347 348–362 363–367 368–370	Hawthorn E.B. Wilson Sharp Stewart Vulcan E.B. Wilson	2 10 15 5 3	Sturrock – 368 and 369 ex-OWWR

The additions to Class 308 included two engines numbered 368 and 369, which had been built by E.B. Wilson to Sturrock designs for C.C. Williams, who had a contract to operate the OWWR. All four OWWR engines were unused when received by the GNR.

January–December 1855

Goods locomotives predominated again in 1855, with total deliveries amounting to twenty-three.

Class	Numbers In Year	Maker	No.	Designer
Class 223 2-4-0	223–228	Hawthorn	6	Sturrock developed from Class 71
Class 308 5ft 3in 0-6-0 Goods	371–380 381–385 386–387	E.B. Wilson Kitson Sharp Stewart	10 5 2	Sturrock

During June and July 1855 nine locomotives were absorbed from the Nottingham and Grantham Railway. All but one were made by Wilson; the nine included three 0-4-0Ts, two 2-2-2s, three 0-6-0s and a single 2-4-0. They were numbered 219–222 and 391–394. In the same year three passenger tender engines and two goods tank engines were taken over from the West Yorkshire Railway – numbers 261–263 and 470–71.

The six Class 223 2-4-0s were all delivered during 1855. Developed from the Class 71 engines, they were designed for passenger traffic on the Leeds, Bradford and Halifax Railway, where the 'small' Hawthorns and the unaltered Sharps were unsuitable for the hilly route. The engines are described as 'handsome' by Bird.

January 1856–April 1860

During a period of four years from January 1856 to April 1860 no new locomotives were delivered, other than the final three 0-6-0 Class 308 Goods engines from Sharp Stewart numbered 388–390.

May 1860–December 1864

It was not until late 1859 that Sturrock was able to persuade the Board that new passenger engines were essential for the increasingly heavy loads. Eleven were delivered in 1860 and one in early 1861.

Class	Numbers In Years	Maker	No.	Designer
Class 229 7ft 2-2-2 Passenger	229–232 233–236 237–240	Kitson SharpStewart R. Stephenson	4 4 4	Sturrock – the last to be delivered from Sharp Stewart was designed to burn coke or coal

In July 1863 six Leeds, Bradford and Halifax Junction locomotives were transferred to the GNR. These included three 0-4-2Ts and three 0-6-0s. Kitson made all but one of the engines, which were numbered 162 and 395–399.

The Class 229 2-2-2s were deemed by Bird as 'Mr Sturrock's masterpiece in designing'. They were the first new passenger engines where we can be certain that a boiler pressure of 150lb was specified. With 7ft driving wheels, they met the needs of the ever-increasing weight of the express passenger trains.

January–December 1865

In 1865 deliveries commenced of the Class 400 0-6-0 steam tender goods locomotives and the Class 241 0-4-2Ts for the growing suburban services. There was some variation in the latter Class between the 241 series delivered largely in late 1865 and the 270 series which commenced delivery in early 1867. Nine tank engines were delivered in the last three months of 1865 as well as forty Class 400s mostly with auxiliary steam tenders.

Class	Numbers In Years	Maker	No.	Designer
0-4-2T Suburban	241–249	Avonside	9	Sturrock
Class 400 0-6-0	400–409 410–419 420–429 430–439	Kitson Hawthorn Neilson Kitson	10 10 10 10	Sturrock

The 0-4-2T Suburban tank engines were intended to work underground and suburban traffic from Hitchin and over the Metropolitan lines to Victoria. The successful 241 series was to be followed by an order for ten more numbered from 270. All the engines used coke as fuel to avoid smoke.

The Class 400 locomotives were developed from Sturrock's 0-6-0 goods locomotives and were built with large fireboxes to provide steam for both the auxiliary steam tender and the engine proper. The grate sloped steeply from back to front. There was some variation in design between engines in the Class. The fireboxes in 400–419 were 7ft 9in outside length, but those in 420–469 were 7ft 2in.

January 1866–December 1866

During Sturrock's final year with the GNR deliveries of his last two passenger designs commenced. Both were 2-4-0s. More Class 400 goods engines also acquired, bringing total deliveries in the year to forty-seven. Two 0-8-0 tank engines were also obtained for trial for local goods traffic around London.

Class	Numbers In Years	Maker	No.	Designer
Class 240 0-4-2T Suburban	250	Avonside	1	Sturrock
Class 251 2-4-0	251–260	SharpStewart	10	Sturrock
Class 264 2-4-0	264–266 267	J. Fowler Yorkshire	3 1	Sturrock
Class 400 0-6-0	440–449 450–455 456–460 461–469	Neilson Vulcan Avonside Hawthorn	10 6 5 9	Sturrock
0-8-0T	472–473	Avonside	2	Firm's standard

The first of two Classes of 2-4-0s, numbers 251-260, were used largely for secondary passenger working in south Yorkshire. They were acquired at the time when the GNR was moving from coke to coal for its passenger services. Sturrock made some modifications during construction to take account of his experience with coal.

Sturrock's final design was originally intended to be a 2-2-2, but he changed his mind after placing the order, believing that a coupled engine would be more suitable on the stiff gradients on the GNR's main line out of London. Four were delivered in Sturrock's final two months with the GNR and two in early 1867.

To cope with the heavy goods traffic on the steep inclines around London, Sturrock needed powerful tank engines. Avonside's standard 0-8-0T design was modified for underground use.

January–April 1867

These twelve engines were ordered by Sturrock, but delivered in early 1867 following his retirement:

Class	Numbers In Years	Maker	No.	Designer
Class 264 2-4-0	268–269	Yorkshire	2	Sturrock
Class 270 0-4-2T Suburban	270–274 275–279	Neilson Avonside	5 5	Sturrock

The most comprehensive source of information on Sturrock's locomotives is the Railway Correspondence & Travel Society's *Great Northern Locomotive History*, Vol. 1 by N. Groves.

STURROCK FAMILY TREE I

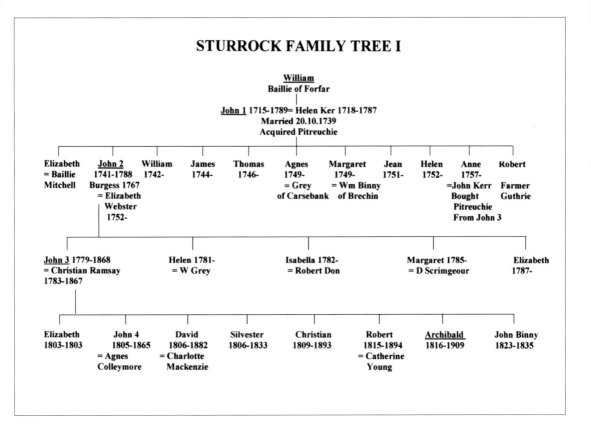

William
Baillie of Forfar

John 1 1715-1789= Helen Ker 1718-1787
Married 20.10.1739
Acquired Pitreuchie

Elizabeth	**John 2**	William	James	Thomas	Agnes	Margaret	Jean	Helen	Anne	Robert
= Baillie	1741-1788	1742-	1744-	1746-	1749-	1749-	1751-	1752-	1757-	
Mitchell	Burgess 1767				= Grey	= Wm Binny			=John Kerr	Farmer
	= Elizabeth				of Carsebank	of Brechin			Bought	Guthrie
	Webster								Pitreuchie	
	1752-								From John 3	

John 3 1779-1868	Helen 1781-	Isabella 1782-	Margaret 1785-	Elizabeth
= Christian Ramsay	= W Grey	= Robert Don	= D Scrimgeour	1787-
1783-1867				

Elizabeth	John 4	David	Silvester	Christian	Robert	**Archibald**	John Binny
1803-1803	1805-1865	1806-1882	1806-1833	1809-1893	1815-1894	1816-1909	1823-1835
	= Agnes	= Charlotte			= Catherine		
	Colleymore	Mackenzie			Young		

STURROCK FAMILY TREE 2

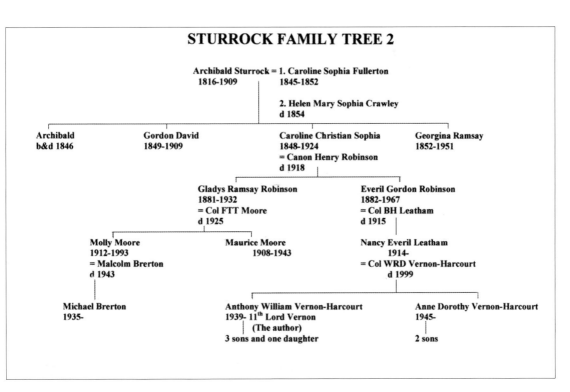

Archibald Sturrock = 1. Caroline Sophia Fullerton
1816-1909   1845-1852

2. Helen Mary Sophia Crawley
d 1854

Archibald	Gordon David	Caroline Christian Sophia	Georgina Ramsay
b&d 1846	1849-1909	1848-1924	1852-1951
		= Canon Henry Robinson	
		d 1918	

Gladys Ramsay Robinson	Everil Gordon Robinson
1881-1932	1882-1967
= Col FTT Moore	= Col BH Leatham
d 1925	d 1915

Molly Moore	Maurice Moore	Nancy Everil Leatham
1912-1993	1908-1943	1914-
= Malcolm Brerton		= Col WRD Vernon-Harcourt
d 1943		d 1999

Michael Brerton	Anthony William Vernon-Harcourt	Anne Dorothy Vernon-Harcourt
1935-	1939- 11th Lord Vernon	1945-
	(The author)	
	3 sons and one daughter	2 sons

REFERENCES

Chapter One

1 'For my children' was dictated by Archibald Sturrock at the age of seventy-six on 9 June 1892.

2 *Doncaster Chronicle* obituary, 8 January 1909.

3 *Engineer* obituary, 8 January 1909.

4 Interview given by his daughter Georgina Sturrock and quoted in F.A.S. Brown, *From Stirling to Gresley 1882–1922*, p.17.

5 C.A. Whatley, *Onwards from Osnaburgs, the rise and progress of a Scottish Textile Company*, Don & Low.

6 The Pitreuchie rent rolls cease in 1805. John Ker is shown as the owner of Pitreuchie on John Wood's plan of Forfar 1822.

7 W. Norrie, *Dundee Celebrities of the 19th Century*.

8 C.W. Munn, *Scottish Provincial Banking Companies*.

9 Niall Ferguson, *Dundee & Newtyle* (Oakwood, 1995).

10 Niall Ferguson, *Dundee & Newtyle*, p.35

11 Nial Ferguson, *Dundee & Newtyle*, p.37

12 James Lowe's *British Steam Locomotive Builders* (1975).

13 Sir Daniel Gooch, *Memoirs & Diary*. (David & Charles, 1972) pp.20–24.

14 Second Statistical Account for Dundee 1833.

15 Sturrock papers.

16 Sturrock papers.

17 James Lowe, *British Steam Locomotive Builders* (1975).

Chapter Two

1 Sir Daniel Gooch, *Memoirs & Diary* (David & Charles, 1972) p.34.

2 E.T. Macdermot, *History of the Great Western Railway*, p.751.

3 A reproduction Firefly Class locomotive can be seen in operation at the Didcot Railway centre on a short stretch of broad-gauge track.

4 *Rail* 253/107.

5　　Sir Daniel Gooch, *Memoirs & Diary*. (David & Charles, 1972) p.27.

6　　M. Sharman, *The Crampton Locomotive*.

7　　*Rail* 1008/83, 3 July 1841.

8　　Sir Daniel Gooch, *Memoirs & Diary*. (David & Charles, 1972) p.43.

9　　*Rail* 250/2, 6 October 1840.

10　　*Rail* 250/2, 20 April 1841.

11　　John C. Bourne, *History of the GWR 1846*. (David & Charles Reprints).

12　　*Swindon Advertiser* 31 July 1871.

13　　*Rail* 1149/7, 19 January 1843.

14　　J. Cattell and K. Falconer, *Swindon Legacy of a Railway Town*, p.42.

15　　John C. Bourne, *History of the GWR 1846* (David & Charles Reprints) p.48.

16　　Edward Snell's UK diaries are being edited for publication by John Cattell, joint author of *Swindon: Legacy of a Railway Town*, who kindly enabled me to look at typescript of the diary for references to Sturrock.

17　　Snell UK diary.

18　　Snell UK diary.

19　　*Rail* 250/573c and 250/122, May to July 1843.

20　　*Rail* 250/122 and *Devizes and Wilts Gazette*, February 1844.

21　　*Rail* 250/122, December 1843.

Chapter Three

1　　*Illustrated Exhibitor and Magazine of Art*, p.102.

2　　*Locomotives of the GWR* vol.2 p.B20 RCTS.

3　　E.T. MacDermot, vol.1 p.200 and *Devizes and Wilts Gazette* 31 July 1845.

4　　Sir Daniel Gooch, *Memoirs & Diary*, pp.50–52.

5　　Sir Daniel Gooch, *Memoirs & Diary*, pp.53–54.

6　　*Locomotives of GWR* vol.2 p.B18 RCTS.

7　　*Railway Magazine*, August 1907 p.90.

8　　*Railway Magazine*, interview p.94.

9　　Rail 250/122, April 1845.

10　　Sir Daniel Gooch, *Memoirs & Diary*, p.53.

11　　Brunel Letter Books at Bristol University 13 August 1846.

12　　*Locomotives of GWR* vol.2 p.B21.

13　　*Locomotives of GWR* ppB21 and 22.

14　　Snell UK diary 5 May 1849.

15　　A.S. Peck, *Great Western at Swindon Works*, p.278.

16　　Gooch's Guard Book *Rail* 253/334.

17　　*Rail* 1008/17.

18　　*Locomotives of the GHR*, vol.2 p.B18.

19　　*Rail* 1008/27.

20　　Gooch's Guard Book *Rail* 253/334.

21　　*Rail* 1005/454 and *Railway Times*, 27 November 1847.

22　　*Rail* 1008/27, 4 August 1849.

23　　*Rail* 1005/454 and B. Darwin, *A Century of Medical Fund Service*, 1947.

24　　Brunel letter books Bristol 20 December 1848.

25　　*Rail* 1008/17.

26　　Brunel Diaries at Bristol University and letter book reference 7/143.

27　　*Rail* 250/4, May 1850.

Chapter Four

1   N. Groves, *Great Northern Locomotive History*, vol.1 provides comprehensive information on all GNR locomotives acquired between 1848 and 1866, when Sturrock retired.

2   *Railway Times* 31 August 1850, p.882.

3   *Rail 236/71* 13 August 1850.

4   The origin of the use of the word 'Plant' to describe the Doncaster locomotive facilities is uncertain. For details see F.A.S. Brown, *Great Northern Locomotive Men,* vol.1 pp.20–22.

5   *Doncaster Gazette*, 3 June 1853.

6   A copy of the 1855 edition of this booklet is available in the Institute of Mechanical Engineers' Library and the introduction quoted is taken from this edition.

7   *Rail 236/71* 14 January 1851 and locomotive engineer's report of 11 January 1851.

8   *Rail 236/39* 17 and 20 May 1851 and June, July and August 1851.

9   *Rail 236/16* 24 October 1850.

10   *Rail 236/16* 18 August 1851.

11   *Rail 236/17* 27 October 1851.

12   *Rail 236/18* 25 January 1853.

Chapter Five

1   Half-year report to shareholders, 31 December 1856.

2   *Railway Times*, 28 August 1852, p.866.

3   *Railway Times*, XIII 1850, p.774.

4   Sturrock memorandum.

5   C.H. Grinling, *GNR History*, p.92 and *Illustrated London News*, 10 August 1850, p.116.

6   *Rail 236/71*, 17 September 1850.

7   *Rail 236/71*, 24 September 1850.

8   N. Groves, *Great Northern Locomotive History* Vol.1 p.50 and *Rail 236/71*, 10 and 13 December 1850.

9   Sturrock memorandum.

10   *Rail 236/39*, 3 January 1851.

11   *Rail 236/39*, 17 February 1851.

12   *Rail 236/39* Traffic Committee 7 February 1851 and *Rail 236/71* Executive Committee 11 February 1851.

13   N. Groves, *Great Northern Locomotive History*, vol.1. p.69–70.

14   *Rail 236/206.* 6 January 1851 and *Rail 236/71*, 7 January 1851.

15   C. Hamilton Ellis, *Twenty Locomotive Engineers.* pp.55-63 and M. Sharman' *The Crampton Locomotive.*

16   *Rail 236/71*, 3 December 1850.

17   *Rail 236/16*, 29 April 1851.

18   *Rail 236/72*, 1 July 1851.

19   C.H. Grinling, *GNR History*, p.104.

20   *Illustrated London News*, 30 August 1851.

21   6 September 1851.

22   *Rail 236/206*, 8 and 22 November 1851.

23   Charging to capital was important to Sturrock. If charged to revenue, it would have affected his running costs per mile. Sturrock had a number of disputes with the Board as to what should be charged to capital.

24   *Rail 236/73*, 13 January 1852.

25   N. Groves, *Great Northern Locomotive History*, pp.60-65.

26   Sturrock memorandum.

27   *Rail 236/70*, 16 April 1850.

28   *Rail 236/70*, 17 May 1850.

29   *Rail 236/70*, 25 May 1850.

30   *Rail* 236/70, 2 July 1850.

31   *Rail* 236/71, 19 November 1850.

32   *Rail* 236/206, 4 January 1851.

33   *Rail* 236/71, 25 February 1851.

34   *Rail* 236/206, 5 April 1851.

35   *Rail* 236/206, 3 July 1851 and 236/72, 5 July 1851.

Chapter Six

1   E.L. Ahrons, *British Steam Railway Locomotive*, vol.1. p.95–96.

2   *Rail* 236/18, 27 July 1852.

3   *Railway Magazine*, August 1907, p.93.

4   Hamilton Ellis, *Twenty Locomotive Men*, p.70.

5   Harry Webster, *Railway Motive Power* p.62.

6   Bird, p.24; N. Groves, *Great Northern Locomotive History*, p.66.

7   C. Stretton's *Development of the Locomotive*, 1903 edition, p.107 and 216.

8   *Rail* 236/675/1.

9   *Rail* 236/206, 29 August 1853.

10   N. Groves, *Great Northern Locomotive History*, vol.1, p.68.

11   N. Groves, *Great Northern Locomotive History*, vol.2, pp.59–62.

12   *Rail* 236/275, 6 August 1852 and Carriage & Wagon register 236/686.

13   *Rail* 236/206, 20 October 1852.

14   *Rail* 236/276/8.

15   *Rail* 236/206, 9 October 1852 and 236/18, 12 October 1852.

16   *Rail* 236/75, 22 March 1853 and 236/276/19, 22 December 1853.

17   *Rail* 236/275/25, 13 July 1853.

18   *Rail* 236/19, 10 January 1854.

19   John Thomas, *History of the North British*.

20   *Rail* 236/21, 20 November 1855.

21   The Leeds, Bradford & Halifax Junction had received its Act in June 1852. It was opened on 1 August 1855 with rolling stock supplied by the GNR.

22   *Rail* 236/207, February 1855.

23   *Rail* 236/206, 10 March 1855 and *Rail* 236/78, 13 March 1855.

24   *Rail* 236/20, 27 March 1855,

25   *Rail* 236/78, 10 April 1855, 236/207, 14 April and 5 May 1855, 236/20, 17 April 1855, 236/20, 8 May 2005.

26   *Rail* 236/78, 11 September 1855.

27   *Rail* 236/207, 15 September 1855.

28   *Rail* 236/21, 18 September 1855.

29   *Rail* 236/207, 15 September 1855.

Chapter Seven

1   *Rail* 236/699 Table of costs per train mile from 1856–66.

2   *Rail* 236/227, 9 June 1856, 236/207, 28 June 1856, 236/22, 1 July 1856 and 236/227, 23 July 1856.

3   *Rail* 236/22, 7 October 1856, 236/207, 1 April 1857, 236/22, 21 April 1857.

4   *Rail* 236/27, 22 May 1860.

5   *Rail* 236/22, 15/16 September and 7 October 1856.

6   *Rail* 236/23, 5 and 18 May, 16 June and 18 August 1857.

7   *Rail* 236/281, 26 August 1857 and *Rail* 236/24, 17 October 1857.

8   *Rail* 236/207, 26 September 1857, 236/24, 29 September 1857 and *Doncaster Gazette*, 25 September 1857.

9   *Rail 236/207*, 31 October 1857 and 236/24, 3 November 1857; N. Groves, *Great Northern Locomotive History*, vol.1. p.24.

10   *Rail 236/207*, p.82.

11   *Rail 236/25*, 11 March 1858.

12   *Rail 236/40*, August 1858 to May 1859.

13   *Rail 236/227*, 18 February 1858, 236/25, 18 February 1857.

14   *Rail 236/282/12*, 19 April 1858, 236/25, 30 March, 27 April, 10 June 1858,236/84, 6 July 1858.

15   *Rail 236/25*, 11 May 1858, *Doncaster Chronicle*, 30 April 1858, Brown p.84, 236/26, 19 February 1959.

16   *Rail 236/207*, 7 January 1859.

17   *Rail 236/207*, 2 July 1859.

18   *Rail 236/89*, 24 April 1863.

19   *Rail 236/85*, 3 May 1859 and 236/26, 10 and 19 May 1859.

20   *Rail 236/26*, 19 February 1859.

21   *Rail 236/27*, 18 October and 1 November 1859.

22   *Doncaster Chronicle*, 6 April 1860.

23   Bird, p.31.

24   *Rail 236/28*, 31 July 1860.

25   *Rail 236/207*, 7April 1857.

26   *Rail 236/207*, 6 September 1860.

27   *Rail 236/283*, 29 August 1860.

28   *Rail 236/31*, 9 February 1864.

29   *Doncaster Chronicle*, 25 May 1860.

Chapter Eight

1   *Doncaster Gazette*, 12 March 1852.

2   *Doncaster Gazette*, 25 April 1856.

3   This quotation and information on the history of adult education in Doncaster is taken from a paper by Alan Thrall available from Sheffield University library.

4   *Doncaster Chronicle*, 31 December 1858.

5   Information on fee levels proved elusive. The OWWR Board agreed a fee not exceeding 50 guineas for McConnell to inspect the rolling stock on 20 February 1856, PRO *Rail 558/2*.

6   General background on the MSLR was taken from Great Central by George Dow.

7   *Rail 463/3*, 15 January 1857.

8   R.A. Cook & C.R. Clinker, *Early Railways Abergavenny to Hereford*.

9   E.T. Macdermot, *History of the GWR*, vol.1. p.526 to 537.

10   *Rail 513/7*, 10 November 1854.

11   *Rail 513/3*, August 1854 to November 1855.

12   The National Museum of Wales holds 5 NAHR carriage drawings signed by Sturrock.

13   PRO *Rail 236/78*, 29 December 1854 Sturrock's salary for the quarter was £235 8s 4d, plus expenses of £13 2s 6d.

14   *Rail 513/7*.

15   *Doncaster Gazette*, 21 November 1856.

16   B. Jones and D. Dunstone, *Vale of Neath Railway*, p.89 (Gomer Press, 1996).

17   E.T. Macdermot, *History of GWR*, vol.1. p.457–526.

18   *Rail 558/907*.

19   *Railway Magazine*, 1908 vol.23, p.228 and Sturrock interview with *Railway Magazine*, 1907. Sturrock remembered the differential to be £15,000.

20   *Rail 500/2*, 15 April and 22 June 1857; *Rail 500/107* 17, 24, 25 April and 8 May 1857.

21   *Rail 500/36*, 10 June 1857.

22   *Rail 734/68*.

Chapter Nine

1   *Rail* 236/207, 29 August 1861 and 236/87, 9 August 1861.

2   *Rail* 236/207, 11 January 1862 and 236/29, 14 January 1862.

3   *Rail* 236/207, 17 May 1862.

4   *Rail* 236/30, 28 October 1862.

5   *Rail* 236/207, 30 May 1861 and 236/87, 31 May 1861.

6   *Rail* 236/30, 11 and 25 November 1862.

7   *Rail* 236/207, 29 January 1863 and 236/30, 4 February 1863.

8   *Rail* 236/207, 3 March 1863, 236/30, 13 March 1863 and 236/207, 6 April 1864.

9   Patent No.1135 submitted 6 May 1863 and sealed 2 November 1863; the *Engineer*, 8 January 1864; the *Engineer* 17 January 1919 gives full technical specification; the *Engineer*, 9 May 1919.

10 J.F. McEwan, *Locomotive Magazine*, July 1941 and British Locomotive Catalogue vol.4, pp.47 and 53.

11 The financial benefits of the steam tender are set out on p.889 of the Minutes of Evidence of the Royal Commission on Railway Charges published 1867.

12 *Rail* 463/7, 28 August 1863.

13 *Rail* 236/687, 5 August 1864.

14 *Rail* 463/7, 28 September 1864.

15 *Rail* 236/207, pp.192–196.

16 *Rail* 236/31, 28 December 1863.

17 *Rail* 236/31, 11 January 1864.

18 *Rail* 1008/83, 30 December 1863 and 9 January 1864.

19 *Mechanics Magazine*, 19 February and 19 August 1864.

20 *Rail* 236/31, pp.317-9.

21 *Rail* 236/90, 17 June 1864.

22 *Rail* 1008/1, 23 July 1864.

23 *Rail* 236/207, 7 October 1864.

24 *Rail* 235/285, 23 January 1865.

25 Groves, pp.105–116.

26 *Rail* 236/33, 11 April 1865.

27 *Rail* 236/296/11 and 236/33, 11 April 1865.

28 *Rail* 236/296/11.

29 *Rail* 236/33, 10 January and 21 March 1865; Groves pp.101-105.

30 See chapter 7 above.

31 *Rail* 236/675/4.

32 *Rail* 236/32, 10 January 1865.

33 *Rail* 236/296/19, 236/208, 8 November 1865, 236/33, 14 November 1865.

34 *Rail* 236/33, 25 July 1865.

Chapter Ten

1   *Rail* 436/8, 17 January 1866.

2   Royal Commission on Railway Charges XXXVIII minutes of evidence pp.879–888, 31 May 1866.

3   *Rail* 236/298, 29 January 1866 and *Rail* 236/34, 6 February 1866.

4   *Rail* 236/296, 17 February 1866, 236/296, 20 February 1866.

5   *Rail* 236/194, 10 March 1866.

6   *Rail* 236/34, 10 and 24 April 1866 and 236/194 23 April 1866.

7   *Rail* 236/208, 7 April 1866.

8   *Rail* 236/194, 1 October 1866.

9   *Rail* 236/208, pp.33–36.

10 *Rail* 236/194, 17 December 1866.

11   A.R. Bennett, *Chronicles of Boulton's Sidings*, p.170.

12   *The Locomotive*, 15 September 1928. pp.290–291.

13   Edward had also been Sturrock's pupil at the GNR. He worked as assistant to Budge. He served as locomotive superintendent on the East Kent line and had been a locomotive engineer in Australia.

14   YE Board minutes are in the Sheffield archives.

15   N. Groves, *Great Northern Locomotive History*, vol.2. pp.8–11.

16   Board minute 17 September 1868.

17   R.A.S. Hennessey, *Transcaucasian Railway*, 2004. pp.17–19.

18   For a fuller account of the history of the first Yorkshire Engine Co., see *Back Track*, 2 December.

Chapter Eleven

1   *Doncaster Chronicle* and *Doncaster, Nottingham and Lincoln Gazette*, 22 February 1867.

2   *Doncaster Chronicle*, 27 March 1868.

3   *Doncaster Chronicle*, 10 November 1871.

4   *Doncaster Chronicle*, 21 December 1877.

5   *Doncaster Gazette*, 31 January 1879; Sturrock's speech at the mayor's banquet.

6   Peter Tuffrey, Town & Country Houses of Doncaster.

7   *Doncaster Chronicle*, obituary, 8 January 1909.

8   History of the Badsworth Hunt Ralph Greaves 1949: Badsworth Hunt Song Book William Sheardown: Bell's Life, 28 December 1872.

9   *Doncaster Chronicle* and *Doncaster Gazette* various dates in August and September 1871 to 1879.

10   *Doncaster Chronicle*, 15 November 1867, 31 January 1868, *Doncaster Gazette*, 22 March 1889.

11   'Aspects of Doncaster', article by Brian Barber.

12   *Doncaster Gazette*, 25 January 1883.

13   *Doncaster Gazette*, 6 April 1886, *Doncaster Chronicle*, 20 March 1885, 26 March 1886 (Church Defence Association), 3, 10, 24 February 1888.

14   Doncaster archives DS/DX 61034, 27 April 1879.

15   Charles Jackson, *Doncaster Charities*, 1881. Sturrock was a subscriber to the book. *Doncaster Gazette*, 4 May 1883.

16   *Doncaster Chronicle*, 9 April 1886.

17   *Doncaster Chronicle*, 20 December 1878 and *Doncaster Gazette*, 17 January 1879.

18   Quoted in the *Doncaster Chronicle*, 24 August 1888 and taken from *Railway News*.

19   *Doncaster Chronicle*, 26 March 1886.

20   *Doncaster Chronicle*, 28 December 1888.

21   C. Hamilton Ellis, *Twenty Locomotive Men*, p.74 and F.A.S. Brown, *Great Northern Locomotive Engineers,* vol.1. p124.

BIBLIOGRAPHY

Ahrons, E.L., *British Steam Railway Locomotive* vol.1 1825-1925 1969 impression
Bird, G.F., *Locomotives of the Great Northern Railway*
Bourne, J.C., *History of the Great Western Railway 1846* (David & Charles Reprint)
Brown, F.A.S., '1846–1881', *Great Northern Locomotive Engineers*, vol.1
Brown, F.A.S., 'From Stirling to Gresley', *Great Northern Locomotive Engineers*, vol.2
Buchanan, A., *Brunel*
Cattell, J., and Falconer, K., *Swindon Legacy of a Railway Town*
Clark, D.K., *Railway Machinery*
Cook, R.A., and Clinker, C.R., *Early Railways Abergavenny to Hereford*
Darwin, B., *Century of Medical Fund Service*
Dow, G., *Great Central*
Durie, A.C., *Linen Industry*
Ferguson, Niall, *Dundee & Newtyle Railway*
Gooch Sir Daniel, *Memoirs and Diary*
Greaves, R., *History of the Badsworth Hunt*
Grinling, C.H. *History of the Great Northern Railway*
Groves, N., '1847–1866', *Great Northern Locomotive History*, vol.1
Hamilton Ellis, C., *Twenty Locomotive Men*
Hennessey, R.A.S., *Transcaucasian Railway and the Royal Engineers*
Jackson, C., *Doncaster Charities 1881*
Jones, B., and Dunstone, D., *Vale of Neath Railway*
Lowe, James, *British Steam Locomotive Builders*
MacDermot, E.T., *History of the Great Western Railway* (1927 edition)
Marshall, J., *Biographical Dictionary of Railway Engineers*
Miskell, L., Whatley, C.A. and Harris B., *Victorian Dundee Image and Realities*
Munn, C.W., *Scottish Provincial Banking Companies*
Nock, O.S., *History of the Great Northern Railway*
Norrie, W., *Dundee Celebrities of the 19th Century*
Peck, A.S., *Great Western at Swindon Works*
Railway Correspondence & Travel Society, *Locomotives of the GWR Part Two Broad Gauge*
Rosling Bennett, A., *Chronicles of Boulton's Sidings*
Sharman, M., *The Crampton Locomotive*
Simmons, J. and Biddle, G., *Oxford Companion to Railway History*
Snell, Edward, *Diary: Life and Adventures in Australian Colonies 1849–1859*
Stretton, C., *Development of the Locomotive* (1903 Edition)

Thomas, John, *History of the North British Railway*
Tutton, M., *Paddington Station 1833–1854*
Whatley, C.A., *Onwards from Osnaburgs, the rise and progress of a Scottish Textile Company Don & Low*
Wrottesley, J., *History of the Great Northern Railway*
Tuffrey, P., and Roe, M., *150 years of Doncaster Plant Works*
Tuffrey, P., *Town and Country Houses of Doncaster*
Webster, Harry, *Railway Motor Power*

The following archives and libraries provided assistance:

Bristol University	Special Collections Library for Brunel papers.
British Library	Newspaper Library at Colindale.
Cambridge	University Library for finding innumerable books.
Doncaster	The Doncaster archives and Doncaster local library provided material about Doncaster in the nineteenth century.
Dundee	Central Library and the archives of St Paul's Episcopal Cathedral, where Sturrock's father was treasurer.
English Heritage	Photographs from Images of England website.
Forfar	Angus Archives at Restenneth contained information on the Sturrocks in Forfar in the eighteenth century.
Great Northern Railway Society	Photographs of Sturrock locomotives.
National Archives at Kew	Principally items in the RAIL series for Great Western and Great Northern Railways.
National Museums and Galleries of Wales	Collections Centre, Heol Crochendy, Parc Nantgarw for Sturrock's rolling stock drawings for the Newport, Abergavenny and Hereford Railway.
National Railway Museum York	Photographs and background information on Sturrock's time at the GNR.
Sheffield City Archives	Records and photographs of the Yorkshire Engine Co.
Stephenson Locomotive Society	Photographs of Sturrock locomotives.
Swindon	Swindon Museum and Art Gallery and STEAM Museum of the Great Western Railway for Edward Snell's drawing of Swindon works and other papers on the early history of the GWR.
Tyne & Wear Museum Service	Hawthorn drawings of Sturrock locomotives.
Winchester College	Sturrock's personal record of locomotives designed during his time with the GNR.

INDEX

If you are interested in purchasing other books published by Tempus
or in case you have difficulty finding any Tempus books in your local bookshop
you can also place orders directly through our website

www.tempus-publishing.com